Riding Pretty

Women in the West

Renée M. Laegreid

Riding Pretty

Rodeo Royalty *in* *the* American West

University of Nebraska Press
Lincoln & London

Parts of chapter 1 originally
appeared as "Rodeo Queens at the
Pendleton Round-Up: The First Go-Round,
1910–1917," *Oregon Historical Quarterly*
104 (Spring 2003): 6–23.

Parts of chapters 3 and 7 originally
appeared as "'Performers Prove Beauty
and Rodeo Can Be Mixed':
The Return of the Cowgirl Queen."
*Montana: The Magazine of Western
History* 54, no. 1 (2004): 44–55.

Library of Congress
Cataloging-in-Publication Data
Laegreid, Renée M.
Riding pretty: rodeo royalty in the
American West / Renée M. Laegreid.
p.   cm.—(Women in the West)
ISBN-13: 978-0-8032-2955-6 (cloth: alk. paper)
1. Women rodeo performers—West (U.S.)—History.
2. Cowgirls—West (U.S.)—History.
3. Rodeos—West (U.S.)—History.
I. Title.   II. Series.
GV1833.5.L34   2006
791.8'40973—dc22
2006044454

Contents

Illustrations

Maps

Acknowledgments

The old adage "writing is a lonely business" certainly does not apply to this book, the success of which involved interactions with people and institutions across the West. I would like to begin by thanking some of the people at the University of Nebraska–Lincoln who were instrumental in helping cultivate the idea for a book on rodeo queens and shaping its progress: Benjamin Rader, John Wunder, Charlene Porsild (now at the Montana Historical Society Library), and Timothy Mahoney in the Department of History; and Maureen Honey in the Department of English. Through their insightful suggestions and rigorous criticisms, they encouraged me to think about how rodeo queens fit into a larger context of culture, gender, and the West. I am grateful to the Center for Great Plains Studies for generous grants in 2000 and 2001, to the Center for Graduate Studies for a Day Fund grant in 2000, and to the University of Nebraska–Lincoln Department of History for numerous travel fund grants.

I owe a special thanks to the people who provided assistance at research institutes, museums, and libraries: Charles Rand, archive director at the National Cowboy and Western Heritage Museum in Oklahoma City, Oklahoma; Ruth Karbosh and Jennifer Nielson, past archivists at the National Cowgirl Hall of Fame in Fort Worth, Texas; Matilda Bolin at the Stamford Chamber of Commerce, overseer for the Texas Cowboy Country Museum in Stamford, Texas; and John Gavin, curator of collections at the Cheyenne Old West Museum in Cheyenne, Wyoming. Shirley Flynn, Cheyenne historian, also deserves a word of thanks for directing me to new sources. Members of the Round-Up Hall of Fame in Pendleton, Oregon—

Bonnie Sager in particular—gave me enormous assistance over the years. Michelle Desrosiers, curator for the Umatilla County Historical Society, lent her expertise as well on several occasions. And a special thanks to the librarians who helped with this project: Dennis Miller at the Abilene Public Library and Mary Finney at the Pendleton Public Library. And last, but definitely not least, a special thanks to Mary Ann Dobrovolny at the Perkins Library at Hastings College.

I would like to thank all the women who answered questionnaires, and especially Susan Talbot, Leah Conner, Jean Dearinger, Julie Kilkenny, Ann Smith, and Jeannette Rutledge, who allowed me to interview them and who shared their memories, stories, and scrapbooks.

Completing this book has been made more enjoyable by friends and colleagues who offered to read and discuss the manuscript at various stages. Antje Anderson, at Hastings College, cheerfully took the time to read a number of the chapters, all of which benefited from her sense of structure and her prodding to clarify some of the rodeo terminology for non-rodeo readers. Andrea Radke, at the University of Idaho–Rexburg, also deserves a very special word of thanks for her rigorous criticisms, insightful comments, and unfailing sense of humor.

My family played no small role in the success of this book, and I would like to thank them for bravely enduring all manner of inconveniences. My sons, Carl and Peter, showed remarkable patience and grace, and my husband, Will, readily took on additional family responsibilities so that I could pursue this venture. Truly, his encouragement, moral support, and technical assistance ("Computers have *two* kinds of memory . . . ") made it all possible. It is to them I dedicate this book.

Riding
Pretty

MAP 1. The communities of Pendleton, Oregon; Stamford, Texas; and Cheyenne, Wyoming, played significant roles in the development of the rodeo queen phenomenon in the American West.

Introduction

In the summer of 1910 Bertha Anger, dressed in a cowgirl outfit, stood on a float and waved to the crowds lining the streets. Anger had won the honor of reigning as queen over the first Pendleton, Oregon, Round-Up celebration, which entitled her to reign over its Westward Ho! parade and rodeo. In reality she really had very little to do with the rodeo; her only assignment was to look as regal as possible as her parade float bounced along Pendleton's rough streets. Yet Anger's new position as queen broke the tradition of hiring cowgirl athletes to promote rodeos, endowing Anger with the honor of being the first community-sponsored rodeo queen. Over time, the role of community queen that began in Pendleton evolved into a remarkable phenomenon, one that spread throughout the American West.

Anger's position as Round-Up queen, like the Round-Up itself, had been hastily put together. Only two months earlier several of Pendleton's leading citizens hit upon the idea of holding an annual booster celebration in Pendleton.[1] Settling on a theme for the new celebration was easy: It would focus on Pendleton's frontier past. It would be, according to Pendleton's paper, *The East Oregonian*, a "mosaic of honest pieces rescued from such little corners of the Old West as still survive, these pieces, melded into a great, dignified, and very stirring spectacle."[2] The new celebration would have a rodeo, featuring "bad horses and good riders" and cowboys and cowgirls. Native Americans, members of the Umatilla, Walla Walla, and Cayuse tribes on the nearby Umatilla Reservation, would also have a prominent role. And, of course, there would be a parade. But not just any parade—one that highlighted the heroic saga of American progress as it marched westward across the nation. Once the idea was announced the entire community worked to make the celebration come together. In only two months the Round-Up went from an idea to a reality.

But who would reign over the celebration? No community festival would be complete without a lovely young woman to preside over the events. Following the long-established tradition in America, young women served as festival queens and, in this capacity, acted as a symbolic representation for their communities' values and expectations.[3] Perhaps the Round-Up directors, pressed for time, followed the tradition of Pendleton's Fourth of July goddess of liberty parade queens. The role of the new queen, following the goddess tradition, was limited to a parade appearance. The selection process for the new Round-Up queen—a ticket selling competition—also imitated Pendleton's goddess of liberty tradition. Results from the first Round-Up queen competition came in too late to print the winner's name in the paper, but there was indeed a first queen of the first Round-Up. Bertha Anger, wearing a cowgirl costume and surrounded by her royal court, waved to the thousands of spectators who witnessed the first Westward Ho! parade.

This book examines the history, evolution, and significance of the community-sponsored rodeo queen, from the introduction of this new phenomenon at the 1910 Pendleton Round-Up to the advent of Miss Rodeo America in 1956. The model for community-sponsored rodeo queens that originated in Pendleton gradually spread to other rodeos throughout the West, providing young women with the opportunity to participate both in rodeo and in their communities. Because the first rodeo queen appeared at the Pendleton Round-Up and Pendleton continued to feature queens, that rodeo plays a central role in the story of rodeo queens. Across the West women selected to serve as queens embodied the ideals and values of their communities. The queens and their communities' values proved to be complex and dynamic. As the phenomenon of rodeo queens spread, each town determined its own criteria for selecting its queen according to local norms and standards. The ability to interpret which characteristics they felt were most important—the ones represented in their choice of rodeo queen—allowed each community to emphasize its own unique character.

In 1956 Miss Rodeo America made her appearance as the national representative for the sport of rodeo. The connection between community rodeo and rodeo queens underwent a significant change. In many cases local rodeos became affiliated with the Professional Rodeo Association circuit, opening the queen competition to young women contestants from outside the vicinity, undercutting the connection between local ideals and values and the girl selected to "rule" the rodeo. The advent of state and national rodeo queen titles also amplified this disconnection between local communities and their queens. However, by closely examining the role of pre-1956 rodeo queens, it is possible to explore the ways in which the rodeo queen position reflected the cultural perceptions of gender within and outside of specific communities. It would be a mistake to consider these women as passive participants in the rodeo queen phenomenon, caught in a web of demeaning feminine roles. Rather, the queens were active and willing participants in the complex and diverse manifestations that the position provided.[4]

Before embarking on the subject of community-sponsored rodeo queens, it is worth contemplating definitions of the word "community." The most commonly studied form of community in western history is a group of people bound by the exigencies of their living together in a particular area.[5] "Community" can also refer to the interaction of diverse kinds of individuals in a common location, such as histories of ethnicity, race, gender, or labor in frontier areas.[6] But "community" can also mean a body of people scattered throughout a larger society who are bound by a common interest. As the history of the rodeo queen phenomenon unfolds, the concept of community expands to include all of these definitions. However, the common denominator for these various definitions of community remains constant: the rodeo queen. She stood as the symbolic representation of the community, whether the community was based in a fixed location, like Pendleton, among groups within a specific location, or a group of individuals, such as the community of cowgirl athletes who worked together to reinstate women's participation in competitive rodeo. Moreover, each of these various communities held its own standard of appropriate gender roles and behavior.

The tradition of having a young woman serve as community representative can be traced to the earliest days of the American republic.[7] But the use of royal figures to preside over civic celebrations, contrasting sharply to the earlier rejection of monarchy in all its forms, has a more recent history. During the mid-nineteenth century, medieval festivals—replete with kings and queens—became a popular form of entertainment in the South. By the late 1890s the idea of a royal figure moved beyond medieval celebrations as individual communities adapted the role to fit celebrations that highlighted local interests. Particularly in the West, as new towns sprang up, celebrations featuring a local queen became a popular form of self-promotion.

The queens for the new festivals were selected as the most

ideal representative for the type of pageant being held. For example, the queen for the Wenatchee, Washington, Apple Blossom Festival had to meet different criteria than did the queen of New Orleans's Mardi Gras or the queen of a children's bicycle and dog parade. However, the role of queen to rule over a specific event became firmly established, as did the royal treatment she received: a coronation ceremony, presentation of a crown or tiara, and a formal ball. The queens, then, were highly visible and celebrated figures, albeit for only a few days. The selection of the queen addressed the idea of community identity, helping answer the question, Who are we and what do we represent?

Robert Lavenda notes that community festivals, especially those that deal with historical themes, disclose more about the aspirations of the town's middle class than they do about the actual history of the town.[8] For example, when Pendleton's town leaders decided to hold their Round-Up celebration, town leaders—merchants, professional people, and political leaders—decided who would be queen. The young women they chose to exemplify their town provided shining examples of the town leaders' middle-class values, which stressed a strong work ethic, high moral standards, genteel behavior, support of higher education, and a commitment to one's community through leadership. The directors of the Round-Up did not set out to find the most beautiful young woman in town; that is, it was not a beauty contest. Rather, they selected a young woman who, in her position as queen, would best represent the overarching middle-class standards and values of the community.

Queens selected by festival committees were not drawn exclusively from prominent families. Nevertheless, the young women represented families committed to upholding the strictures of local, middle-class values. How, then, could a young middle-class woman act as representative for all the diverse inhabitants of her community? Town leaders held the highest posts in the Round-Up organization, but the act of staging a large-scale rodeo in a small town—Pendleton's population ranged from 4,460 in 1910 to 11,774 in 1950—brought the entire town together.[9] Three weeks before the event, everyone in town was encouraged to get into the spirit of the celebration by wearing western clothes; newspaper announcements invited residents to watch the "matinees," where local cowboys tested the bucking abilities of the new broncs; Pendleton residents registered the number of cots they could fit in their homes to rent to out-of-town rodeo spectators; and when the rodeo grounds and town were ready for the show, Pendletonians congratulated themselves with a community dance before the flood of visitors began.[10] The inclusive nature of the celebration allowed all people—not just one segment of the population—the opportunity to participate in the celebration. The process of putting the celebration together fit a pattern that had developed across the country. Community celebrations affirmed "the existence of an intricate web of human relationships connecting parents and children, old people and kids, men and women, tradition and progress—the individual, the family, and the community."[11]

By taking an active part in an organization, the participants adopted the symbols associated with it and gained a sense of belonging by being recognized as fellow members.[12] The queen, then, became more than a representative of the town's middle class. She symbolized the entire celebration and everyone who participated. And while the organizational structure, or ritual, of putting on the annual event perpetuated community standards and power structures, the Round-Up queen symbolized both the collective efforts of the town and the potential for upward mobility in a democratic society.[13]

The major focus of *Riding Pretty: Rodeo Royalty in the American West* is the relationship between rodeo queens and their communities. Within this larger theme two threads—rodeo history and gender history—weave their way through the story. Rodeo became a spectator sport at a critical juncture in American history. In 1890, as the frontier era drew to a close, Buffalo Bill Cody's Wild West Show played a large role in capturing the nostalgia for the disappearing frontier era. Cody's show, which built on a longer tradition of informal cowhand gatherings, "Sunday rodeos," and Indian powwows, formed the basis from which rodeo as a spectator sport emerged; it appealed to an enlarging middle class who had the time and finances to enjoy leisure activities. As soon as rodeo became a popular and profitable spectator event, town boosters quickly sought to create their own rodeos. In the Pacific Northwest alone, there were over fifty rodeos and frontier days celebrations by 1912.[14]

The connection between rodeos and cowboys has been well researched.[15] By and large, the world of the cowpuncher and the rodeo athlete was a male province. The first cowboys came from diverse ethnic backgrounds and performed a variety of tasks related to watching livestock. Many were seasonal cowboys—itinerant wage laborers in the agricultural business who moved with the seasons in search of work.[16] Some cowboys were fortunate enough to find steady work, but many others, called "waddies," were temporary hands hired for the intensive work during spring calving and fall round-ups.[17]

But ranch work was not just for men; women, too, worked cattle, broke horses, and roped steers.[18] The women who worked performed numerous chores on the ranch and were the wives and daughters of ranchers, and occasionally ranch owners; they were not itinerant wage laborers. As with every rule there are exceptions, of course, and several accounts exist of women working as hired cowhands.[19] This is not to deny the work of cowgirls but rather to emphasize the class and gender elements associated with cow punching: It was a male, working-class province. Wage-earning cowboys competed in the informal competitions held during round-ups. Women did not.

When rodeo did become a sport in the late nineteenth century, women had difficulty breaking into this male domain. The problems cowgirl athletes faced were part of an overall struggle for women to enter occupations previously held by men, in that the women were neither welcomed nor integrated into their new professions.[20] Clifford P. Westermeier notes the difficulty the early cowgirl athletes faced, writing, "Though never particularly welcome as participants in the work, they [the women] carved a niche for themselves by sheer audacity, courage, and female persistence, and won the respect of all who have witnessed their daring and skill."[21]

If queens were to be the best representatives of a pageant or public festival, then it only made sense that these rare cowgirl athletes would be selected. Indeed, the first rodeo queens competed in rodeos; promoters hired women as queens and gave them newspaper billing along with famous cowboys and bucking horses. The idea of women competing in the arena with cowboys, riding broncs and roping steers, was quite a novelty, one that rodeo promoters and town boosters capitalized on to attract paying spectators.

By the late 1920s rodeo had evolved into a more organized and professional sport. The Rodeo Association of America, founded in 1929, played an increasing role in deciding which events would be included or eliminated; who was eligible to compete, union or non-union cowboys or both; and whether women riders would be allowed to compete, and if so, in which events and in what capacity, open competition or exhibition. The changing dynamics of the rodeo, in large part shaped by perceptions of appropriate gender behavior, played an important part in determining whether to feature a cowgirl athlete or a community-sponsored queen to draw in the crowds.

This leads to the second thread in the rodeo queen story, the changing discourse of gender. The combination of gender history and the evolution of rodeo as a spectator sport helps answer the question, Who will be queen of the rodeo? by explaining the shift from queens as women participants in rodeo to women who promoted rodeo. Cowgirl athletes at the turn of the twentieth century had benefited from trends that opened opportunities for women to become more active in the public sphere. During the 1880s a noticeable shift in attitudes toward women's traditional roles and restraints on "proper" activities for women occurred. Middle-class women began to move outside their domestic spheres, literally and figuratively, and challenge the distinctions between private, passive female mores and public, aggressive masculine ways.[22] Young women in particular challenged the restrictive virtues of "True Womanhood," characterized by piety, purity, submissiveness, and domesticity.[23] Leaving the sanctity of the home, they entered professions and activities previously open only to men. The number of women entering new professions and activities—including rodeo—constituted a small percentage of the overall American population, only 8.2 percent of working women in 1900.[24] Even so, the diversity of areas that women entered and the rapidity of their advancement created national alarm.[25] Traditionalists maintained that marriage and domesticity were central to most adult women's identity and constituted their most important contribution to society.[26] Modernists argued that all society would benefit if women would think and act for themselves.

Bernarr McFadden, writing in 1901, identified the reform spirit of the times when he argued that women in civilized countries had been "genteeled" into an abnormal and unhealthy state. Women, he argued, needed to adopt reforms in dress and attitudes toward the body—in terms of physical activity and sexuality—to save both men and women.[27] McFadden's voice was but one of many engaged in the debates over the proper role for women.[28] Susan K. Cahn writes that during the first decade of the twentieth century, the number of women engaged in competitive sports was very small. However, the growing popularity among women to engage in sports encouraged athletic women of every class to confront "the contradiction inherent in being both 'woman' and 'athlete.'"[29] Women who participated in sports continued to face accusations of being "unfeminine." However, the persistence of women to continue in sports "contributed to the dynamic image of the 'athletic girl' who refused to be excluded from a domain of masculine privilege and pleasure."[30] The insistence on participating in the masculine realm helped ease the hard lines of the gender binary, which required that women behaved in a manner unbefitting to their sex if they participated in activities considered to belong to men.

Exercise reform was one part of an overall shift in manners and morals, yet, as James R. McGovern writes, "The most significant area of changing manners and morals as they effected the American woman was the decided shift in her sex role and identification of more masculine norms."[31] The manifestation of this shift, the "New Women" of the 1890s–1920s, challenged the distinctions between traditional gender roles and modern views. New Women self-consciously crossed boundaries of traditional behavior to express sexuality, individualism, and self-development. In her work on the New Women and society, Paula S. Fass uses the terms "traditionalist" and "progressive" to help define the kinds of contemporary sensibilities. The traditionalist position, she argues, closely reflected the middle-class values of traditional gender separation and domestic roles and passive behaviors for women. The progressive "voice," seen as a positive force, challenged old values, institutions, and gender restrictions.[32]

In urban areas rapidly changing social conditions opened the doors of opportunity for young women in employment, living arrangements, recreation, and unchaperoned social interactions with men in dance halls, amusement parks, and movie

theaters.[33] For the most part, women in rural areas lagged behind their urban counterparts, as the conservative mores of
small towns were reinforced by the interconnected controls of
family, church, and the watchful eyes of local residents.[34] But
opportunities did exist for these New Women of the West and
often in matters that reflected the unique characteristic and lifestyles of the region. Annie Oakley, for example, performing in
Wild West shows enjoyed "a life of adventure for a young lady
of an otherwise staid Victorian era."[35] By performing western
frontier skills in front of large audiences, Oakley expanded
the boundaries of traditional feminine behavior. While a Wild
West show did not have the same immoral reputation as the
stage, Oakley's "proper" friends would have been concerned
over her skating so close to the edge of the demimonde world
of the theater. Yet her demeanor outside the arena conformed
to Victorian middle-class standards. Women like Oakley were,
as Susan A. Glenn writes, "two women in one," able to move
into the masculine public sphere as professional performers,
while maintaining the womanly virtues associated with traditional femininity.[36]

When western women began participating in rodeos, they
also crossed the boundary into public performance. The first
women's event, the Ladies' Relay Race, was held at the 1899
Cheyenne Frontier Days. In 1904, again in Cheyenne, Bertha
Kaepernick (later Blancett) became the first woman to bronc
ride in open competition.[37] The images of these women competing in rodeo are quite striking: Wearing long skirts and hair
piled up in the fashionable styles of the day, these Victorian
women are hard to picture racing horses and riding "outlaw"
bucking broncos.

Herein lies the paradox: Cowgirls in rodeo both met and
contradicted acceptable norms of gender. Their position as
female athletes in a traditionally masculine sport exemplifies the unsettled discourse of gender between traditionalists

and modernists. Women roping steers, bulldogging cattle, and riding broncs to a standstill countered norms of appropriate feminine behavior, making McGovern's statement on the New Woman, "She had abandoned passivity," seem like an understatement.[38] Yet when women performed in rodeos, written accounts stressed their adherence to commonly held norms of femininity, conspicuously noting their marital status—usually married—and their ladylike appearance.

The appearance of cowgirls, especially their clothing, became an important part of their performance and of the newspaper coverage on the women. As women in general became more active, they had to invent clothing that would accommodate their new activities, and in the process, as Susan Gordon notes, "produced a new conception of what it meant to be feminine."[39] Women designed and sewed outfits not only to allow them to participate in physical sports but also to reassure traditionalists that they remained feminine and had not become "mannish." The designation of "mannish" or "masculine women" developed, as Laura L. Behling notes, "in the Progressive and early modern eras, when the difference between *sex* and *gender* was not as carefully defined as it is now."[40] The phrase, "masculine woman" had pejorative connotations, categorizing women who "performed men's work and assumed their roles, often in men's clothing," while denying their "natural" female roles.[41] At the turn of the century, cowgirl athletes did not dress like cowboys. The women wore corsets, long skirts, and huge bows in their hair.

By the early 1900s the women began designing and sewing clothing more appropriate for their equestrian gymnastics. Cowgirl regalia, based on jodhpurs or gym bloomers, allowed greater freedom of movement, and emphasized a slim, boyish figure. The outfits were flashy too. Trick riders were judged on their costumes as well as their riding abilities, and the three Ss of an eye-catching outfit—silk, satin, sequins—formed the ba-

1. Studio portrait of professional cowgirl performers wearing typical riding costumes, c. 1920. From the Collection of the Cheyenne Frontier Days Old West Museum, Cheyenne, Wyoming.

sis of many a cowgirl's outfit. Prairie Rose Henderson, known for her flamboyant costumes during the 1910s and 1920s, designed one outfit that included silk bloomers trimmed with mink.[42] But the fabric, cut, and often elaborate embroidery on chaps, vests, and skirts maintained a feminine appearance. Gordon notes that a common feature in many children's play-suits, a sailor's collar, was commonly used in women's sports outfits.[43] Wearing a scarf similar to a sailor's collar was also a very popular style among rodeo cowgirls. Although sailor suits and rodeo make an odd combination, by dressing like children, the women, "reduced the threat of their changing behavior."[44] The outfits, while flashy or childlike, were not risqué. The cow-girl athletes dressed in a radically new and feminine manner, yet their costumes were not "immoral," like those worn by stage performers, nor did they appear too "mannish."

The tension between traditionalists and modernists regarding the role of women continued throughout the early decades of the twentieth century. Ella Granger grew up on a ranch near Pendleton and competed in the first three Round-Ups. During a 1982 National Public Radio report, "Cowgirls of Eastern Oregon," she recalled, "the women [riders] who came in with these professional [rodeo] men would play cards and maybe drink and associated with men all the way around more so than we did. . . . We didn't know that kind of life." When asked by the interviewer if these cowgirl athletes were "proper women," Granger whispered, "I don't think so."[45] Ella Granger exemplifies both the expanding opportunities for New Women in the West and the concern over the boundaries of behavior. Granger, a young woman from a prominent Pendleton ranching family, enjoyed the freedom to compete in her hometown rodeo. However, the idea of turning her amateur talent into a professional career—riding the rodeo circuit and the unstructured life that it entailed—crossed her line of appropriate gender behavior.

The cultural debate over appropriate gender behaviors, never resolved, returned to the conservative standard in the late 1920s. Writing on cowgirl athletes in the early twentieth century, Marilyn Burgess states that cowgirls were excluded from competition because, "the visibly butch performances by cowgirls in the rodeo arenas of the first quarter of the century simply exceeded the normative bounds of the patriarchal gender system."[46] But it was not that simple. Until 1929 the boundaries were still in a state of flux. A combination of events that occurred in the late 1920s reversed the trends that allowed women access into the arena as cowgirl athletes. Gender expectations swung back to the more conservative view of appropriate female behavior, signaling an end to the reign of cowgirls as queens and a new beginning for community-sponsored rodeo queens.

Community-sponsored rodeo queens in the twentieth century were not frontier women, urban women, or laborers, which is perhaps why, despite their numbers, they have received so little scholarly attention. The idea behind community festival queens is that they represented the essence of a celebration, which in turn exemplified what was important to the community. Obviously, these are not uniquely western characteristics. Fascination with celebrations and royalty existed across the nation, yet westerners put their own spin on the phenomenon with the invention of a rodeo queen. A rodeo celebrated unique regional occupations: ranching in the arid West and the frontier experience.

But during the late 1920s and into the early 1930s, community-sponsored rodeo queens usurped cowgirl athletes as the royal figure of choice at local rodeos. Cowgirl athletes were by then considered to be riding beyond the pale in terms of mainstream, womanly behavior. With the transition from cowgirl to community-sponsored queens, the connection between distinctive regional occupation skills—roping and bronc riding—and the young women who served as queens was often tenuous. Although a community rodeo queen's family might own a ranch, as a rule the young woman did not ride for a living. A conscious effort was made, therefore, to emphasize the connection between the queen and the town's western heritage.

When announcing the new queen in the local paper, the article would emphasize her cowgirl skills and that hard-to-define "western spirit"—those qualities that made western women unique. She rode western style, a mode that emphasized usefulness and practicality. Riding astride in a western saddle allowed her to gallop "flat-out" and provided a sturdy anchor for her rope and a stable base should she need to rope a calf or shoot from the saddle. It was the antithesis of the English style of riding, which involved balancing oneself precariously on a "pancake" saddle and was only considered appropriate for polite riding in a well-groomed arena. The rodeo queen embodied the image of a traditional frontier woman, showing she could do what needed to be done and do it without losing her feminine qualities.

Family lineage became increasingly important too. How many of her grandparents had settled the area as a pioneer? One such grandparent in the family tree was almost a requirement; two who crossed the Plains was even better. This frontier heritage reflected the fortitude and the spirit of the family, and by extension, of the young woman. Historical connection to the town reinforced the importance of longevity in the area by showing how her family was connected to the unique occupations of the region—cattle ranching, wheat farming, or raising horses—or to the economic development of the town. The days of the Old West were gone, and people knew it, but by consciously reinforcing the connection between the rodeo queen and the frontier past, the queen became the representative of "all the pieces of the West that still exist."[47] Through the queen, the frontier past and the expectations for the future were brought together and celebrated.

During the post–World War II years, rodeos cropped up across the West, and the opportunity to compete for the title of rodeo queen was technically open to any young, unmarried woman who could ride and supply her own regalia. By this time, the role of a community-sponsored rodeo queen had become firmly established. As a young woman who served as both a symbolic representation of the town and a metaphor for western women, her "character was thus a matter of independence, ingenuity and physical skill fostered by the demands of the environment."[48] The queen exemplified the necessary duality of western womanhood: the ability to balance these masculine traits without losing her feminine character. She had the necessary riding skills and spirit to be considered an appropriate representative of the rodeo while, importantly, remaining squarely within the parameters of middle-class respectability.

This genteel cowgirl image was further reinforced with the

introduction of the Miss Rodeo America pageant in 1955. The criteria for winning this prestigious title—horsemanship, appearance, and personality—encouraged a standardization of rodeo queen contests throughout the West. As the national representative of professional rodeo, Miss Rodeo America became a role model for thousands of young women, serving to reinforce a traditional view of western women consistent with postwar concepts of gender behavior.

The Pendleton Round-Up stands as the first community celebration to have local woman serve as queen. The idea that small western towns, while isolated, were not insulated from outside influences is particularly apt in the study of the rodeo queen phenomenon.[49] The concept of a community-sponsored rodeo queen, once invented in Pendleton, slowly spread to other communities. Three particular rodeos, the Texas Cowboy Reunion, Cheyenne Frontier Days, and the Tri-State All-Girl Rodeo, profoundly changed or challenged the rodeo queen role that had originated in Pendleton. Changes in the queen's role initiated at these rodeos influenced the overall history of the rodeo queen phenomenon, and in some cases, the evolution of Pendleton's Round-Up royalty as well.

When Bertha Anger stood on her float and waved to the crowds in 1910, it is unlikely she thought to herself she was blazing a path for generations of women to come. She was having a good time. But there is no doubt that Bertha Anger, first queen of the first Pendleton Round-Up, is the prototypical rodeo queen. From its simple origins, the phenomenon evolved into one that provided an active role for women across the West. Queens would recognize they were, indeed, ambassadors for their community, representing an important part of their town's heritage. Thousands of women would compete for the title of rodeo queen, and for their efforts their community would reward them with heady attention, honors, and a lifetime of recognition.

1. Community-Sponsored Rodeo Queens

Pendleton's First Go-Round, 1910–1917

Whether they were called rodeo queens or the sweethearts of the rodeo, cowgirl athletes like Prairie Rose Henderson, Ruth Parton Webster, and Ollie Osborn belonged to the exotic community of rodeo riders. If there was concern over their status as "proper women," it took a back seat as newspaper articles, ads, and promotional flyers whipped up anticipation to watch cowgirl daring and expertise in the arena. These professional rodeo stars captured the imagination of the townspeople. They rode into town in a blaze of fanfare, wowed the crowd with their stunts, then galloped off in search of another town, another performance, another chance to win the prize money.

When the Pendleton Round-Up held its inaugural show in 1910, it introduced a new dimension to the excitement of frontier entertainment: a community-sponsored rodeo queen. Miss Bertha Anger, first queen of the first Round-Up, was truly a queen of a different sort. She was not a member of the rodeo community. It was anybody's guess whether she could ride a horse, let alone buck one out. In contrast to the attention given to the rodeo star queens, Anger's reign was forgettable—so

2. Bertha Anger, shown here in 1910, was the first queen of the
Pendleton Round-Up. Courtesy of Howdyshell Photography,
Pendleton, Oregon.

forgettable, in fact, that later a dispute arose to contest the
validity of her title.[1] Yet Anger's title at the Round-Up marked
the beginning of a new type of rodeo royalty, one that did not
gallop in and out of town on a horse but was an integral part of
the community. Inauspicious as Anger's reign may have been,
the creation of a community-sponsored rodeo queen was precedent setting. Over time the concept of "local girl as queen"
that originated in Pendleton would develop into the standard
rodeo queen pattern found throughout the West.

The idea of selecting young, local women to represent a town at its own celebration did not appear suddenly; it evolved slowly out of a combination of existing local traditions and national trends. The town of Pendleton provides a case study in the rodeo queen phenomenon, illustrating the intersection of rodeo, gender, and boosterism to create this specifically western phenomenon. Yet the idea of a community-sponsored rodeo queen was not immediately a success. A look at the experiences of the first queens, 1910 to 1917, illustrates their tenuous position within the sport of rodeo. The first Pendleton Round-Up queens did not garner the kind of publicity reserved for cowgirl rodeo stars; nevertheless, traditions surrounding the queen's role developed quietly, setting the stage for later royalty to emerge as prominent and integral figures of the Round-Up.

Situated in the bottom of a canyon in the plains of northeastern Oregon, the Pendleton town site was located along the Oregon Trail route, which ran through Umatilla Indian homelands. The geography and climate of the area proved ideal for raising sheep and cattle, and settlers began to form a town in the early 1860s. In 1893 a wool-cleaning factory opened. Two years later the Pendleton Woolen Mills began making trade blankets based on local Indian designs and marketing them to settlers, tourists, and Indians. In 1868 Pendleton was selected as the Umatilla County seat, and the town was incorporated in 1880. By 1900 Pendleton's population counted 4,406, making it the fourth largest city in Oregon.[2]

But it was the Pendleton Round-Up that put the town on the proverbial map, and the origin story of the Round-Up has become part of the town's collective consciousness. E. N. "Pink" Boylen began his long association with the Round-Up as a young boy in 1911, and he later served on the rodeo board. In his history of the event, he writes, "It is believed and commonly accepted that following a very successful 4th of July celebration in 1909, the potential spark for the Pendleton Round-Up was ignited."[3] Mildred Searcey, a Pendleton historian, describes the 1909 event as a rather unorganized affair that was so much fun that "after the dust had settled and the cowboys had limped up town, the merchants on Main street decided the 4th of July celebration had been a success and should be repeated."[4] Of course, having a good time did encourage the town merchants to hold another bigger and better celebration the next year; if the 1909 Fourth of July celebration had flopped, there is no telling what would have happened. But there was little chance the 1909 celebration would not succeed; the origins of the celebration were not nearly as haphazard as the local lore might suggest.

The Fourth of July had always been a popular excuse for townspeople and ranchers to get together and hold a celebration in Pendleton. In 1877, for example, the town paper, the *Pendleton East Oregonian*, announced, "The coming Fourth of July was to be celebrated in a manner heretofore unexcelled in Eastern Oregon." With the promise of "good speeches," fireworks, and a dance, it was expected that "a general good time would be had."[5] After the railroad arrived in Pendleton in 1884, town boosters moved quickly to capitalize on the new opportunity. The 1885 Fourth of July celebration boasted special excursion trains to bring visitors to Pendleton from throughout the region, and the Pendleton celebration committee designed a slate of new activities to encourage out-of-town visitors to make the trip to their town. By 1888 Pendleton's Fourth of July celebration had made the transition from a local affair to a booster event. Planners anticipated that year's celebration would be the biggest ever, and young men, "rustlers in every sense," sold subscriptions to merchants throughout the city.[6] To recognize those who had subscribed (or perhaps to shame those who had not), the *Pendleton East Oregonian* listed the names of citizens who had helped fund the event. A formal committee organized entertainment for the day, including a sack race, a bicycle race, a greased pig chase, a greased pole climb, and a baseball game.[7] Truly, there was something for everyone. But the boosters had a more serious economic goal in mind as well. As a reporter for the *Pendleton East Oregonian* noted, "The benefits derived from a good rousing celebration in Pendleton are at last beginning to be seen by our businessmen and citizens. They know that every visitor to the city on the glorious Fourth comes with the intention of having a good time at whatever expense, and consequently carries with him a large-sized wallet, well filled with coins of the realm."[8] Better that the visitors spend their money in Pendleton than elsewhere.

In 1910, when the directors of what would become the Pendleton Round-Up decided to hold a frontier-themed celebration, the decision was not based on recollections of spur-of-the-moment good times. The Round-Up was founded on a long-standing tradition of community celebrations and unself-conscious boosterism. The directors made a deliberate decision to shift the town's major income-generating celebration away from a Fourth of July extravaganza—there were too many towns already competing against Pendleton to expect a profitable celebration every year from that event—and to create a celebration unique to Pendleton and its history. The directors ultimately decided that a rodeo, held in conjunction with the upcoming district fair, seemed a perfect match for the town.

Town boosterism involved, as Carl Abbott writes, "the entire process by which business and civic leaders assess the situation they faced, tried to define a coherent economic program to be carried out by public and private actions, and publicized that assessment and program to local and national audiences."[9] In a classic example of boosterism, a reporter for the *Pendleton East Oregonian* assessed Pendleton's place in the region and the town leaders' vision for its future:

Now a word about the frontier celebration and what these behind the move hope to accomplish . . . the company hopes to
pull off an exhibition annually that will be worth coming many
miles to see. It will be a thrilling three days, make no mistake.
. . . The district fair is a valuable enterprise. It shows the progress
of this section in the fields of agriculture, horticulture, animal
husbandry, etc. . . . and the goods that are manufactured at our
mills and factories. *These things represent our industrial activity
and needless to say the hope of the future rests in further progress
along these lines. . . . [However,] in an industrial sense we have
nothing to hope for from the Indian or the cowpuncher. But for
entertainment purposes frontier celebrations are certainly good.*
[People] will come from far and near to see the big frontier celebration this fall and in doing so they will also aid the fair and be
of benefit to the city in general.[10] [emphasis added]

The statement fully embraced the contemporary view of civilization's inevitable advancing across the frontier and the belief
that for the economic basis of a community, it would ultimately
move past the agrarian phase and into the industrial. Yet town
leaders recognized a market existed for entertainment that featured a connection to the not-so-distant frontier past. The Indian and the cowpuncher had been important in the frontier
era of Pendleton. Their day had passed; they could now con-
tribute to the town's future as entertainers in the Round-Up.

The Round-Up directors were well aware of the major
frontier celebrations held throughout the West. Rather than
reinvent the wheel, they sent Mark Moorehouse, a successful
banker in town and the son of Lee Moorehouse, the Umatilla
Indian Reservation agent, to Frontier Days in Cheyenne, Wyoming. There Moorehouse took notes, observing "defective as
well as successful features."[11] They also sent a delegation to
critique the rodeo celebration in Denver.[12] In the final analysis
the directors decided to pattern their celebration after these

rodeos with "exhibitions of bronco riding, steer riding, fancy roping, wild horse races, relays and pony express races, cavalry and artillery drills, fancy shooting, lady races, and other events."[13]

The directors also recognized the importance of Native peoples to the history of the area and to the town of Pendleton. Roy Bishop, owner of the Pendleton Woolen Mills, who had "personal acquaintance with the Indians through his business as manufacturer of Indian blankets," offered to invite tribal members to participate in the first Round-Up.[14] After considering the invitation, leaders of the three tribes at the Umatilla Reservation—the Umatillas, Walla Wallas, and Cayuses—wrote Round-Up director Lee Moorehouse, stating that if "suitable prizes" and arrangements could be made, "They would bring as many friends as possible and [would] include other race horse Indians to bring their animals." They would also "bring their families and [would] camp at the 'celebration' grounds during the 'round-up,' thus insuring an additional attraction of considerable importance." Several weeks later tribal leaders met with Moorehouse again, this time to propose that Indian horse races open the Round-Up and that the races be held every day of the celebration.[15] By negotiating their role at the Round-Up, Native Americans developed what was, and continues to be, a unique feature of the Round-Up.

One of the key elements of the Pendleton Round-Up is its status as a community-based celebration and the fact that local townspeople produced the rodeo. In 1910 this was still a novel arrangement. Although small ranch rodeos still existed throughout the West, the sport of rodeo had become a significant form of public entertainment. Traveling promoters typically approached town officials and offered "to stage a contest for a certain sum of money and promise to assume responsibilities and worries that are connected with this work." The promoters promised to advertise the rodeo "by means of a wide advertising campaign which infected the community and the surrounding districts with enthusiasm in anticipation of the contest."[16]

Contract rodeos had their advantages: advertising was taken care of, and the contract producers, familiar with talented cowboy and cowgirl athletes from outside the town, could provide a more diverse field of riders than would have been available locally. Still, there were drawbacks. By producing the rodeo themselves, Round-Up directors avoided the pitfalls of unscrupulous promoters—legal entanglements over unpaid bills, rodeo cowboys receiving less prize money than promised, and crowds disappointed by top riders who failed to show.[17] In planning their first show, local producers in Pendleton drew upon past traditions while also incorporating community interests and values.

When Bertha Anger became the first rodeo queen of the Round-Up in 1910, she filled a position that also developed out of existing local traditions. An important element of the town's celebrations was its parades; another was having a young woman represent the town during the parades. The Round-Up continued both of these traditions but altered them to fit the new frontier days theme. The new Westward Ho! parade was advertised to be a "great spectacular frontier pageant" designed to showcase the progress of civilization as it advanced across the American frontier.[18]

Parallels between the Fourth of July parade and the Westward Ho! parade are quite remarkable. An article on the 1907 Pendleton Fourth of July parade reported on a car "carrying the Goddess of Liberty, Miss Pauline Jones and her 50 attendants, representing the different states."[19] The first Pendleton Round-Up Westward Ho! parade in 1910 also involved "fifty girls in costume."[20] The float that carried the Round-Up queen and her court, "festooned with red, white, and blue bunting, looked very much like the Goddess of Liberty float."[21] Physical resemblances aside, the directors understood the importance of a good parade for the success of their new celebration. They designed the Westward Ho! parade to be an enormous spectacle.[22]

The decision of the directors to have a community queen for the Round-Up was based on the goddess of liberty figure who headed local Fourth of July parades. For the Westward Ho! parade, however, the Round-Up directors decided on a queen rather than creating a "goddess of the rodeo." In spite of ideological difficulties—the connection between the politically inspired goddess was perhaps too well ingrained to make a leap into a rodeo celebration—precedence existed for parade queens in the region. Round-Up directors could follow the example of Portland's first Rose Parade in 1909. The Round-Up could have a queen.

To help explain the interest in having a queen figure to preside over local events, even a cursory review of local papers in the early 1900s turns the question, Why a queen? on its head to, Why *not* a queen? The *Pendleton East Oregonian* was a small paper, usually eight pages in length. As a subscriber to a wire service, it kept readers abreast of the latest national and international news and included a surprising amount of information on royal families from around the world—and there was a good deal of royalty in the early 1900s. At least once a week readers were updated as to who among this elite group was getting married, having an anniversary, or celebrating a birth.

It is also worth noting how the royals were depicted in the press. One 1910 article, for example, reported on Queen Margherita of Italy and her children, who enjoyed the new roller skating fad by zipping down the palace halls. Readers also learned of how King Edward's favorite terrier, Caesar, mourned his master's death. And they must have been amused at the story of a young prince, tired of all the pomp of his position, running off to play "Injun" for an afternoon.[23] The royals were obviously important and respected for their status, but they also seemed approachable, connected with their communities, and involved with the concerns, even popular trends, of everyday people. Community queens in America were European royalty writ small and democratic. Select young women could be exalted, honored, and admired, not because they were so much better than their communities but precisely because they were of them.

Anger's position of queen fit right in with the bourgeoning acceptance of celebration queens, of elevating local women to royal heights, albeit for a few days. Searcey's description of the rodeo queen riding on a float stressed the regality of the queen's position: "A horse was not regal enough for this first court. They rode on a float, trimmed in evergreen trees from the Blue Mountains."[24] Creating a royal persona justifies the pageantry that evolved with community-sponsored rodeo queens and foreshadows a disconnect that developed between community-sponsored royalty and the itinerant rodeo crowd.

Anger's position as the first queen of the Round-Up opens a window into exploring the connection between queens and their communities. Anger probably moved to Pendleton shortly before 1910 with her mother, Alice Anger, and an invalid brother. Alice Anger was remembered as "an expert seamstress," and Bertha was employed as a sales clerk of the People's Warehouse department store.[25] Her name first appeared in the *Pendleton East Oregonian* in June of 1910, when the town of Stanfield held a goddess of liberty contest for a Fourth of July parade.[26] The contest was open to any young lady from the county; the winner would be determined by who sold the most tickets. Along with the coveted title of goddess of liberty, the fortunate young woman would also win a one-hundred-dollar diamond ring.[27]

Bertha Anger did not fare well in the competition, and a few

Returns of the Jeffries-Johnson Fight will be received
at Stanfield, and bulletins will be posted during each
round on a bill board at the base ball grounds.

Spend July the 4th at
STANFIELD

VOTE FOR THE QUEEN
OF THE DAY

She Will Receive a Beautiful
$100.00 Diamond Ring

and with every vote purchaser receives one ticket towards
an elegant gold watch. Votes on Sale at

Pendleton Drug Store and Donaldson's Drug Store

Ball Games and Other Sports

Dancing and Fire Works at Night. Music All Day

By United Band and Orchestra
of Pendleton and the Echo Band

3. Queen contests, such as the Stanfield contest advertised in this
photo, encouraged young women from nearby towns to enter
the competition as a way to increase out-of-town ticket sales
(*Pendleton East Oregonian*, June 1, 1910).

days later her name disappeared from the list of competitors.[28]
Later that summer, when the Round-Up directors scheduled a
queen contest—again with ticket sales to determine the winner—things turned out differently. This time, backed by her
employer, the People's Warehouse, Anger won.

A young woman living in a rural western town, Anger challenged the assumption that the New Women phenomenon remained a urban experience. Her "out-and-about" attitude is a fine example of a late-nineteenth- and early-twentieth-century young woman, whose "salient traits [were] boldness and radiant vigor."[29] The same cultural shift that allowed shop girls and cowgirl athletes to operate outside the restrictive parameters of late Victorian gender assumptions also helped young women like Anger to expand their opportunities. Moving beyond roles that promoted passivity, self-sacrifice, and gender separation, young women pursued their own interests, interacted in broader social circles, and began to enter the workforce.[30] The income these women earned allowed them to negotiate freedoms with their families and to participate in activities and amusements that would have been unthinkable a generation earlier. In larger urban areas, entertainment might include evenings or weekends at amusement parks.[31] In Pendleton young women who found employment as clerks could engage in goddess or queen contests.

As a Pendleton Round-Up queen, Anger stands as a bit of an anomaly—she was the only queen to win her title through ticket sales. This, combined with the fact that there is no mention of her as the first queen until six years later, led to a contentious discussion over whether or not she was, indeed, the first queen. A reporter covering the "first queen" controversy years later speculated that the directors waited until a final tally for all the tickets before awarding the title.[32] But the question remained: Did selling tickets qualify Anger as the first queen, or was she just a crackerjack ticket seller? The question sheds light on later perceptions of the queen contest. First was the assumption that every queen had to be selected by the Round-Up board. The question over the validity of "winning" a title also shows a misunderstanding of the primary function of a good queen, which was, and still is, promoting the rodeo. Whether a cowgirl rodeo star or a latter-day community-sponsored rodeo queen, the queen's main role is to promote her rodeo, which all boils down to selling tickets. As the idea of having community-based rodeo queens gained popularity across the West, ticket-selling competitions became a popular method to determine who would serve as queen.

The controversy over Anger's position as the first Round-Up queen relates to her and her family's position in Pendleton. Specifically, it raises the question of whether it was too risky to use ticket sales as the criteria for selecting a queen to represent the community. Anger did not have a long history in Pendleton, and her family was not counted among area merchants, ranchers, or community leaders. Although she must have been an acceptable candidate for the position—after all, her employer backed her bid for the title by selling tickets for her—there may have been concern that not everyone who entered the queen competition would be so worthy. With so little time to prepare for the show the first year, it is likely the directors simply used the same method they had always used to select the goddess of liberty. By the next year, however, new criteria were in place and the Round-Up directors appointed the queen based on the young woman's family position and ties to the Round-Up.

Anger was not the only queen to reign in relative anonymity. In the early years of the Round-Up, the queens were not nearly as important as the bucking horses, who were advertised months in advance of the show, and the cowboys who attempted to ride them, the cowgirls who thrilled the crowds, or the Indians who raced horses and displayed regalia. What did the rodeo queens do? Not much. In all honesty, a queen's publicity was equivalent to her importance and participation in the Round-Up. The names of the queens were announced only days before the rodeo began and their role was to adorn a float. Unlike other town rodeos, which opened the festivities with a parade, the Westward Ho! parade was held on the last day of the Round-Up, further inhibiting the queen's visibility.

4. 1911 Round-Up queen Laura McKee and her princesses, posed on horseback in front of the special trains that brought visitors to Pendleton from all over the Inland Empire. Photo courtesy of the Pendleton Cowgirl Company, Inc. All rights reserved.

The Pendleton Round-Up's second queen, Laura McKee, did make the papers. An article describing the Westward Ho! parade reported, "Other floats throughout the course of the parade were the 'Queen of the Round-Up.' Miss Laura McKee, surrounded by her maids, Misses Genevieve Clark, Iva Hill, Norma Alloway, and Muriel Saling."[33] This was the second and final year for a Round-Up court. Between 1912 and 1917 a queen alone presided over the events.

The newspaper coverage for the 1912 Round-Up queen did not increase much. The headlines for the September 28 *Pendleton East Oregonian* announced, "Second Day Round-Up Feats Entrance 25,000 Spectators," "Cowboys and Cowgirls Make Reckless Bids for Death," and "Increased Attendance, More Lively Show." Two small references to the queen appeared, both buried in the coverage of the Westward Ho! parade. The

SHOW THEM THE GLAD HAND NOT THE BIG MITT

MISS PENDLETON

WELCOME!

5. This cartoon was the first image of a Round-Up queen published in the *Pendleton East Oregonian*, September 10, 1913.

evening edition of the paper reported, "A beautiful float bearing Miss Muriel Saling, queen of the Round-Up, was greeted with enthusiastic cheers, as was the Cowboy Band, which followed it."[34] It was not until 1913 that an image of the Pendleton queen made an appearance in the *Pendleton East Oregonian*. Although the paper carried numerous photos of cowboy and cowgirl athletes, the queen—Gladys McDonald—was depicted in the form of a cartoon showing a pretty young woman, kerchief at her neck, holding a lariat in her gloved hand. Her hat bore the title "Miss Pendleton." According to Searcey, McDonald "could ride like the wind," and she set a precedent by actually riding her horse in the Westward Ho! parade rather than standing on a float. But nowhere in the newspapers, not with the cartoon image nor with the description of the parade, is McDonald's name mentioned as Round-Up queen.

In 1914 the *Pendleton East Oregonian* carried a noticeable increase in the number of photographs, especially before the outbreak of World War I. As the annual Round-Up date grew closer, more and more photographs appeared of the cowboys and cowgirls who would perform in the rodeo. The 1914 Round-Up queen, Lula Matlock, did not experience quite the same anonymity as her predecessors. One of the reports described her role in a booster delegation that traveled to Spokane, Washington, to advertise the show. The *Pendleton East Oregonian* reported that as the delegation "paraded through the streets, their official *mascot*, Miss Lula Matlock, was one of the notable hits" (emphasis added).[35] Although Round-Up queens would not travel to promote the rodeo again until later in the 1920s, Matlock's inclusion with the traveling delegation set an important precedent for future community rodeo queens.

In 1915 the Round-Up queen began to draw more attention. That year the *Pendleton East Oregonian*, featured Doris Reber on the front page, identifying her as "Queen of the Round-Up."[36] The reporter described the float on which she rode as "a huge replica of the first prize saddle, perfectly designed, perfectly stamped and adorned, and forming a fitting throne for the sovereign of the great frontier festival."[37] To this point Round-Up queens had been mere appendages of the celebration. Selected a few days or, at most, a week or so before the celebration, they played a minimal part in the Round-Up, primarily waving to the crowds during the parade on the last day of the show. Then in 1916 Muriel Saling made a return to queen status, four years after her previous crowning, and threw the nicely constructed pattern completely askance. Saling was awarded her title well before any previous queen, her picture appeared in the paper three times, and a special coronation ceremony was added to the Westward Ho! parade in her honor.

A full month before the 1916 Round-Up a large photo of Saling, accompanied by a lengthy article, appeared on the front page of the *Pendleton East Oregonian*. The paper reported that Saling had reigned as queen of the Portland Rose Festival and the Columbia Highway Festival earlier in the year and that she had just been named queen of the Astoria, Oregon, Regatta. One of Pendleton's own daughters, the *Pendleton East Oregonian* boasted, would have the "unprecedented distinction of reigning over the three largest municipal festivals of the state this year."[38] There was no question who would reign over the Round-Up that year: The directors immediately named Saling to that position and arranged for her to receive both the Regatta and the Round-Up crowns at the same time. A few days later, the *Pendleton East Oregonian* carried a photo of Saling at the Regatta coronation, swathed in an extravagant white dress and wearing an impressively large crown. Her celebrity continued during the Pendleton Round-Up, and the paper devoted two half-page articles, as well as numerous smaller ones, to her reign. The paper also announced that because of her unusual rank as queen, a special coronation event would be added to the Westward Ho! parade. No queen had ever had received so much attention.

The attention Saling received did not reflect changing attitudes toward the queen's role, at least not permanently. Rather, the attention was generally considered "a natural consequence of her other regal honors."[39] Members of the Astoria commercial organization contacted Pendleton boosters as soon as she had been elected, writing that having Saling represent their Regatta would "strengthen the bonds between the Inland Empire and Astoria. It was also suggested that such an arrangement

6. Muriel Saling, who reigned as queen of the Pendleton Round-Up in 1912 and 1916, shown atop a huge saddle in the 1916 Westward Ho! parade. Courtesy of Howdyshell Photography, Pendleton, Oregon.

would serve to exploit the Round-Up."[40] In true boosterism spirit, Round-Up directors used Saling's celebrity status and publicity from the Astoria Regatta as a vehicle to promote their own celebration.

From all accounts, the town was extraordinarily proud of

their queen, and they described her virtues with the enthusiastic rhetoric typical of the day:

> Shakespeare in making his historic observation about "the head that wears a crown" took cognizance only of those European kings and queens whose right to rule rests upon the fact that their father or mother ruled before them. Had he lived to note the institution of queenship in America, *he might have modified his poetic utterances to the extent of including those sovereigns who are enthroned by popular choice to symbolize the spirit of an occasion.* . . . *With no claim to royal lineage,* she [Muriel Saling] has nevertheless in this democratic commonwealth of Oregon been crowned four times within the past year . . . can any other Oregon girl claim such a manifold right to the title of queen?[41] [emphasis added]

American queens *were* different from European royalty. They reigned, as the article makes clear, for a specific occasion, and the selection of the queen depended on the type of celebration she represented. But the article ignored the promotional aspect of the queen's role completely. Portland opened up the queen's competition to women from outside their city that year, and following standard democratic practice, the title would be awarded to the young woman who sold the most tickets. Saling's crown was secured less by popular choice than by some very shrewd ticket-buying strategies among Pendleton's town leaders. The selection process was only truly democratic if one sidesteps the commitment to a true meritocracy and acknowledges the capitalist influence of buying power—crowns included.

The article also sidestepped the fact that there was indeed a lineage to Saling's queenship, one based on her family's history and standing in Pendleton. This lineage was reported in 1917, along with the history of some of the other former queens. Laura McKee, for example, married a popular Round-Up performer, "one of the best bucking broncho riders in the country. . . . Queen Gladys of the fourth Round-Up . . . pretty daughter of a well-known stockman . . . bec[a]me the bride of Richard Thompson, brother of the husband of Queen Laura, and another prominent arena assistant of the Round-Up. . . . Miss Lulu Matlock is a granddaughter of former Mayor Matlock, one of the best known pioneers of eastern Oregon."[42]

In reality, the Round-Up created its own dynasty. This is in large part the most important reason for the controversy over whether Bertha Anger or Laura McKee served as the first queen. Anger's family was not from Pendleton, and she left the community shortly after her reign, while McKee married a Thompson (the Thompsons, one of the oldest families in town, had been active in the creation of the Round-Up).

When Lula Matlock was named queen of the Round-Up for a second time in 1917, press coverage reverted back to its pre-Saling levels. A photo of Matlock, appropriately attired in cowgirl regalia, announced her selection as queen three days before the Round-Up festivities began. But Queen Lula's reign in 1917 signaled the end of Pendleton's first go-round with rodeo royalty. The terse announcement in the paper read, "The Pendleton Round-Up Board has gone on record as being opposed to royalty and this year the big show will be conducted as an institution of the common people. This will be the first time the Round-Up has been without its queen."[43] Even a year earlier there was an indication that all was not well with the royal institution when the paper noted, "There will be a queen of the 1917 Round-Up, all statements to the contrary notwithstanding."[44] These were the World War I years; the paper was filled with reports of the war in Europe and anti-German slogans. It is possible that the decision to cancel the Round-Up queen position and the reference to the "institution of the people" were in protest to the role of the European aristocracy during the war. If so, what better way for Pendleton residents to show support for their republican system of government than to oust any semblance of aristocracy from that most "American" sport—rodeo.[45]

The repudiation of Round-Up aristocracy, however, most likely had its roots in circumstances closer to home. There were still numerous positive human interest stories on European royalty. In fact, immediately above the announcement of the discontinuation of Pendleton royalty was a rather exuberant article on a countess coming to watch the rodeo.[46] If there was discontent with Round-Up royalty among the 1917 directors, the sudden resignation of one of the old directors and the replacement with a new director most likely played a role. It would have been out of character for the directors to argue publicly over whether or not to keep the role of queen. When they reached their decision they released a simple statement to the paper: They ceased to support the role of a Round-Up queen, and that was it.

In his semi-fictionalized account of the 1911 Round-Up, *Last Go-Round*, Ken Kesey provides a clue as to why queens were eliminated from the celebration. He described one of the Round-Up princesses as "the pampered daughter of a small-town merchant."[47] Kesey's novel is too fictionalized to use for evidence; he also wrote that royalty was won by a popularity contest and that Prairie Rose Henderson was queen of the Round-Up, both untrue. His insight, however, seems to hit the mark. Enthrallment with European royals aside, it appears that the creation of a royal elite from daughters of powerful local families had grown a bit much for the town. In the eight years that the Round-Up had been in existence, the honor of reigning as queen or princess had revolved around an elite group of young women.[48] It would appear that the argument was not over foreign royalty but rather over "aristocracy" of the local sort. If queens were selected according to the type of celebration they represented, why celebrate a pampered local girl as a representative of Pendleton's frontier past? The lack of a queen "will be no appreciable loss," the article continued, "as there will be any number of candidates to prove themselves entitled to proclaiming themselves queen of relay riders, bucking bronchos, or other stunts that come in the life of the range."[49]

The Pendleton Round-Up, its origins based in community traditions, gradually evolved gradually from a small, local affair into one of the largest frontier days rodeo celebrations in the country. Within the context of the celebration, Round-Up queens evolved too. Pendleton applied the concept of festival queen or goddess to the sport of rodeo for the first time; Anger and the other young women were experimental figures in the early phenomenon of rodeo queens. These young women had no real connection to rodeo; their part, much like that of the goddess of liberty, was to wave from a parade float. Selected by town leaders, they imitated the itinerant cowgirl athlete and reigned over a constructed frontier celebration.

Between 1910 and 1917 Round-Up queens were, for all practical purposes, dispensable. A rodeo without cowboys and cowgirls would have been unthinkable, but a queen? One could easily do away with the queen role, so the directors did. From 1918 to 1920 there were no queens at the Round-Up, whether community sponsored or cowgirl athletes.

The idea of rodeo royalty did not disappear, though. As suddenly as they vanished, and with as little explanation, Pendleton rodeo queens reappeared in 1921. When they did make a return, their role became much more visible. The success of Pendleton's queens in promoting rodeo caught the attention of rodeo directors throughout the West and became the model for other communities who wanted to establish a rodeo queen role for themselves.

2. "Who Will Reign as Queen?"

*Community Queens Return to the Pendleton
Round-Up, 1921–1929*

When the Pendleton Round-Up abruptly eliminated royalty in 1918, the explanation given was that a queen's role seemed anathema for that "institution of the people," the rodeo.[1] Cowgirl riders, so able to compete for that title in the arena, made artificially chosen queens unnecessary. Yet three years later, in 1921, the rodeo queen figure inexplicably reappeared, and the *Pendleton East Oregonian* reported, "Who will reign as queen of Let 'Er Buck City during Round-Up is question confronting association members."[2] The queen came back and so too, for the first time since 1911, did the royal princesses to attend her.

At first glance it would appear that rodeo queens in the 1921 to 1929 era fulfilled a role similar to that of their predecessors, one in which the rodeo queen and cowgirl athlete operated in dynamic opposition to one another. In other words, the more important the cowgirl athletes were to the success of the rodeo, the less important the queen's role, and vice versa. This concept of dynamic opposition illustrated the two options for women—one based on traditionalist behaviors, the other on modernist views. Indeed, the dates that bracket this era reflect an unspoken contest over who would rule the Round-Up. The contest to determine who would represent western womanhood, played out in the rodeo arena, represented a microcosm for the larger cultural debate over the role of women in America. As noted earlier, in 1921 community-sponsored rodeo queens returned to the Round-Up, while 1929 marks the last year cowgirl athletes were allowed to ride rough-stock in open competition in Pendleton. Despite the occasionally "brilliant" stars who reigned as queen between 1921 and 1929, the role of community-sponsored queen could only develop fully when rodeo policy changed after the 1929 rodeo, gradually excluding cowgirl athletes from all competition in the rodeo arena.

The question of whom to choose as queen that confronted Round-Up directors makes the history of Pendleton queens difficult to analyze—there was no standard format for determining whom the directors would pick next. The concept of rodeo queen was well defined: The young lady selected to represent Pendleton would have some connection to the town, no matter how tenuous; she would welcome important visitors; and she would exhibit the manners and mores associated with respectable middle-class citizens. Within these general parameters, however, the directors experimented with a number of different examples of queens—movie stars, an Indian woman, a cowgirl athlete, and young women from the community—and some of these queens received far more attention than the cowgirl athletes.

The difficulty in settling on a queen suggests that this was a transitional era in rodeo queen history. The directors experimented with how best to use the queen's position to advertise the Round-Up, as part of a move to professionalize Round-Up booster techniques. As the Round-Up promotional efforts became more sophisticated, queens were included in these promotional strategies in a more organized and pointed fashion. This elevated them from their original relatively minor role as a parade queen to a position of prominence in the Round-Up.

The 1920s also witnessed a significant transition in attitudes toward liberated New Women. In the late 1910s and into the mid-1920s, newspapers like Pendleton's *East Oregonian* voiced both excitement and concern over women's increasingly visible roles. By the mid-1920s the discourse of gender, which in the newspapers appeared as a verbal tug-of-war over women's place in American society, shifted from supporting new roles for women to a return to the more traditional views on a woman's place. This included a dramatic change in the discourse on the cowgirl athletes who boldly played out the challenges to normative female expectations in rodeo arenas. The juxtaposition of queen and cowgirl athletes in the local paper became a vehicle for exploring the discourse of gender in the 1920s. As cowgirl athletes became less acceptable, the community-sponsored rodeo queen, who represented traditional views of feminine behavior, began to rise in prominence. Despite the inconsistency of who was selected to "rule the Round-Up," rodeo queens became a more prominent and important figure in terms of promoting the rodeo.

Who, indeed, would reign as queen of the 1921 Round-Up? After the initial question appeared in the *Pendleton East Oregonian*, residents were kept in suspense for nearly a month. On September 22, the first day of the Round-Up, residents learned that "Queen Helen of the Round-Up and her maids" would reign over the show. The text accompanying the full-length photo of Helen Thompson in her cowgirl costume reported, "Miss Helen Thompson, who Buckaroos of Eastern Oregon say is 'some rider . . . ' is not only that, but she is a noted rifle shot, recently winning the shoot at the Washington State University in competition with all other entrants, men as well as women."[3] This description emphasizes Thompson's frontier skills, her shooting and riding abilities. The designation as "some rider," like that of one who admits to being able to "ride some" was (and still is) code for real riding skill.[4] There is an old saying that to be a real cowhand one has to be able to rope, ride, shoot, and spit—and to do these things well. Assuming the last requirement did not apply to ladies, Queen Helen was on her way to real cowhand status. The image of Thompson showed her in traditional cowgirl dress, with a fringed skirt, embroidered vest, and hat. With her hands on her hips and a stern expression, she looked like a rough rider, ready to step into action, not some hot-house noble. Here, indeed, was one of the rodeo crowd. Well, sort of.

While the emphasis on both written and visual descriptions of Queen Helen portrayed her as someone who was not above the masses, she was not exactly one of the rodeo crew either. The glowing account of her shooting ability included the fact that she was a co-ed at Washington State University. Her name alone would have been recognized by anyone in town as a member of one of the two founding families of Pendleton. The community enjoyed watching this member of the elite's moment of fame; by accepting the position, she acknowledged the attention. Susan A. Glenn writes that respectable middle-class women often took pleasure in observing the spectacle of New Women performing in the public sphere, relishing "the pleasures and dangers of those often daring female performers from a safe distance across the footlights and still maintaining their own pretense to respectability."[5] In the case of community-sponsored rodeo queens, they could enjoy watching the cowgirl athletes from a safe distance—on the other side of the arena fence. The queen could get down off the parade float and up into the saddle to "play cowgirl" in a genteel, refined fashion. This modification of masculine cowgirl characteristics allowed the rodeo queen to meet the expectations of a western woman's abilities yet remain within normative constructs of gender.

Under the photo of Queen Helen were studio portraits of her "maids." As had been the tradition since the first community-sponsored queens, the young women lived in or near Pendleton, but this was the first time princesses had their photos in the paper. Like Thompson, all the princesses were wearing large cowboy hats. The Round-Up directors clearly looked to the cowgirl athletes of the day to set the standard for royal outfits: "Queen and maids," the *Pendleton East Oregonian* announced, "will wear cowgirl costumes."[6]

The paper's description included a subtle but important distinction in language: Cowgirls wore "regalia," a style of clothing that indicated membership within a particular group. The queen and her court did not wear regalia. Rather, they wore "costumes" in imitation of the distinctive attire of professional performers. Queen Helen and her maids would not ride broncs or bulldog steers, but, dressed like cowgirls, they would ride at the head of parades. Thompson, wearing a black hat and astride a white horse, would be surrounded by her princesses wearing white hats and riding black horses. They would make a stunning display, safely within the parameters of traditional feminine behavior.

Aside from their style of dress, cowgirl athletes influenced the court in other areas as well. During the early years of rodeo royalty it was not only the queen's position that was in a state of transition but the court's as well. This is seen in the description of court members—indiscriminately alternating between "maid" and "princess"—and the composition of the court. For example, a married woman, Mrs. Leslie Gibbs, served as one of Queen Helen's "maids." The choice of a married woman to attend the queen likely reflected the reality of married cowgirl athletes, especially those like Mabel Strickland, Bertha Blancett (who first rode to fame as Bertha Kaepernick), and Tad Lucas, who received a great deal of attention from the Pendleton press during the Round-Up. In terms of re-negotiating gender roles, married cowgirl athletes put themselves on display—participated in female spectacle—and yet maintained, to use Glenn's words, "virtues associated with true or traditional femininity."[7] Gibbs, a young, upper-class married woman from a small, conservative town, could dress in cowgirl costume and imitate the professional athletes for a few days without risk to her reputation.

In August of 1921, when the Round-Up directors announced the return of royalty by asking "Who will reign as queen?" they set the question to the town a full month before the start of the celebration. Round-Up directors had begun planning for the queen further in advance than ever before. This did not translate into using the queen's position to advertise the Round-Up in advance of the show—not yet at least. Thompson was not introduced as queen until the first day of the Round-Up.

In 1921, the same year that the queen and court reappeared, the Round-Up board hired Arthur Rudd as a professional booster. Rudd began new promotions to enhance boosterism efforts and, hopefully, the success of the celebration. Under Rudd's watch, the queen's role in promoting the Round-Up increased. Prior to hiring Rudd, the Round-Up booster season typically began immediately after the Fourth of July, whether Pendleton held a patriotic celebration or not. Sometime toward the end of July articles would begin to appear in the *Pendleton East Oregonian* to keep the Round-Up foremost in the town's mind. Articles might describe new bucking horses purchased for the rodeo or top riders who had agreed to participate in the Round-Up. Usually in August booster caravans would head out to the larger urban areas, such as Portland, Oregon, or cities in Washington State, such as Walla Walla or Spokane. The informal and often impromptu caravans were great fun but perhaps not the most effective method of promoting the Round-Up.

In 1921 Arthur Rudd devised a "Let 'Er Buck" campaign,

which "extended over 10 weeks time and hundreds of miles of territory, including Denver, Salt Lake, Ogden, Pocatello, Weiser, Baker, La Grande, Walla Walla, [and] The Dalles."[8] Rudd's professional and systematic approach to advertising the Round-Up paid off. On June 5, 1922, the *Pendleton East Oregonian* reported that requests for information on the 1922 frontier days celebration were already coming in, much earlier than usual.[9] The day after that announcement in the paper, the *Pendleton East Oregonian* ran a photo of a champion cowgirl trick rider who had previously performed at the Round-Up to reinforce the early interest in the upcoming celebration. Photos of cowgirl riders, along with blurbs on cowboys and famous bucking horses, updated Pendleton residents on the upcoming event. In the early 1920s cowgirl athletes figured prominently as a promotional strategy, while community-sponsored rodeo queens did not. Rudd began a serious analysis of successful promotional strategies, considering new methods and new "stars" to advertise the town's celebration, which opened the door to consider the queen's position as an innovative way to promote the Round-Up.

When Thelma Thompson was announced as the 1922 Round-Up queen, the notice in the paper came a full month before the show—earlier than past queens, although it appeared almost two months after the first advertisement for a cowgirl athlete.[10] A studio portrait of Thompson, wearing the requisite ten-gallon hat, accompanied the following article, which reported on the queen's qualifications:

> [The daughter of] Mr. and Mrs. William Blakeley, Umatilla county pioneer, has been chosen as queen of the 1922 Round-Up. Miss Thompson will ride at the Round-Up each day and will ride in the Westward Ho! parade. Miss Thompson is a young lady of much charm and manner and is an expert horsewoman. She is a graduate of the University of Washington. Her father is one of

the Round-Up directors and her grandfather was formerly sheriff of Umatilla county. She is a cousin of Miss Helen Thompson, last year's queen.[11]

This brief article contains a wealth of information on the evolution of the queen's position and an indication of her expanding role. Previously, the queens had only been involved in the Westward Ho! parade. But as this article makes clear, in 1922 the queen and her court became involved with the rodeo itself. When Queen Thelma and her court walked their horses into the arena, they began one of the most important rodeo queen traditions: riding into the rodeo arena at the beginning of each rodeo performance and being introduced to the rodeo spectators as the reigning monarch of the show.

The text also describes Thompson as someone who embodied middle-class attributes, noting she was "a young lady of much charm and manner" and that she was a college graduate. A great deal of attention is given to her family's position and history in town, which not only serves to justify the board's choice of queen but also, in effect, publicly establishes the standards for future queens. With few exceptions, the board would expect their queen and court to come from long-established, elite families with strong ties to the Round-Up.[12] Thompson's place in the royal lineage is also mentioned—her cousin Helen was the 1921 queen.

The article closed by reporting, "Miss Thompson's maids will be four in number and will be selected within the next few days." As mentioned earlier, the size of the queen's courts varied considerably and so did the amount of press coverage the court received. Adeline Scroggins, from La Grande, Oregon, was the only princess to have a photo and a brief article in the paper. Scroggins, "chosen by the Pendleton Round-Up Association as a representative of her city," was described as "entirely at home in the saddle" and "a University of Oregon girl," which established her qualifications for the position.[13] Scroggins's appointment to the court had several important implications for Pendleton rodeo royalty and for future rodeo queens. First, it set the precedent of placing a young woman from outside the town of Pendleton as part of the Round-Up boosterism strategy. Secondly, it changed the traditional selection process for court members.

In terms of booster strategy, the standard method for a town to advertise its celebrations was to advertise the "extravaganza" in other towns' newspapers. Earlier in 1922, Dayton, Washington, boosters published an article in the Pendleton paper, writing, "We've been coming to your Round-Up by the thousands for several years, and we'd like to have you come up here and help up enjoy our races and pageant." Dayton boosters felt justified in admonishing Pendletonians to visit their show: "Good horses and harness races, bucking contests and some other wild west stuff" would reward Pendleton residents for their trip to Dayton.[14] Moreover, by encouraging reciprocal celebration hopping, Dayton hoped to recoup some of its residents' money spent at the Pendleton Round-Up. Pendleton continued to advertise its Round-Up in newspapers, but by incorporating an out-of-town princess the directors gave people a reason to travel to Pendleton. It encouraged her relatives and townsfolk to travel to see "their girl" in the honored position of Round-Up royalty. Scroggins was the first in a succession of out-of-town young women invited by the directors to participate as royalty.

Despite the increase in visitors an out-of-town princess might encourage, Scroggins, like the other non-local royalty that followed, was not chosen for completely mercenary reasons. Her rise to the Round-Up court and the "new tradition" it engendered indicated that the Round-Up community was growing. Bonnie Sager, president of the Round-Up Hall of Fame, notes that the Round-Up was (and is) "such a big event and it takes so many volunteers that I think they [the directors] have always had to keep in mind the fact that we have volunteers from other ranching communities as well."[15] Beginning in 1922 the directors rewarded out-of-town families for their participation in the event by appointing their daughters to participate on the royal court.

Secondly, by taking an active role in selecting the queen's court, the Round-Up directors also changed the traditional method for selecting princesses. Up until 1922 princesses were selected by the queen, which helps explain the small number of Pendleton women who continually appeared and reappeared on the court. When the Round-Up directors entered into the selection process, they added an element of mystery as to who was really making the decisions for the court. Kathryn Furnish, a 1929 Round-Up princess, recalls that all the princesses were appointed to the court, but who made the appointment was not clear. "I don't know how I got to be princess," Furnish says. "Kathleen was queen, and I was her friend. Maybe she picked me, but I just don't know."[16] The decision of the Round-Up directors to become involved in court selection, whether selecting a princess as to reward a family for their efforts or to attract a wider audience, indicated the growing connection between boosters and community-sponsored rodeo royalty.

Just as 1922 saw changes in Pendleton's rodeo queen court, it was also a year for extraordinary changes in how women were depicted in the press. The *Pendleton East Oregonian*, subscribed to a wire service and carried stories and photos from around the nation and the world. During that year, women were given more exposure in the press than ever before. Articles featured stories on women in new professions; there were more photos and articles on women's fashion and on women in sports, business, and activities traditionally performed by men.[17]

Although the papers enthusiastically reported the new liberating fashions, not all articles were positive: clearly, the traditionalists harbored deep concerns. News stories and cartoons covered some of the disconcerting effects and trends of liberated women. The sentiment was that while it was great (well, mostly great) that women were striding into quarters traditionally occupied by men, there were likely to be repercussions. In Detroit, for example, a story about the havoc created by a pretty new clerk at a municipal tax office made national news. Men, "swarming like bees" to pay their taxes, created a huge line at the woman's desk, while the male clerks were ignored.[18] Placing a large pasteboard map in front of the lower part of her desk hid her dainty feet and ankles from view and helped even out the workload among the clerks, but the experience demonstrated the disruptive potential of a pretty woman in the workplace.

When describing New Women in the press, "exposure in the press" truly became a key phrase. Previously unseen parts of the female anatomy, and not just dainty ankles, suddenly cropped up everywhere. There was both titillation and concern over the amount of heretofore prohibited views of female parts. What had started out in the immediate postwar years, rather innocently, as photographing women athletes in the new sport of competitive swimming, threatened to get completely out of control. During the summer of 1922 the *Pendleton East Oregonian* ran wire photos of women in bathing suits on beaches, in beauty contests, and even on horseback—a very untraditional riding outfit, worn by a wealthy socialite galloping along a Washington DC bridle path.[19] The taboo of showing women in bathing suits had been breached, and in the early 1920s any excuse to show a woman in a bathing suit seemed to be a good one. As Angela J. Latham notes, "No particular fashion aroused more anxiety and strife than did swimwear," and New Women, flouting traditional ideas of modesty by showing off their limbs in public and the press, seemed to many "a visual synopsis of all that was morally wrong with American women."[20]

Considering the ambiguity over the status of the New Woman, it is remarkable that cowgirl athletes were treated as positively as they were in the press. These women had definitely invaded traditionally male territory. Yet, not only were they celebrated in the newspapers but the language in the press specifically connected the positive attributes of cowgirl athletes to community-sponsored rodeo queens, and vice versa. Readers were told how the queens embodied true cowgirl characteristics, just as they were told how womanly and feminine the cowgirl athletes were.

Newspaper stories did stress the femininity and middle-class attributes of the cowgirl athletes like world champion trick rider Bonnie Gray. The *Pendleton East Oregonian* reported that "Bonnie Gray is a graduate of the University of Idaho and a postgraduate of the University of Chicago, but she didn't learn the above trick at either school. She won the women's championship of the world for trick riding at the Pike's Peak rodeo."[21] Perhaps this was an effort to recognize a stratification of propriety among the New Women. Some behaviors represented direct challenges to traditionalist understanding of womanly behavior—women theater performers, women boxers, women who displayed too much of their bodies—and some behaviors were less threatening. The description of cowgirl athletes suggests that while they were definitely involved in a masculine realm, they had not lost their femininity. Their masculine ways were based on real and necessary activities grounded in the western tradition, where it was a matter of survival for women to step outside gendered boundaries and perform necessary tasks. Moreover, cowgirl athletes did marry, have children, and dress in a feminine manner. The inclusion of cowgirl athletes into the ranks of the middle class indicates that the term "middle class" itself was less monolithic than commonly supposed and was open to local interpretation.[22]

In 1923 Jessie Drumheller was selected as the Round-Up

queen. Earlier that year a new trend appeared in newspapers, in which a large photo of a woman was featured on the front page. In fact, everywhere women were on display, and remarkably more so than just a year earlier. But the Round-Up queen and her court were not on display; she received significantly less attention than the preceding two royals.

Drumheller's name did not appear in the paper until she selected her court. Even then, the headline for the article announcing her court sidestepped the queen altogether when it revealed, "Thelma Thompson Chosen to Attend Round-Up Queen."[23] The two princesses—the perennial royal Thelma Thompson and Elizabeth Hailey of Portland—are mentioned in the paper before the queen. While the ebb and flow of rodeo queen publicity is nothing new, during the entire three days of the Pendleton Round-Up only one brief line appeared to describe the queen and her court's appearance in the Westward Ho! parade.

What makes the lack of attention for Jessie Drumheller so noteworthy, considering the contemporary newspaper discourse of gender, is the amount of attention given to other women vying for titles, and not just rodeo titles, although more information appeared on the cowgirl athletes—background, family, and reason for their entrance into their careers—than on the queen and her court in the paper. The number and diversity of contests reported in the newspapers all across the country is absolutely staggering: coiffure contests, hat contests, contests for the most beautiful girl in a state or the most beautiful girl of her type, even a "50 contest"—a bathing beauty contest for Rubenesque women with waistlines larger than fifty inches. There were contests for specific body parts too: sweetest smile, loveliest back, prettiest arms. It would appear that once the barrier that prohibited women from venturing into the public sphere was breached, there was no keeping them, or their various parts, out of the limelight.

The Round-Up queens remained relatively anonymous because the title was not based on a contest. It remained an appointed position and as such did not involve the problematic requirements of competing in public for the position. The queen and her court were not professional or even amateur performers. They were private women elevated into the limelight for a few days to perform the civic duty of promoting their town. As non-public women, their private lives were kept just that—private. Whether or not the queens wanted the position or lobbied behind the scenes to get an appointment for themselves or a friend is another story.

As the 1924 Round-Up season approached, the directors were again facing the question of who to chose as queen. So far the directors had not been overly innovative when it came to the task of appointing a queen. Since 1921 there had been three queens and queen's courts, and although there had been two non-Pendletonian princesses, the growing tendency toward an inbred Round-Up dynasty seemed to threaten local interest once again. But a radical shift in the royal lineage occurred in 1924 when the directors selected an actress, Josephine (Josie) Sedgwick, to be queen of the Round-Up.

One of Pendleton's first all-around cowboys, Hoot Gibson, came back to Pendleton to shoot his silent movie *Let 'Er Buck* accompanied by Sedgwick, the leading lady in the film.[24] Gibson was a hero in the town, and by shooting a film about the Round-Up, he was helping put Pendleton in the national spotlight once again. Perhaps the Round-Up directors considered it a logical step to place a member of Gibson's "family" on the court. This time, though, the directors selected Sedgwick, the out-of-towner, to reign as the queen, not as a princess. They saw an opportunity to add glamour to the rodeo, invigorate the queen's position, and gain nationwide attention for the show. And their decision paid off. The news of Josie Sedgwick as rodeo queen hit the national wires, and stories about this film star–turned-queen were reported from California to New York and as far north as Anchorage, Alaska.[25]

Not only did Josie Sedgwick find herself in the papers more often than past queens, she also brought a bit of notoriety to the position. Glenn writes that women in theater lived outside normative parameters; the public rather expected actresses to exhibit outrageous behaviors.[26] Sedgwick's choice of court members, if not outrageous, was certainly shocking. Papers around the country ran the news that "Miss Josie Sedgwick, queen of the Pendleton Round-Up, broke with the precedent of years when she selected two husky cowpunchers for personal attendants instead of the customary maids of honor."[27] It was a daring move for this queen to select men for her court, even though the "cowpunchers," had competed at the Round-Up and belonged to Gibson's motion picture "family." But this sort of reckless flouting of royal tradition would have been unthinkable for a young woman from Pendleton. The enormous amount of publicity generated by Sedgwick in 1924 marks a watershed year for rodeo queens. From this point on, rodeo queens, famous or not, would have a more visible role in promoting the Pendleton Round-Up.

A real breakthrough in the position of rodeo queens occurred the next year, with the 1925 reign of Mildred Rogers. The reign of "Queen Mildred I" marks the first time a sort of symmetry existed in the amount and kind of press coverage cowgirl athletes and rodeo queens received. Both royalty and athletes garnered attention in the press. It seemed entirely possible that the two could happily coexist, but 1925 was, in fact, the first real firm footing for community-sponsored rodeo queens and also the final hurrah for unqualified acceptance of the cowgirl athletes in the press.

The year 1925 marks the first time a queen made an appearance in the paper before any cowgirl athletes and indicates an important change had occurred. The *Pendleton East Orego-*

nian also honored Rogers with three front-page articles and, shortly before the Round-Up began, with a large portrait of "Queen Mildred I of the Round-Up" dressed in her cowgirl costume.[28] The first article was careful to announce Rogers's pioneer pedigree, noting she was "a native daughter of Umatilla county and whose grandparents crossed the plains over the Old Oregon Trail" and that "Miss Rogers, who is the daughter of Mr. and Mrs. L. L. Rogers, prominent Pendleton residents, is the great granddaughter of the late Nicholas DuPuis, who in early days was a Hudson Bay company scout and who guided emigrants across the plains."[29]

Having settled the issue of her pioneer lineage, the papers went on to describe Rogers's personal attributes. The *Pendleton East Oregonian* reported, "She is an accomplished horsewoman, and at Oregon Agricultural College, from which college she was graduated this year, she was in charge of the woman's division of the military tournament this year. In addition to her skill as an equestrienne, Miss Rogers is a fine swimmer and at O.A.C. held the championship for the long dive. She was active in college activities and most popular on the campus."[30] Rogers was the offspring of a pioneer family who had succeeded. From their inauspicious origins in America as a scout to one of the leading families in the county, the Rogerses, and by extension their daughter, exemplified the pioneer dream of working their way up the social ladder.

The second article on Rogers announced the selection of her court: "Miss Agnes McMurray, of Portland . . . *and Miss Doris Churchill, queen of the Ellensburg fair this year*, have been chosen as attendants for Miss Mildred Rogers, queen of the Round-Up. They are in addition to Miss Mary Clarke and Miss Catherine McNary, Pendleton girls who are attendants. . . . *Miss Rogers with Miss Clarke and Miss McNary donned cowgirl costumes yesterday and rode in the parade at the Spokane Fair.* They were introduced as the Round-Up queen and

attendants and were well received" (emphasis added).[31] Queen
Mildred and her court started a new tradition when they rode
in the Spokane Fair. In 1914 Round-Up queen Lula Matlock
had accompanied a booster caravan to Spokane, but she had
no specific role and was introduced as a "mascot" rather than
as the queen.[32]

In 1922 a photo of a bobbed-haired young woman made the
front page of the *Pendleton East Oregonian*. Under the headline "Bears Bid to President," the caption explained that the
lovely young woman, Mary Harrington, had been "picked as
a representative of Western womanhood to travel 3,000 miles
to Washington D.C. to invite President Harding to the Reno
Round-Up. She presented the president the executive with a 10
gallon hat."[33] It is quite likely Arthur Rudd or another Pendleton booster saw this story and recognized the merit of sending
a lovely young lady out of town as a representative to advertise their Round-Up celebration. The idea to send queens out
of town to generate interest in the rodeo was a strategy that
worked well and a good example of the kind of idea-borrow-
ing common among rodeo producers.

The article on court selection also mentioned that Princess
Doris Churchill was queen of the Ellensburg Fair. Out-of-town
court members may have served as queens in their own hometowns; however, this is the first instance of highlighting that
fact about a court member. The emphasis on a princess's previous royal status signaled the beginning of the "visiting royalty"
phenomenon. In rodeos throughout the West, traveling to other
rodeos to promote her own would become one of a community-sponsored rodeo queen's most demanding responsibilities.
During the opening of the rodeo, the presentation and introduction of royalty—both hometown and visiting—became an
integral part of the rodeo performance.

Queen Mildred's and her court's involvement in the rodeo,
limited as it was, foreshadowed the gentrification of the cowgirl

athlete. Boosters encouraged community rodeo queens to have a larger presence in the rodeo arena at roughly the same time that cowgirl athletes started to become less acceptable. While an equilibrium between cowgirl athletes and community-sponsored rodeo queens existed in 1925, each doing well within their own sphere, the scales begin to swing toward the gradual exclusion of the cowgirl athlete from competitive activity in the arena. The community-sponsored rodeo queen rose to prominence as the genteel version of a cowgirl athlete.

In 1925 all still seemed well for the cowgirl competitors. The *Pendleton East Oregonian* souvenir edition featured the women riders in a full-page spread under the headline "Prowess of Girls Shown in He-Man Sport of Rodeo: Mabel Strickland, Fox Hastings, Lorena Trickey, and a Host of Young Women Real Athletes." The first paragraph of the article was particularly flattering, reporting that "the American woman who proves herself to be adept in cowboy sports is to be found at the Pendleton Round-Up. She is an exponent of modernism and proves that the Victorian era is quite in oblivion, and that the woman of today is a true athlete."[34] But 1925 was also the first year that the *Pendleton East Oregonian* published a number of articles emphasizing a return to traditional femininity. The debate over appropriate feminine behaviors began to encourage women to return to traditional feminine ideals. That year saw the emphasis on photos and articles gradually encouraging the return to long feminine locks, highlighting famous women, especially movie stars, who decided to let their bobbed hair grow long.[35] A year earlier, in 1924, an article on cowgirl athlete Prairie Rose Henderson reported, "The curls, by the way, are bobbed, for Prairie Rose has followed the example of other cowgirls who consider long hair the opposite of chic in making up a modern cowgirl ensemble."[36] Yet only a year later, the tide had turned. The reorientation toward more conservative mores did not begin, as is commonly thought, with the

Great Depression but was already moving in that direction as early as 1925.

While newspaper discourse emphasized a connection between long hair and traditional concepts of femininity in the general population, the association of long braids with traditional Native American culture remained firmly fixed in the popular imagination. In 1924 Esther Motanic, from the Umatilla Reservation, five miles from Pendleton, competed in the American Indian Beauty Contest, held in conjunction with the Round-Up, and won the title in 1924.[37] The *Pendleton East Oregonian* reported, "For the dark-eyed maidens who are the pride of the Cayuse, Umatilla and Walla Walla tribes are getting ready for the most unique beauty contest in the world. It is not for bathing beauties of America; no indeed, it is pure blooded American beauties, and only full-blooded Indian girls may compete in the Round-Up's American Beauty contest. Girls in the contest must have long hair, too; no bobbed-haired beauties need apply."[38] It is unclear when American Indians began holding their own beauty contests, but it appears that by 1926 the Round-Up was only one of many.[39] In 1926 Motanic reigned as "Queen Esther I of the Round-Up." The *Pendleton East Oregonian* noted that "Pendleton 'started something' when it chose Esther Motanic, Indian beauty, as queen of its annual Round-Up and announced her as the loveliest Indian girl in America."[40] Motanic did not have a court. During the Round-Up Jessie Jim, "Princess America who was chosen at the national Indian Congress in Spokane, Washington," accompanied Motanic in the Westward Ho! parade.[41]

If Native American beauty contests were becoming more common, the idea for a Native American rodeo queen remained unique to Pendleton. The *Pendleton East Oregonian* announced Motanic's appointment with a large photo of her on horseback wearing traditional regalia and her horse with beaded trappings. The honor of the position, the paper noted, had gone "in years past to socially prominent, beautiful white girls, and one for which all of them assiduously seek and fervently hope."[42] When the directors selected Motanic to rule the Round-Up, they began a tradition of recognizing young Indian women from the Umatilla Reservation who met traditional middle-class norms. The *Pendleton East Oregonian* listed Motanic's qualities, proving she earned the right to wear a royal crown: "Motanic combines rare beauty with high intelligence. Well educated, a brilliant conversationalist and writer, this maid attracts attention wherever she goes. . . . She has the full confidence of her people, and of the Indian services of the government, and is doing valuable work among the Navajo in Arizona."[43]

Motanic's selection by the Round-Up board adds a new dimension to the discussion of community. The connection between Pendleton and the Umatilla tribal community was strong, and the three tribes on the Umatilla Reservation played important roles in the Round-Up since its beginning. Motanic reigned as the first of five Native American queens in Pendleton and set the precedent for later all-Indian courts.[44] In the mid-1940s and into the early 1950s, several Native American young women served on mixed-ethnic courts at other rodeos. But the Pendleton Round-Up made a distinctive contribution to the history of community-sponsored rodeo queens with the introduction of Native American royalty.[45] Until Native Americans began holding their own rodeos in the 1970s and selecting their own royalty, no other organized rodeo ever selected Native American women to serve as their queens.

Motanic's family, like many Umatilla Indians, participated in the Round-Up for many years. It was a way for the Native Americans to share in traditional cultural activities, especially those associated with ranching and horses. Horses, introduced into the area circa 1730, evolved into an important part of tribal culture. As Peter Iverson writes, "Horses symbolized the power and ambition of Native groups. . . . On horseback, Indian men performed acts of great skill and courage in hunt and in war. Even when the peoples were confined to the prisons the white people called reservations, horses remained living embodiments of better days and future possibilities."[46] In the 1890s the Umatilla Reservation was the leading livestock producing reservation in the United States. Ranching and horse herds declined after passage of the Dawes Act in 1887; however, ranching—and all the ranch hand skills required for the job—and horses remained on the reservation and an important element of their culture.[47] Although tribal members were given token compensation for participating in the Round-Up, their motivation had more to do with a forum for maintaining their own traditions. Indeed, Native American determination to participate in rodeos played an role in their efforts to resist assimilation.[48] Motanic, as the first "True American Queen," celebrated the connection between Pendleton and the Umatilla Reservation, while allowing each group to emphasize characteristics and values they shared.

The Round-Up directors' decision to create an all-Indian court indicated their willingness to expand past the traditional concept of Euro-American royalty. Yet this flash of innovative thinking did not extend to allowing cowgirl athletes to expand their range of competition. In 1926 Mabel Strickland petitioned the Round-Up board to be allowed to compete against men in the steer roping event. She had set a world record time for steer roping the previous year, and since she was one of the very few women who roped steers, she wanted to test her skills in real competition against the cowboys. Even though the *Pendleton East Oregonian* claimed in a headline, "Slender Girls Vie with Men at the World's Greatest Frontier Exhibition and Often Come Off with First Honors," women did not compete directly against men. The events—bucking broncs, bull riding, bulldogging, roping, and relay races—were separated by gen-

MABEL STRICKLAND
QUEEN OF THE
PENDLETON ROUND-UP
- 1927 -
(DOUBLEDAY)

7. Champion cowgirl athlete Mabel Strickland reigned as queen of the 1927 Pendleton Round-Up. Doubleday Photo [79–26.1790], National Cowboy and Western Heritage Museum, Oklahoma City, Oklahoma.

der.[49] Despite Strickland's petition, they declined to change the rules.[50] It was one thing for her husband, cowboy athlete Hugh Strickland, to teach his wife to rope steers and for her "to show prowess in those fields," but it was another thing to publicly embarrass the cowboys by out-competing them in the arena.[51] And so, as *The Dalles (OR) Optimist* reported, "Chivalrous Round-Up cowboys decline to compete against pretty girl who beats them."[52]

Strickland's failed petition and the changing language about cowgirls in the *Pendleton East Oregonian* suggest that cowgirl athletes were not as welcome as they were only a few years earlier, a fact that might make the 1927 queen selection seem a bit odd. But really, there was nothing odd at all in the directors' decision to have Mabel Strickland reign over the Round-Up. Strickland, called "Pendleton's Darling," garnered more press than any other performer. She was, perhaps, the most successful New Women role model of rodeo, combining traditionalist values and modernist ambitions.

Mabel Delong grew up in Walla Walla, Washington, less than forty-five miles away from Pendleton. Her father was a bootmaker, and it was through him that she was introduced to the world of rodeo. She began her rodeo career when she turned sixteen, and two years later she married Hugh Strickland, "one of the important competitors and managers in pre–World War II American rodeo."[53] Michael Allen notes that even before her marriage to Hugh, the diminutive, beautiful, and modest Mabel was a "seasoned and crowd-pleasing rodeo star."[54]

Excerpts from an interview with Strickland, published in the *Pendleton East Oregonian* during the Round-Up, highlight both the modern and traditional nature of the star athlete. She acknowledged, "You think I'm a paradox. But I belong in the saddle, for I've been there since I was three. I love the open, dogs, horses, a gun, and the trees . . . Still, I love dresses and everything that goes with them. I can't stand tolerate the mannish woman any more than I can stand the womanish man."[55] Well known for her feminine taste in arena-wear, Strickland considered those outfits were her "work" clothes. Outside the arena she wore fashionable and feminine styles of the day. When asked how a celebrity such as herself could be happily married, she explained what she called her "religion on marriage": "Now, here's the way it is with Hugh and me: He's a one woman man, and—well, I'm a one-man woman. My home is my heaven. . . . Hugh's my husband, and that doesn't mean maybe; he's my manager, and he's a bird; he's my daddy sweetheart and we're pals right down to the last old heel of our boots. And when you slide in my baby girl, April, there you have it, full and complete, hog-tied and ready for any old judge to look 'em over."[56]

Her response is a delightfully personal description of a rather new and radical approach to marriage, hotly discussed among social scientists, religious figures, and feminists at the time. Companionate marriage, as it was called, rejected the strictly economic basis of marriage, focusing instead on "the democratic doctrines of individualism in which the woman can make a contract on equal footing with the man; the scientific treatment of sex activities as natural functions; and the economic pressure which renders early marriage with the immediate bearing and rearing of children an utter impossibility."[57] While intellectuals hashed over the pros and cons of companionate marriage in academic circles, New Women like Strickland embraced the change and discussed its benefits in terms most readers could understand.

Her concerns and future plans for her daughter, April, were also mentioned in the interview. When asked if she hoped April would become a cowgirl athlete like her famous mother, Strickland replied, "I don't want her to follow my game. It's too hard for a woman, and then, maybe when she is old enough, there won't be any contests."[58] Instead, Strickland encouraged her daughter to follow a more traditional path, including dance and piano lessons and keeping a distance from the rodeo crowd.

Strickland's dress, her career, her success, and her comfortable relationship with men as well as women all pointed to the expanded opportunities progressives had hoped women could experience and enjoy. Yet for all her progressive tendencies, Strickland adhered to strong traditionalist values of home, morality, and motherhood. Here was an example that the modernist and traditionalist worlds could collide without causing the destruction of American civilization. It is no surprise that Strickland's successful balancing act endeared her to Pendletonians as no other cowgirl athlete had or would, and they celebrated her success by making her their queen.

In 1928 Pendleton was again the site for a new motion picture. The *Pendleton East Oregonian* reported that "for the first time in motion picture history, Pendleton's annual Round-Up will be both heard and seen on the screens of the world."[59] Movietone introduced sound to the big screen, and the Pendleton paper proudly announced this would be the first big western film to have sound. Producer Edward Sedgwick had returned to Pendleton to shoot the film. Considering the close relationship the producer had established with the town and the luck Pendleton had had with its 1924 movie star queen, Josie Sedgwick, it is hardly a surprise that the star of this new film, Mary Duncan, was chosen to rule the 1928 Round-Up.

There are two items of note in Duncan's reign. First was her court. Unlike Sedgwick, Duncan did not have cowboys as attendants. The Round-Up board of directors appointed a traditional court: two princesses from Pendleton and two from the surrounding area.[60] The front page of the *Pendleton East Oregonian* featured two large photos—a glamorous photo of Duncan coyly peeking out from behind a large cowboy hat and, above that, a group photo of her "attendants" dressed in matching hats, silk shirts, and black ties.[61] Traditional femininity was definitely back in style.

The second noteworthy aspect of Duncan's reign involved the emphasis on the trappings of royalty. The *Pendleton East Oregonian* announced, "Her Majesty, Queen Mary I of the Round-Up Dynasty, will wield the scepter over her cowboy and cowgirl kingdom during the 1928 show."[62] Was this hyperbolic emphasis over her royal status because this article had been juxtaposed next to a story on the queen of England at the time—also a Queen Mary?[63] American fascination with royalty continued unabated throughout the 1920s, and on the local level, royal visitors to the Round-Up were always big news.

The connection between royal trappings and rodeo queens would continue to develop.

The amount of attention Queen Mary of the Round-Up received highlights the lack of attention cowgirl athletes received that year. Mary Lou LeCompte writes that it was not until 1929, when Bonnie McCarroll caught her foot in a stirrup while bronc riding at the Pendleton Round-Up and died several days later, that the move toward removing cowgirl athletes from rodeo began in earnest.[64] Although there do not appear to have been any orchestrated movements toward removing cowgirl athletes until after 1929, the mood toward the cowgirls had already changed. With the exception of Mabel Strickland, there is a remarkable absence of information on the cowgirl athletes.

Beginning in 1926 the daily reports on rodeo performances seldom mention the cowgirls other than to list their standings in their events. The only mention of the cowgirl athletes in 1928 was a negative comment on their performance before the cowgirl relay races. The paper reported, "It took the cowgirls in the relay race some time to get off to a start and considerable criticism was heard from the stands . . . why, oh why, do these excellent horsewomen always hold up the show when it comes to getting the relay started? Finally matters were adjusted to suit the foibles of the female mind." Even Strickland did not escape public censure when she neglected to pin her contestant number on before the start of the race.[65]

During the Round-Up, an article appeared on a new cowgirl athlete in Pendleton. Under the headline "Books? Great Stuff. But Give Claire Belcher a Buckin' Bronc in the Great Outdoors," readers were introduced to a new rider to the circuit. Belcher had been reared in Texas and Oklahoma, a rider all her life, but as the paper reported, "Her parents wanted more advantages for their little girl than a life in the saddle roughing it." Belcher recollected her parents' attempts to introduce her to a genteel, middle-class lifestyle by sending her to college: "At first I liked the novelty of wearing frills every day and learning how to go to teas and art exhibits and symphony concerts and all that sort of thing. . . . But when I actually got into college and had to study hard I began to long for my pie-faced pony, 'Pal' out home. . . . So I ran away. I've spend my time ever since riding, roping and now bulldogging in rodeos. I just love it."[66]

Only a few years earlier Belcher's escape to freedom would have received enthusiastic support, but there is a tone of disapproval throughout the article. Belcher rejected gentility, ran away from the opportunity for a college education, had no interest in getting married, and favored the most physically demanding sport in all of rodeo—bulldogging. Bulldogging, or steer wrestling, is a rough sport: riders gallop their horses alongside a running steer, then jump onto the steer and "wrestle" the animal to the ground. Mabel Strickland considered this event "the most desperate thing a man or woman can do."[67] It was a dangerous enough sport for men, but it was also more than a little unladylike to roll around in the arena dust trying to twist a beast's head until it fell over onto its back. The only other woman who bulldogged at the time was Fox Hastings, whose decidedly unfeminine performances in the arena led consternated newspaper reporters to compensate by emphasizing her domestic skills at home.[68] Belcher enjoyed her rodeo life. In fact, she was quite pleased with it, saying, "I wouldn't trade my lot in life to be the wife of the Prince of Wales."[69] Belcher had placed herself squarely on the side of modernists, and while her behavior was still within the norm for cowgirl athletes, she would not be considered in the same class as Mabel Strickland. Belcher would not have met the criteria for queen material— not for the boosters, and probably not for the Prince of Wales either, had that opportunity arisen.

In 1929 Kathleen McClintock, who had served as princess

Fox Hastings

"Bulldogging"

Round Up 1924

Pendleton

8. Fox Hastings, known as the only lady bulldogger in the world, at the
1924 Pendleton Round-Up. Hastings earned the reputation as
"unfeminine" for engaging in this dangerous event. Courtesy
of Howdyshell Photography, Pendleton, Oregon.

for Mary Duncan in 1928, was elevated to the queen's position. Press coverage for Queen Kathleen was limited, with just
the traditional front-page photo and caption to announce her
appointment and a small article several days later.[70] Aside from
the fact that McClintock was a local girl rather than a famous
movie star or cowgirl athlete, one of her princesses, Kathryn
Furnish, recalled that the queen's and court's activities were
very limited. "There was no travel that year," she said, "no
pictures taken. There was a queen's dance the week before the
Round-Up—they don't do that anymore. But those were hard
times."[71]

The queen and her court did ride in the Westward Ho! parade and in the rodeo's grand entry. Their increased presence in

9. Mabel Strickland, "Wears Fifth Avenue Clothes and Can Punch Cows." Photo taken by Ed McCarty, c. 1920. Courtesy of Jean McCarty Dearinger, private collection, Laramie, Wyoming.

the arena also increased pressure on the young women to live up to their "excellent horsewoman" reputation. Furnish, who lived in town all of her life and did not own a horse, had to borrow a mount from her cousin for her term as princess. She was not alone in her anxiety over how well she would ride in front of the large audiences. "Queen Kathleen and her attendants for the 1929 Round-Up," the *Pendleton East Oregonian* reported, "are spending a good deal of time on horseback these days. Her highness and the four princesses are taking morning canters and ride at other times of the day as well."[72]

In terms of riding ability, a real disconnect developed between community-sponsored Round-Up queens and the cowgirl athletes. The Pendleton queens rode—and some rode well—but not all had "ranch hand" skills. The queens dressed in cowgirl costume, but they wore a conservative imitation of the regalia the cowgirl athletes wore. Cowgirl athletes were known for their distinctive and innovative style of dress. Trick-riding, in particular, required garments that allowed unrestricted freedom of movement, and trick-riding events were judged, in part, on the athletes' costumes. Since the return of the queen and court in 1921, there had been an emphasis on creating a conservative, uniform appearance for Round-Up royalty.[73]

The most important distinction between the cowgirl athletes and the queens rested in their relationship to the town of Pendleton. The queen and members of her court had a direct connection to the community, whereas cowgirl athletes rode into town for a few days, then left. The cowgirl athletes, Furnish remembers, "were just part of the entertainment," whereas, "being selected to the court was a real honor in the town. At that time, everybody knew everybody. . . . The court has always been important, it's always been an honor and I've always felt honored." When asked if she and the other members of the court experienced any pressure to live up to their royal position, she replied, "We had to act like ladies as we were representatives of the court. There was more emphasis on manners. As far as I'm concerned, I felt I needed to watch my p's and q's. You're *still* watched, you know, still representing the Round-Up."[74]

From the reintroduction of a community-sponsored rodeo queen in 1921 through 1929, the Pendleton Round-Up directors presented the most diverse group of rodeo queens in the history of the entire celebration. It was indeed a transitional phase, in large part due to the new strategies for promoting the Round-Up.[75] Part of the promotional campaign involved learning to pay attention to the subtleties—making advantageous connections between important towns, placing certain daughters on the court, or paying attention to the swings in popular attitudes toward feminine behavior.

It is this latter connection, where concerns over the role of women found expression in the newspaper discourse, that it is possible to evaluate the role of community-sponsored rodeo queen as a dynamic opposite to the cowgirl athlete. By tracing the amount of press coverage, one gains a sense of who was most important to the success of the rodeo, the cowgirl athlete or the rodeo queen. The 1920s began with the emphasis on athletes. By the end of the 1920s, conservative mores had prevailed. As Mabel Strickland had predicted, opportunities for professional cowgirl athletes in the rodeo arena were in decline. As the number of cowgirl athletes, never very large to begin with, diminished, the importance of the rodeo queen expanded. The decade ended with queens reigning over the rodeo, genteel versions of cowgirl athletes complete with "royal" trappings. The success of the queens at the Pendleton Round-Up set as a model for other rodeos—both new and established—throughout the West.

3. A New Kind of Community Rodeo Queen

Sponsor Girls at the Texas Cowboy Reunion

In the fall of 1930 plans for the Pendleton Round-Up were moving forward, but things were not exactly "business as usual." The economic fallout from the 1929 crash on Wall Street had a profound effect on the Round-Up. Although the board directors did not cancel the celebration, they were concerned there would not be enough spectators to cover expenses. They were right. The show ended in a deficit. The banks agreed to advance the Round-Up board money to meet their financial obligations, with the stipulation that they reduce their budget.[1] Well before the disappointing ticket sales were totaled, the board began cutting costs where it could. Mildred Hansell, a 1930 princess, recalls that while the Round-Up board gave each member of the court an official shirt and skirt, as was the norm, they asked court members to return the outfits so they could be used by the next year's royalty. Even the traditional leather gauntlet gloves were considered too extravagant; board members purchased white canvas gloves and painted them to look like the beaded leather gloves worn by past royalty.[2]

Despite the Depression and the effect it had on established rodeos, new rodeos cropped up throughout the West. The surge

MAP 2. Stamford, Texas, home of the Texas Cowboy Reunion
and the sponsor girl contest.

in new rodeos can be attributed, in large part, to a combination of local boosters hoping to bring income into their towns and people looking for distractions.[3] During these economically hard times, Americans found "the diversions of popular culture and amusements were just as absorbing as the latest unemployment figures."[4]

One of these new rodeos began in the West Texas town of Stamford. In this High Plains town leaders looked to established rodeos, like the Pendleton Round-Up, for ideas on how to hold a successful event themselves, picking and choosing elements that would suit local interests. Although Pendleton originated the community-sponsored rodeo queen, the Stamford rodeo transformed that model. In Stamford the tradition of young women "sponsored" by their hometowns and sent out to represent it at various civic functions in the surrounding area became intertwined with rodeo. Two aspects of the Stamford sponsor girl idea in particular would have far-reaching implications for the future of rodeo queens across the West. The first involved a competitive rodeo event to select the rodeo queen.[5] The second added feminine appearance as a category in the rodeo queen contest, an addition that both highlighted the evolving beauty culture in America and profoundly influenced the rodeo queen phenomenon.

In 1930 the town of Stamford, located in the northwest corner of Texas, was struggling. Located in Jones County, 190 miles west of Fort Worth and 40 miles north of Abilene, the town was founded in 1899 as a Texas Central Railroad town. Named after the railroad president's hometown of Stamford, Connecticut, the new Texas town became a retail, banking, and commercial center as oil, cattle, cotton, and wheat farming developed in the region. As these industries prospered so too did Stamford; by 1930 the population reached nearly 4,500, and the Stamford Chamber of Commerce reported that the "West Texas Chamber of Commerce was housed here for all of West Texas."[6] This remote region of the West did not escape the downward spiral affecting the national economy. The timing for the first Texas Cowboy Reunion (TCR), then, was not incidental. Like so many other communities, Stamford's leaders searched for ways to keep its businesses going.

Holding a rodeo, especially in this West Texas region, was a familiar way to encourage business. Stamford had staged rodeos in the past, albeit without any permanent organization or regularly scheduled dates.[7] But the number of rodeos already operating in Texas combined with the tight economy meant that Stamford would have to offer something unique. Tom Upshaw, one of the founders of the TCR, recalls, "Some of us stumbled on the idea of Stamford sponsoring an annual get-together of working cattlemen and cowboys of West Texas past and present and building around that an attraction that would be different from those in other communities."[8] Professional riders would not be allowed to compete, "although their presence as visitors was encouraged."[9] The idea of holding a rodeo with only hired hands set Stamford apart from other rodeos and generated a great deal of attention from the press.[10]

In 1930 the Stamford Chamber of Commerce sent invitations to ranches within a one-hundred-mile radius of the town, asking that they send their top hands and their "wildest outlaw horses and steers."[11] The ranches, which included a number of large-scale corporate ranches such as the Matador Ranch, the 6666, and the T Diamond, employed enough wage-earning cowboys to put on a good show. The Stamford rodeo directors were not so much interested in joining the community of organized rodeos, like the Rodeo Association of America, as they were in putting on a show that captured a way of life in Texas that to many seemed to be fast disappearing.[12]

The emphasis on a cowboy-only rodeo meant that this first Texas Cowboy Reunion did not include cowgirl athletes. With the requirement that only ranch hands could participate as rodeo contestants, the likelihood of a cowgirl athlete to diversify the contestant pool was low. Although there was no shortage of women who were skilled riders and ranch hands in West Texas, they were usually the wives and daughters of ranchers or ranch owners themselves, not hired hands, which disqualified them from participating.[13] The requirement that all competitors had to be working cowhands also excluded the possibility that women would participate in exhibition, trick-riding, or cowgirl relay riding events that were still commonly staged throughout the West. The Stamford rodeo did not even have a queen that first year to lead the pre-rodeo parade. If one considers the traditional role of a cowgirl athlete hired as queen a woman who would compete with or alongside the men in the rodeo, the theme of the new Texas Cowboy Reunion precluded such a position.

On the surface, excluding women appeared to be just a natural consequence of recreating an "authentic" old-time working rodeo, the kind of event that took place out on the range and in which women had not participated. But this was no casual get together. An organized, income-generating (they hoped) spectator sport that emphasized a nostalgic look to the frontier past, highlighted the success of working hands, and banned cowgirl athletes suggests the confluence of harsh economic times and the always controversial dynamics of gender. During the Depression, the effects of widespread and lengthy unemployment had a profound impact on men throughout the country. As E. Anthony Rotunda shows, masculinity "defined by notions of success at work" came under fire when men lost jobs and created tensions over gender expectations.[14]

Although a new concept of masculinity based on athletics emerged during the early years of the twentieth century, not until the Depression did success in sports rise up to replace success in employment as a basis for defining masculinity.[15] The early-twentieth-century attitude toward sports, to use Michael

S. Kimmel's apt phrase, "both reflected and illuminated" the qualities men needed to succeed in life: "coolness, steadiness of nerve, quickness of apprehension, endurance against hunger, fatigue and physical distress and—above all—courage."[16] This new concept of rugged masculinity dovetailed nicely with the romantic ideal of the frontier, "where manhood was tested, where, locked in a life or death struggle against the natural elements and against other men, a man discovered if he truly was a real man."[17] The unique format of the Texas Cowboy Reunion combined this new vision of competitive sport with the romantic aspect of the frontier. A rodeo staged for cowboys only could help shake off the debilitating effect of the Depression and the threat it posed to concepts of masculinity. But why exclude women competitors entirely? As Kimmel notes, "Violence, aggression, extreme competitiveness, a gnawing insecurity—are also the defining features of compulsive masculinity, a masculinity that must always prove itself and that is always in doubt."[18] Women competing in the same venue as the men would only exacerbate that sense of doubt. Excluding women athletes from the TCR, then, can be understood in a larger economic context that created a "Depression psychology which sought to bring women out of the work force."[19] Although the decades-old debate over women's position in society had edged toward the conservative camp since 1927, after 1929 the movement became increasingly pronounced. The advances the New Women made into traditionally male occupations were viewed in a different light during the Depression, and all across the country women were asked, if not forced, to give up their positions to allow men the jobs or return home and provide moral support for their families.[20] At the Texas Cowboy Reunion, women athletes found themselves barred from competition and relegated to a non-threatening, supportive role.

One example of focusing on positive elements of working men was the Texas Typical Cowboy contest. Nominations for this award were submitted to the TCR Association, along with a photo of the cowhand in his working garb; the winner was announced during the rodeo. At the third TCR, a photo of a cowgirl appeared in the *Fort Worth (TX) Star Telegram* under the headline, "Eligible for Cowgirl Contest." The article reported that while women were not allowed to participate in the Typical Cowboy contest, "if such is permissible, then Mrs. Irene Betsill of Vernon [Texas] is the first nominated as an entry in this division."[21] Apparently it was not. No contest emerged to honor the women who worked the range for a living. The rodeo specifically focused on the cowboys.

Excluding working cowgirls did not mean women were unwelcome at the rodeo, just that their participation would conform to more traditional views of feminine behavior. The Texas Cowboy Reunion directors apparently noticed something missing the first year of the show. According to the Stamford paper, the TCR directors had traveled to the Pendleton Round-Up to scrutinize the success of that show; they would have witnessed the promotional benefits of a community-sponsored queen.[22] In 1931 TCR organizers decided to invite young women to participate in their rodeo in a limited fashion. As Texas Cowboy Reunion historian Hooper Shelton reports, these "young ladies, 16 years or older, led the opening day parade, participated in special features of the rodeo, and took part in special events planned for them. The main purpose of the sponsors was to add a little charm and glamour to the previously masculine rodeo."[23]

The local newspaper, the *Stamford American*, reported, "One of the most outstanding features of the opening day parade will be a group of cowgirls that will lead it. Tayman [chairman of the parade] . . . asked Chambers of Commerce in all West Texas towns and also in all the large cities of the state to designate a young lady from those communities to come here and act as sponsor for the pioneer cattlemen from the areas served by

10. Mrs. Frank Morrow, first Stamford Texas Cowboy Reunion hostess.
Courtesy of the Texas Cowboy Country Museum, Stamford, Texas.

those towns during the Reunion."[24] A second article appeared in the society section of the same paper, expanding on what the young women could expect at the TCR, noting that each girl would be expected to bring her own horse, saddle, and "ranch costume" with her and that she would "be given numerous courtesies by the reunion association." The article continued, noting, "special social events for the sponsors will be arranged on each day of the reunion" and closed with the statement, "The affair is being staged for the entertainment and enjoyment of the pioneers of the cattle range days of this area."[25] The inclusion of the women, then, was not as an acknowledgement of the women who helped make the cattle business a success in the area, nor were the women invited to participate in rodeo events. Rather, they were included as a social nicety, a separate addition to the rodeo to add glamour to the otherwise all-masculine event.

The development of the visiting sponsor contest led to the creation of three official roles for women outside the traditional realm of rodeo: hostess, Stamford sponsor, and visiting sponsor.[26] The first role, the hostess, found its precedence in similar activities associated with sporting events. During the 1932 Summer Olympics in Los Angles, a select number of society women were honored with the title of hostess and given the responsibility of organizing social events for the athletes.[27] Similarly, in Stamford the honor of the hostess position was bestowed on a married woman "of standing" from the community. The Chamber of Commerce selected a woman capable of organizing social events, registering the out-of-town sponsors, and arranging their housing. As Shelton notes, "The avowed purpose of the official hostess is that every visiting sponsor have a good time . . . striving to see that there are no dull moments for the many girls who come here."[28]

Zelma Morrow served as the first Texas Cowboy Reunion hostess. As her studio photo makes clear, she is hardly one to participate in the dusty workings of the rodeo or be seen out "workin' doggies."[29] The power of her position, in fact, rested in her very traditional role. As Estelle B. Freedman notes, despite the possibilities New Women enjoyed for expanding their roles outside of the private sphere, "most women were not interested in rejecting their deeply rooted female identities." For the traditionally minded women, the evolution of "True Womanhood" into an updated "New Womanhood" involved "the process of redefining womanhood by the extension, rather than the rejection, of the female sphere." Participating in civic activities in a way that reflected traditional feminine roles allowed women like Morrow and the succeeding hostesses "strength, power, and public recognition for their efforts within their sphere."[30] The Stamford hostesses did indeed receive public recognition for their work. During the rodeo the hostess was awarded "a prominent place in the big street parade and . . . a place of honor in the judges stand at each rodeo performance."[31]

The second role for women at the Stamford rodeo was for a young, unmarried women—a sponsor—who would represent the town during the rodeo. At a closed-door meeting Chamber of Commerce members debated the qualifications (and family connections) of potential sponsors before announcing who would act as sponsor for that year's rodeo. The role involved both private and public responsibilities. Working behind the scenes, the Stamford sponsor helped the hostess plan and assisted at all the social events.[32] Writing on the anti-modern inclinations of southern women during the 1920s, George Britt noted that a young woman might like to "have her fling, but the ideal in the back of her head is a nice house in the home town and a decorative position in society."[33] Indeed, the sponsor position became a rite of passage into Stamford's elite circle and job training for the hostess position many of the sponsors would hold in the future.

The Stamford sponsor role involved significant public exposure as well. Before the rodeo the young woman traveled to nearby towns as part of a caravan to advertise the show. During the rodeo the Stamford sponsor was "very much in the limelight," riding in the parade and grand entry.[34] Stamford's sponsor also made highly visible appearances at the sponsor contest. Although she did not compete against out-of-town sponsors for the title of queen, she set the pattern for the barrel race, in effect showing the others how it was done.

The third role for women at the Stamford Texas Cowboy Reunion involved women from outside Stamford who competed in a newly contrived event that appeared at the 1932 rodeo. The *Stamford American* reported, "Prizes will be given to the two sponsors having the most attractive riding outfits, the best mounts, and showing the best horsemanship."[35] Although not exactly a rodeo event, the sponsor contest became the only TCR event in which women would be allowed to participate. Mary Lou LeCompte writes that in 1939, "a crowd of more than 20,000 saw Mrs. Christine Northcutt take the women's calf roping title from a field of thirty at the famous Stamford, Texas Cowboy's Reunion where the sponsor contests had begun eight years earlier."[36] While it is quite possible that Christine Northcutt participated in an informal calf roping contest outside the purview of the TCR, neither Northcutt nor any other women registered as a contestant in the rodeo.[37] Northcutt did, however, win the TCR sponsor contest in 1940—from a field of thirty contestants.

Northcutt's experience, both as a TCR sponsor contest winner and roper, illustrates the talent of women in the area and their willingness to compete in traditional rodeo events and provides an example of women getting caught in the traditionalist/modernist debate over proper roles for women. Women who enjoyed the opportunities to compete in sports during the earlier part of the decade did not easily relinquish their athletic ambitions. As support for New Women waned, however, the acceptability of their athleticism began to focus on feminine qualities, such as physical attractiveness. Susan K. Cahn writes that sports competitions involving women athletes continued at the high school and college level, but by the late 1920s the competitions downplayed women's athletic, or more troubling, "mannish" accomplishments.

In a bizarre twist, the image of female athletes became linked with beauty queens. For example, "the AAU national basketball tournaments and other independent championships crowned tournament beauty queens. The winners took their place of honor alongside other players selected for all-star teams and most-valuable-player awards."[38] In the Southwest, local concepts of acceptable feminine activities—riding, roping, competing—became caught up in changing national trends that downplayed real athletic ability and focused on beauty and femininity, which encouraged the growth of the sponsor contests. From a rodeo director's point of view, the fact that young women eagerly participated in these contests seemed to indicate that they had accepted their place in society, as helpmates rather than competitors. For the young women, however, the change was not so much giving in as accommodating new demands in order to continue competing.

From the very beginning the success of the sponsor contest at the Texas Cowboy Reunion was a testament to the support it received from other communities—the towns and ranches that agreed to send a sponsor. Between 1932 and 1949, 167 different towns and 28 ranches sent sponsors to the TCR.[39] The concept of sponsor girls as a means of town boosterism had been firmly established before the Stamford Chamber of Commerce co-opted that idea and turned it into a rodeo event. In a sort of booster reciprocity, towns eagerly exchanged sponsors to promote each other's events. Newspapers in the West Texas area abound with examples of sponsor girl activities. The Graham paper, for example, reported, "So many calls for beautiful young ladies for events in this part of Texas have been made on the chamber of commerce, the Publicity Committee, 'Pic' Larmar, chairman, decided to stage a bathing beauty revue at the Graham Municipal Swimming Pool. . . . Events to which Graham has been invited to send young ladies are the Mineral Wells Health Festival, the Sweetwater Water Carnival and Beauty Revue, and the Texas Cowboy Reunion at Stamford."[40]

The town of Sweetwater, Texas, selected three sponsor girls in 1938. One young lady was assigned to a bathing revue in Eastland, one to a bathing revue in Cisco, and the third, Miss Louella Headrick, was assigned to the Texas Cowboy Reunion. In Abilene, a call for sponsors hit the press with the headline article "Pulchritude in Absentia—City's in a Jam!" Abilene had committed itself to sending sponsors to a number of events—more events than one girl could handle. The article noted, "Bathing beauty is needed right away—in fact, today, tomorrow and Sunday—to enter the beauty contest at Fort Stockton's annual Summer Water Carnival, sponsored by that city's Chamber of Commerce . . . then there is the Texas Cowboy Reunion. . . . It is imperative that Abilene be represented."[41] Thankfully, for the honor of the town, it was. An article in the *Abilene Reporter News* announced that "Dorothy Comer, a brunette with dark eyes, gained the title 'Miss Abilene' Wednesday evening" and went on to say that she would represent the town at the TCR. The article was accompanied by a photo of Comer wearing a bathing suit and heels in a classic "cheesecake" pose.[42] Throughout the area, selecting young women to send off as local representatives to other towns was de rigueur, which helps to explain the success of the Stamford sponsor contest. It was a source of civic pride to be able to send a young woman who, in her youthful beauty "embodies what local people believe to be the best of themselves."[43] She represented both the town's history and aspirations for the future. Her accomplishments were an indicator of the promise of the town itself. Likewise, sponsor contestants from the ranches also were connectors to the past and the future, reinforcing the importance of their place in the community and the continued value of the cattle industry.

The roles for Stamford's own sponsor girl and of the out-of-town contestants remained separate. A clear distinction between the Stamford sponsor girls and the winners of the TCR sponsor contest can be seen in the official rodeo programs.[44] Every year since 1932, sponsor contest winners have been prominently featured in the official TCR program. Rather than giving the winning girl a title associated with her hometown, Miss (your town here), or with her own name, Miss or Mrs. (your name here), the women have always been referred to by the year they won the sponsor contest: Miss 1932, Miss 1933, and so on, preventing confusion between the Stamford sponsor girl and the visiting young woman who competed in the contest and won the title.

The actual sponsor contest was based on the idea that women had competed in the arena since the early 1900s. But the design of the sponsor contest maintained clear gender distinctions between the activities the cowhands participated in and those available for the women. The sponsor contest itself was designed to mimic regular rodeo events. The competition was spread over the course of the rodeo—three days of contests before announcing the winner on the last day of the rodeo. And, as in regular rodeo events, the prize fit the rodeo theme: the winning sponsor girl took home a beautifully tooled saddle; runners-up were awarded bits, spurs, or other pieces of riding equipment. But unlike regular rodeo events that pitted the skills of the cowboy or cowgirl against the clock, this competition had less to do with ability than appearance. The young women were subjectively evaluated according to best horse, most attractive outfit, and horsemanship. A newspaper explained, "In determining the winner, the girl's personality will count 15 percent; her riding togs and equipment 15 percent and riding ability 30 percent. The mount will also be scored, conformation and appearance counting 10 percent, equipment 10 percent and the animal's performance 20 percent."[45]

The emphasis on riding togs played an important part in the contest and contributed to the development a distinctive style of western attire for women in rodeo. The fancier and more "western" the costume, the higher the potential score in that category; conversely, a penalty was imposed on any contestant who competed wearing blue jeans—an unlikely scenario, since the penalty would effectively eliminate all hopes of winning the title. Contestants understood they needed to "dress" for the event. As late as 1957 the Texas Cowboy Reunion program stated, "Sponsors to the TCR were introduced in 1931 to lend glamour to the Reunion and sponsors are still depended upon to add the beauty and charm of the western pioneer woman to the reunion. The girls jealously guard that privilege so that the ten-second penalty for wearing blue denims in the arena has never had to be imposed. The girls know they are expected to be beautiful as well as good riders."[46]

If this invention of a special event, a feminized view of rodeo women outside the realm of traditional events, was not enough to distance the women "competitors" from the cowboys and the traditional rodeo events, then the social functions sealed the deal. The hostess and the Stamford sponsor girl kept the visiting young women occupied with a whirl of social events. From the legendary Chuck Wagon dinner to the slate of teas and luncheons (in which each year the hostess presented sponsors with unique mementos of their participation in the sponsor contest), the young women were engaged in events outside the realm of rodeo.[47] A particularly good example was the formal dance, where admittance was "by card only."[48] The young women, "wearing their prettiest gowns," gathered in a specially constructed pavilion, where "the sponsors and their escorts and other invited guests . . . dance[d] to orchestra music."[49] Rather than participate in the general dance, a standard feature at rodeos across the West, the young ladies and their escorts were removed from the boisterous activities of the cowboys and the crowd. At other rodeos, cowgirl athletes were an integral part of the rodeo community; at the Texas Cowboy Reunion, the young women were consciously removed from it. In this respect, the Stamford sponsor contest is the first recorded contest to make such a clear distinction between women who promoted the rodeo—queens, or to use West Texas nomenclature, sponsors—and the community of rodeo athletes.

The focus on beauty and femininity opens the discussion on changing patterns in the American beauty culture. Beauty culture involved, to use Kathy Peiss's apt description, "a system of meaning that helped women navigate the changing conditions of modern social experience."[50] The influence of equating beauty with femininity was particularly useful in the late 1800s, when middle-class women began to venture out into the public sphere.[51] The industry-driven belief that with the right products any woman could make herself beautiful usurped the old notion of beauty as an inner, moral quality. Urban women were the first to engage in the new beauty trend. The New Women of the 1920s—single, self-sufficient, a little bit wild— eagerly picked up on the availability and increasing acceptance of cosmetics. Maintaining the connection of femininity and beauty allowed women to enter masculine spheres without the threat of women becoming too mannish, unfeminine, or threatening. Rodeo cowgirls wore makeup when they performed in the arena; the *Pendleton East Oregonian* published a charming image of Mabel Strickland powdering her nose while awaiting her turn in the arena.[52] By the end of the decade cosmetic companies had successfully convinced women that "being 'painted' was not only respectable, but a requirement for womanhood," and even rural areas became engulfed in the beauty culture.[53]

During the Depression cosmetics sales increased market-wide.[54] The economy-induced resurrection of the domestic ideal reinforced the notion that, married or single, beauty was an essential sign of femininity.[55] The intensification of beauty culture during the Depression influenced rodeo queens on two levels. First, the old caveat "beauty sells" was applied to rodeo tickets: the prospect of thirty or forty beautiful young women, displayed in parades and in the arena as they competed for the crown, could draw spectators to the show—a message not lost on rodeo directors deeply concerned with bringing in large crowds during economically tight times. More importantly, however, the new emphasis on appearance, if not totally replacing riding skills, entered the picture in an unprecedented manner, reinforcing the traditional, domestic view of women and initiating "beauty" as one of the defining characteristics of a rodeo queen.

It would be unfair to say that the sponsor contest was just a beauty contest on horseback. As the representative of a western way of life, the expectation that the queen would be a competent rider continued. The sponsor contest, therefore, was not strictly a beauty contest, nor was it strictly a riding contest, an ambiguity that left open the possibility for interpreting the most important characteristics of a rodeo queen. A reporter for the *Waco (TX) Tribune-Herald* wrote, "Many cowgirl beauties, some of whom actually will compete in the hard-riding dangerous rodeo events [at other rodeos] were delighted to represent their respective Texas cities at the Reunion."[56] While it was acknowledged that some of the contestants were skilled riders, it was also understood that they would not be competing in these dangerous events at the TCR. And yet, organizers of the rodeo did not want to make the sponsor contest appear too easy either, as the following news release makes clear:

All of the 49 sponsors entered this year are qualified for the role. It might be explained that being a sponsor to the cowboy reunion is nothing like the role of May Queen. *These are hard riding lassies as well as representative beauties of West Texas. . . .* In the preliminary tests, the sponsors were required to ride in between and around three barrels set in a straight line and 46 feet apart. The horse must change his lead five or six times to make it, and skillful handling is necessary. All of the sponsors will appear again in the finals Wednesday, with the barrels moved so that they will be only 36 feet apart. *How the judges scored the preliminary contest was not revealed.*[57] [emphasis added]

The sentence "These are hard riding lassies as well as representative beauties of West Texas" emphasizes the dual nature of the contest. "Hard riding" and "beauties" used in the same sentence indicates a melding of elite and working-class characteristics: glamorous young women performing demanding ranch work. While sponsors came from both towns and ranches, between 1931 and 1959 the towns supplied the overwhelming majority of contestants. Only 59 of the 621 women who participated, less than 10 percent, were sponsored by ranches. The number of ranch sponsors did not begin to rise significantly until 1945.[58] Granted, some of the towns were quite small, and it is possible that towns sponsored young women from surrounding ranches. The expectation, though, was that women entering a rodeo event, even if it included non-traditional elements like appearance and personality, should be able to ride.

The statement "How the judges scored the preliminary contest was not revealed" could mean that the judges had scored the riders but had yet not made the scores public. It also indicates an element of ambiguity in the evaluation process. Regular rodeo events held to a more objective standard. A rider had to stay on a bull or a bronc for a specified amount of time. If the time requirement was met, then judges further evaluated the rider by noting specific requirements: Were the rider's spurs above the animal's shoulder when leaving the chute? Did the rider keep one hand free at all times? Steer and calf roping, as well as bulldogging, were even more straightforward: The contestant who got the job done in the fastest time won. But sponsor contestants did not have the same means for objectively evaluating the contestants—the winning sponsor was awarded the title based primarily on the subjective evaluation of the male judges.

In the TCR sponsor contest, riding skills were only part of an overall package, which opened up the definition of "cowgirl" to interpretation.[59] Was a cowgirl someone who grew up on a ranch, familiar with cowhand skills? A town girl who knew how to ride? Or simply someone from the region who dressed in western costume? The difficulty in interpreting the designation "cowgirl" appears in a newspaper report covering the Sweetwater, Texas, sponsor: "Miss Louella Headrick will be the representative to Stamford, competing in the cowgirl beauty contest."[60] This description as a beauty contest, fighting words among rodeo queens even today, seems quite at odds with the description of "hard riding lassies."

The most noticeable difficulty in defining a sponsor girl contestant came from the community papers writing about their sponsors. It is not surprising that towns tended to emphasize a young woman's appearance, social pedigree, education, and social groups or activities she enjoyed. Women sponsored by ranches were most likely to be described as "expert riders," and descriptions often included how active and useful these women were on the ranch: helping with round-ups, riding fence, cutting cattle, and completing other ranch chores. It is interesting to note that during the early years of the sponsor contest both married and unmarried women competed, with little difference in the percentage of married women from ranches compared to those from towns. Of the forty-five sponsors from ranches, one-third were married. Similarly, for town contestants, nearly one-third were also married. That married women entered sponsor contests could again be a reflection of older traditions where cowgirl athletes hired to serve as queens were often married.[61]

Whether married or single, the winner of the TCR sponsor contest took home the title of queen. Again, this reflects the tradition of hiring professional cowgirl athletes to reign over rodeos as queens, where the novelty of feminine women performing wild and exiting riding skills was a real ticket seller. There are two significant differences here. The first is that the women did not engage in wild and exciting riding events. These women, as with their Pendleton predecessors, had been selected by their community based on conservative, middle-class standards. They offered a genteel, non-threatening interpretation of rodeo athletes, consistent with the reinvigorated emphasis on feminine beauty rather than athleticism. More importantly, the women chose to enter the contests; they were not hired for the position nor were they appointed by a board of directors. The voluntary entry into a rodeo queen contest marks an important break from past selection processes and an important step in the evolution of the rodeo queen phenomena.

It is difficult to know what the sponsor contest personally meant to the women who chose to compete. Records show how often women appeared at the Stamford contest, an indicator of their interest.[62] For city girls, winning the title Miss (your town here), a prerequisite for entrance into the TCR sponsor contest, meant community-wide recognition and being the center of attention—no doubt heady business and a welcome break in the usual summer routine for most young women. For those sponsored by a ranch, a chance to travel to Stamford and participate in social events would have been plenty of enticement. Mary Ellen "Dude" Barton, the 1941 sponsor girl from the Matador Ranch, explains, "Things were pretty boring during those times. I lived on a ranch twenty miles from town, and the town only had a population of about 500 people or so. We looked forward to any sort of recreation."[63]

While there are no newspaper interviews with the sponsor contestants, the newspaper articles do provide some useful background, giving a sense of who the contestants were, where they came from, and even, as noted above, how many were repeat performers. The women who were sponsors at the TCR constituted a fairly mixed lot: high school beauty queens, college girls home for the summer, and daughters and occasionally wives of local ranchers. What they have in common is that they were all from middle- to upper-class families. This pattern is similar to that found in Pendleton, where Round-Up directors selected local "girls of standing" to reign over their show. In West Texas, as elsewhere across the country, the image of respectability and beauty remained fixed in middle-class beliefs and aspirations. Although in Pendleton, Native American women were selected to reign as queens, it is worth noting the absence of African American and Hispanic women in the sponsor contest; their lack of participation stands as silent commentary on prevailing racial attitudes and the dominance of upper-class white culture in West Texas.

While the sponsor contest undoubtedly meant many things to many people, it is also worth considering what the introduction of this contest meant in a larger cultural sense, in terms of what it says about the role regional culture played in the origins of the sponsor contest in West Texas. The young women who participated in the sponsor contest from 1931 to 1949 came from towns from Wichita Falls to Midland, Texas, and from Cross Roads, New Mexico, as far east as Dallas. Regionalism in the West is not a new idea; Texas historian Walter Prescott Webb published his theories on what he considered a Texas culture in 1931. Webb believed the Plains environment responsible for creating what he recognized as the cowboy and the cowboy culture—masculine, violent, and fiercely independent. He describes the typical western cowboy as someone who "lives on horseback . . . swears like a trooper, drinks like a fish, wears clothes like an actor and fights like the devil. He is gracious to ladies, reserved toward strangers, generous to his friends, and brutal to his enemies."[64] This image of Texas cowboys, perpetuated by Hollywood movies, remains locked in the popular mind.

Webb paid scant attention to women in this region, other than to note cowboys were gracious to them. By focusing so heavily on environmental factors, he failed to consider that the immigrants who settled this area of West Texas might have carried these traits with them. David Hackett Fischer's work on American folkways does address this question. His research indicates that Scots-Irish immigrants originally settled in the "Backcountry," the mountainous areas of Maryland, Virginia, and the Carolinas, in an area that expended from the Appalachia Highlands into much of the Old Southwest.[65] Later, members of this group migrated to West Texas, southern Oklahoma, New Mexico, and Southern California.[66] Fischer describes as distinctive Scots-Irish characteristics their warlike behavior, strong sense of family, fierce loyalty, and independence, the very traits Webb finds so distinctive with the Texas cowboys. And gender roles exhibited in Scots-Irish culture were strikingly similar to the attitudes reflected in West Texas toward women.

Scots-Irish families were "decidedly male-dominant—much more so than in New England or the Delaware Valley."[67] While local concepts were strictly patriarchal, it was expected that women would work alongside their fathers or husbands doing work that would not have been considered appropriate in other regions. The women worked in the fields, tending livestock and even slaughtering cattle.[68] At the same time, a great deal of weight was placed on femininity and attention to sensual female dress. Western regalia, what Webb describes as "dressing like an actor," originated among the Scots-Irish. The trademark tight fitting pants, open collar shirt, and bright colors worn by the sponsor contestants reflect back to the Scots-Irish tradition of wearing clothes that accentuated the female form (by contrast, Pendleton queens kept their conservative, buckskin cowgirl costume until 1944).[69] It is this dual expectation, to be both "hard riding" and a "beauty," that suggests the sponsor contest did not originate in Stamford by happenstance. Rather, the contest was readily accepted throughout the region because it paralleled local cultural concepts of gender expectations.[70] Adding to this cultural predisposition in West Texas for a contest that emphasized femininity was the Depression. The economic downturn acted as a catalyst, reinforcing traditional views of femininity and masculinity.[71]

When Stamford decided to stage a rodeo in 1930, it created a pleasant distraction from the effects of the Depression and, unwittingly, made an important contribution to the rodeo queen phenomenon: a queen contest in which beauty factored as a criterion for winning. The intention, to introduce a bit of femininity to counter the masculine nature of an all-male rodeo, completed the transformation of cowgirl athlete from the athletic, competitive New Woman into a more acceptable and less threatening figure. While the cultural characteristics in the West Texas region arguably predisposed the members of the Stamford Chamber of Commerce toward inventing this contest, the new queen competition captured a shift in gender expectations occurring across the nation, one that stressed a more traditional role for women and a heightened emphasis on beauty as an essential expression of femininity. During the conservative renaissance of the 1930s and 1940s, the independent lifestyle of the rodeo cowgirl was replaced by the traditional virtues embodied in the figure of rodeo queen: beautiful, young, gracious, and charming, presiding over the world of rodeo, not in it.

Despite Stamford's remote location, the strategy to attract spectators by advertising a rodeo with only "real cowboys" worked. Twelve thousand visitors attended the first year; fifteen thousand, the next.[72] By 1938 the town braced itself for an expected seventy-five thousand spectators from around the country.[73] National presses covered the show, as did western-oriented publications.[74] As new rodeos developed throughout the West, rodeo directors could look to Stamford's contest based on a combination of riding skills and appearance as an option for selecting their own rodeo queens.

4. Riding Pretty

The Glamour Years Begin, 1930–1941

In 1931 the front page of the *Pendleton East Oregonian* printed two photos from the Fresno, California, rodeo. Under the headline "Ups and Downs of Rodeo," Pendleton residents saw an "up" photo, the Fresno rodeo queen confidently astride a rearing horse; and a "down" photo, a cowboy heading back to earth, thanks to the efforts of his mount. The action shot of the cowboy and bronc parting ways was rather commonplace, but the image of the queen on a rearing horse was revolutionary. So too was the tone and language of the caption under her photo: "Maudine Creason . . . can ride prettily as well as looking that way."[1] This image introduced Pendletonians to a new concept: a glamorous queen. It is quite fitting that their introduction came by way of a California rodeo, since the new emphasis on appearance, or more accurately, glamour, rested in large part on Hollywood's expanding movie industry.[2]

The influence of glamour on Pendleton's rodeo queens increased dramatically between 1930 and 1941. During this time, community-sponsored rodeo queens stepped confidently into the limelight as cowgirl athletes faded from rodeo competition. This shift reinforced the dynamic opposition theory, suggesting as it does the idea that only one vision of female identity—cowgirl athletes or rodeo queens—could dominate the rodeo arena at a time. But taking control of the arena was only the beginning for rodeo queens. As witnessed throughout the entire queen phenomena, the role itself was sensitive to changing currents in national cultural trends. During the 1930 to 1941 phase, the queen's role evolved into a more dynamic and self-conscious role, showing both an increasing emphasis on community-sponsored rodeo queens as representatives of true western womanhood and the influence of the new glamour culture that swept the nation.

With minor exceptions, the move that began in 1925—transferring roles from cowgirl athletes to community-sponsored rodeo queens—was complete: the genteel version of the cowgirl ruled the rodeo arena. Shelley Armitage, writing on the role of the western woman in film and literature, notes, "During the 1930s, just following the peak years of women's star performance in the rodeo, cowgirl movie heroines were 'more self-reliant, more athletic, and even sexier,' but seldom the central figure of the film."[3] When community-sponsored rodeo queens took over the role of cowgirl in the arena, they too were portrayed as more self-reliant, athletic, and yes, even sexy. Unlike the silver screen cowgirls, however, the queens did play a central part—they were the stars of their community, even if they were not star performers of the rodeo.

As cowgirl athletes faded from the arena, community-sponsored rodeo queens were increasingly expected to show their riding skills. In 1929 cowgirl athletes rode rough-stock in the arena for the last time. In 1930 rodeo queens moved the exhibition of their riding skills up a notch. Mildred Hansell, a Round-Up princess in 1930, notes that theirs was the first royal court to gallop into the arena. Hansell was not terribly thrilled to be a part of this ground-breaking tradition. Although reared

11. Mary Robison, 1936 Round-Up queen, displaying her riding skills, in one of her many promotional appearances. Courtesy of Howdyshell Photography, Pendleton, Oregon.

on a ranch, Hansell suffered a fall from a horse at an early age and became, as she puts it, "horse shy"; her most memorable experience as princess was "being scared to death most of the time," hoping the horse she galloped into the arena would not run away with her in front of thousands of spectators.[4] Warned to keep a tight rein on the horse, Hansell held him under such tight control that her mother, unable to recognize her daughter down in the ring, later remarked on how well one princess in particular managed her horse. Hansell recalls, "She was surprised when I told her it was me!"[5]

The next year, 1931, marked the beginning of rodeo queens appearing astride rearing horses. Just exactly where this idea came from—if, for example, a specific movie started the trend—is not clear. What is clear is that this representation of western womanhood swept through the rodeo community that year; rodeo queens, waving their hats from the backs of rearing horses made a sudden and stunning appearance across the West. In July 1931 Cheyenne's first rodeo queen, Jean Nimmo, posed for a publicity photo on a rearing horse. In August, the *Pendleton East Oregonian* ran a photo of the Fresno, California, rodeo queen on her rearing horse and, later, of the Ellensburg, Washington, rodeo queen doing the same.[6] Pendleton queens joined the trend a little later: In 1934 Shirley Thompson became the first Pendleton royal to appear on the front page of the *Pendleton East Oregonian* waving her hat and smiling from the back of her near-vertical mount, followed by Mary Robison (1936) and Jean McCarty (1938).

Not all Round-Up queens mastered the art of rearing horses. Some, like Hansell, were competent, if cautious, riders. Others who grew up on ranches rode with confidence and skill. Despite the range of riding abilities among early queens, by the mid-1930s Pendleton's newspaper emphasized the importance of riding and ranching skills. One of the articles on the 1936 Round-Up queen, Mary Robison, began this way: "Can you ride? Are you young? Attractive? Do you know how to smile? Do you like crowds? Are you gracious and charming to everyone you meet? Oh yes, and CAN YOU RIDE? . . . only in the past few years has the Round-Up demanded that queens and attendants be expert horsewomen. Of course, cowgirl monarchs have ridden nicely in parades, but now they must be real hands if they wish to be members of the Round-Up dynasty."[7] The article employs a new definition of the word "cowgirl." The term had previously applied to cowgirl athletes who competed in rodeo events; however, as their presence in the rodeo arena and press declined, the word took on a broader meaning, including "cowgirls" of the silver screen and women who vacationed at dude ranches dressed in "western" garb. As the 1936 article indicates, the word "cowgirl" had been relaxed to mean any young woman who could stay put in a saddle. The term "real hands" came into use to replace "cowgirl" and applied only to proven riders—those who lived on ranches and participated in ranch work. The image of rodeo queens on rearing horses—exhibiting calm and confidence while controlling a potentially dangerous animal—became one way to show that they belonged to the real western world at the same time that they reflected the new, glamorous image of cowgirls found in movies and dime novels.

Along with showing the queens in a more active manner, the tone and language newspapers used to describe community-sponsored rodeo queens underwent a significant change in the 1930s. During the first twenty years of the rodeo queen phenomena in Pendleton, newspaper discourse in the *Pendleton East Oregonian* described young women who reigned over the show in terms of their family histories, civic service, middle-class attributes, and connections to the Round-Up. Little attention was paid to their looks. Rodeo queens, as representatives of the town, exhibited what Robert Lavenda described as "the best of themselves: talent, friendliness, commitment to the community, and its values, upward mobility"[8] And so appearance was discretely ignored. Round-Up queens, like brides and babies, were de facto considered beautiful. But all this began to change in the 1930s. The emergence of a rodeo queen contest at Stamford's Texas Cowboy Reunion, discussed earlier, provides one example of the shift toward the emerging beauty culture and the glamorization of rodeo queens.

The word *glamour* itself, although ancient in origin, emerged in newspaper discourse in the late 1920s.[9] The original meaning of the word, centered on mysteries and occult practices, shifted in the early twentieth century to mean "magical or fictitious beauty" before shifting again to mean "fashionably attractive." The big shift in meaning—from magic/spell to fictitious beauty—occurred in the late 1920s to early 1930s, but the implications of something contrived remained associated with the word.

Taking a broader cultural view, Robert H. Haddow writes that the word *glamour* "symbolized the new streamlined look in the 1930s and 1940s developed by new industrial designs."[10] The new look, Art Deco, represented a vision of a style that encompassed industrial design, home interiors, cars, and most important for this discussion, fashion. Linking the historically adversarial relationship between art and capitalism, Art Deco, with its shiny surfaces and thin veneers, emerged as the representation of modern commercial style.[11] Business leaders across the country made the increasingly obvious connection that when it came to selling goods a flashy package was more important than what the package contained.[12]

The importance of packaging for a consumer market found a ready audience with the movie industry during the early 1930s, a time when theater entertainment increased in popularity. With the stock market crash in 1929 and the ensuing Depression, "Americans looked for something to relieve the debilitating effects of want, idleness and gloom. They went to the movies by the tens of millions weekly."[13] The frustration and confusion of daily life, as historian Terry A. Cooney notes, could be "set against visions of a more cohesive, more romantic, and more purposeful past," where movies like *Gone with the Wind* connected "the epic of nation-building" with romance and "offered an extended relocation into worlds of dramatic events, controlled sexuality, and colorful heroes and heroines."[14] The created images on the screen encouraged the viewers to misperceive reality, which they willingly did. And the actresses and actors, those manufactured beauties of the silver screen, mass-produced by motion picture studios, were part and parcel of the glamour spell. Well-packaged and streamlined in appearance, their fictitious beauty—a shiny veneer of make-up, costume, and carefully coiffed hair—covered up who-knew-what physical flaws or character flaws (or both).

Images of scantily clad women, mostly movie stars and entertainers, found their way into newspapers year-round. From the late 1930s until the outbreak of World War II, the number of these images continued to increase as the square inches of fabric on the women decreased. Along with a new emphasis on costume (or lack thereof) a new camera angle came into use during this time: the camera, held on or near the ground, shot up at the subject, creating what can best be described as "crotch shots." These photos would be considered inappropriate for contemporary newspapers; however, in the 1930s photographs of women from this camera angle or in risqué poses was acceptable if the women were posing as part of their profession. For example, under the title, "Hold That Pose! And She Did," Olympic figure skater Audry Peppe, wearing a short skating skirt, is photographed doing the splits, mid-air (the photographer would have been lying on the ice, photographing mostly legs and underwear).[15]

Lois W. Banner argues that the display of women's bodies, made acceptable through their participation in beauty contests and the legitimization of modeling and acting careers, encouraged the proliferation of such "cheesecake" shots.[16] For the most part the images were publicity shots, used to advertise an upcoming film or keep the star in the public eye. By the mid-1930s glamour completely dominated the media—in the movies, in magazines, and in newspapers. The message spread through the media was that anyone could be beautiful—glamour was not just for the rich or famous. Joan Jacobs Brumberg writes that improvements in home sanitation, particularly modernized bathrooms with mirrors and electric lights, allowed women to scrutinize their looks more carefully. By the 1930s, "Self-scrutiny—perhaps even with a dash of vanity—was now considered healthy and productive."[17] In the *Pendleton East Oregonian*'s Social and Club News section, dedicated to women's issues, readers learned how to accentuate their looks and dress more fashionably at minimal cost.

Movie stars, who governed the definition of ideal beauty, shared their secrets on how they achieved their sophisticated look in the women's sections of newspapers.[18] By heeding these tips even women in rural areas could keep up with the latest trends in feminine style, learn to fix their hair for a party on short notice, and pick up helpful hints, such as when wearing spring hats, hair curled in soft rolls at the side of the head would "fill in that awkward empty space directly behind the ears."[19] The Oregon State College home extension service got into the beauty business, traveling to rural counties around the state, teaching women how to make creams and lotions from common kitchen items, care for skin, and do home manicures.[20]

The emphasis on looks was not entirely influenced by the movie industry, although the movie industry did set the standard. There was a political element to the developing beauty culture as well—a positioning of the benefits of the American capitalist system against Russian communism. Elaine Taylor May notes the perception in the 1930s and 1940s that "Soviet women, as workers and political activists, desexualized themselves" and quotes a *U.S. World and News Today* article describing Moscow as "a city of women—hard-working women who show few of the physical charms of women in the West."[21] An example of the masculinizing effect of communism appeared in the *Pendleton East Oregonian* under the headline, "It's a Man's Job Done by a Girl." The photo's caption reads,

"A young Russian woman girl trimming a tree which she has felled. Note her heavy boots and masculine attire, except for the shawl around her shoulders."[22] Thanks to the fruits of the American capitalist system, American women, "unlike their 'purposeful' and unfeminine Russian counterparts," had the freedom to "cultivate their looks and their physical charms, to become sexually attractive housewives and consumers."[23] The trend toward attractiveness, the new fascination with glamour and starlike qualities, and the concept of a pretty package useful as a marketing tool all converged on the image and role of rodeo queen.

When the rodeo queen phenomena first emerged it was based on precedents set by European royals. Using symbols of royalty had practical advantages: it gave the rodeo queen's role some parameters on ceremony and regalia; it allowed town people to emphasize the qualities of royalty they found acceptable, such as lineage, class status, and connection to civic duty; and it came with a solid, serviceable vocabulary with words like *reign*, *rule*, *regal*, and *scepter*. The connection between royalty and rodeo queens, so much a part of the early years of the phenomenon, underwent a change in the 1930s. European royalty was in trouble. Articles in the *Pendleton East Oregonian* reported divorces, deaths (car accidents seemed to be a leading cause of royal death), and political trouble in this elite circle. The number of articles celebrating Americans marrying into nobility became less frequent. The decline in interest in European royalty corresponded with the increased interest in Hollywood movie stars. It could be that movies were ubiquitous, interesting, and available or that during the international crisis surrounding World War I Americans turned away from the previously fascinating European leaders. Or it could be an example of American pragmatism: only a small number of marriageable princes and princesses existed, whereas jobs in the movie industry were increasing—and according to the papers, with good wages.[24]

Whatever the reasons, movie stars passed European royalty in the rags-to-riches fantasy. The oft-told Cinderella fairy tale was updated: wishful thinking, unpleasant stepmothers, and waiting for a kindhearted fairy godmother to save the day became passé; the new fairy tale involved individual initiative, talent, and living in the spotlight of Hollywood stardom rather than tucked away in some prince's drafty old castle. News stories in the *Pendleton East Oregonian* such as "Today's Cinderella," in which an average young woman was "discovered" and rocketed to fame and fortune, became common items.[25] Often the swift elevation to stardom involved being in the right place at the right time, but one had to be prepared; one had to pay careful attention to grooming and dress at all times so as not to miss that once in a lifetime opportunity.

The new fascination with glamour and movie stars did not sever the connection between royalty and the Pendleton rodeo queen role; rather, the two images combined. A 1931 article in the *Pendleton East Oregonian* noted, "Royalty all the world over may totter on its throne, but not at the Round-Up, where every year a charming girl is chosen to hold sceptered sway over the Western realm."[26] Despite the trouble plaguing European royalty and the lure of glamour, the connection between royalty and the Round-Up was far too entrenched for it to disappear completely. Instead, the regal traditions combined with the sparkle, glitter, and public persona of glamorous Hollywood stars, initiating a new incarnation of the rodeo queen phenomena.[27]

In 1932 Melissa Parr became the second Native American queen to reign over the Round-Up and the first to demonstrate the marriage of glamour and royalty. Parr was a descendant of Chief Joseph, and some articles focused on the "blue blood of the first Americans" that flowed through her veins.[28] Cooney writes that during the Depression an idea developed, stressing America "deserved to be measured on its own standards, not according to borrowed [European] standards—attention

12. Melissa Parr, the second Native American queen to reign over the Round-Up, shown here with her court in 1932. Courtesy of Howdyshell Photography, Pendleton, Oregon.

needed to be paid to what made America America."[29] Parr represented a part of American cultural history—Native American royalty—that was distinct from Europe. Some newspaper articles focused on the Round-Up queen's beauty.[30] Parr had the reputation as an exceptional beauty, one validated by her winning the American Indian Beauty Contest at the Pendleton Round-Up five times. After her fifth victory in 1930, she was barred from ever competing again so that other young women might have a chance at the title.[31]

Although the *Pendleton East Oregonian* mentioned that Parr was a beauty contest winner many times over, the paper never actually described her features. Rather, her appearance was described in general terms as "real American beauty" and her demeanor as "gracious." The 1933 queen, Jean Frazier, was the first to have her physical characteristics publicly men-

tioned in the press. The language used illustrates both the fascination with portraying Round-Up queens as royalty and the
shift toward glamorizing the position: "Queen Jean was born
and reared in Pendleton and is of such charm that ever since
she was a baby she had been mentioned as a prospective queen
of the Round-Up. 'We've just been waiting for her to grow up,'
said the directors when they chose her to wield the scepter of
this year's show. Described as having a lovely smile, sparking
brown eyes and dark hair (its wave is one of those secured
from a fairy godmother and not from a beauty shop), she likes
to ride and golf and swim."[32] The article clearly reflects previous descriptions of queens, showing Frazier's lineage, connection to the town, and symbols of royal reign. At the same
time it includes physical descriptions of the queen—her smile,
sparkling eyes, and dark hair. The new interest in appearance is
included in the article but not without qualification. Unlike the
glamorous stars on the silver screen, Frazier was not a created
or fictitious beauty. She came by her good looks honestly.

The lure of glamour aside, Frazier's story provides two clues
as to why the movie star image would not displace royalty in
the arena. First, movie stars were considered morally suspect.
Real members of the royal class might suffer an indiscretion
now and then, but in the theater moral impropriety had a
long and titillating history.[33] Actors and actresses commonly
portrayed good, upstanding characters on screen, but a quick
check of the newspapers told of multiple marriages, adulterous
affairs, and just plain bad behavior. But a more important reason that the rodeo queen persona held firm centered on the fact
that screen stars lacked one essential element associated with
royalty: lineage. Movie stars skyrocketed to glorious heights
but could just as easily fall from sight. There was no sense of
permanence, no bloodlines connecting people to one another
over time, within and across communities. The emergence of
glamour, then, did not depose the concept of royalty from the

arena. Instead, the traditional image of regality broadened to encompass the physical attractiveness of screen stars. The ideal for a rodeo queen was readjusted to fit the changing times and entered a new and enduring phase.

Hollywood and the fictitious quality of glamour influenced one other aspect of newspaper discourse on rodeo queens—the distinction between public and private life. Historically, theater people had an image problem, and this influenced perceptions of screen stars as well. By the mid-1930s the movie industry was in a fight to improve its own image and that of its actors and actresses. Industry-driven news stories and press releases highlighted the fact that the sultry, scantily clad beauties that appeared daily in the newspapers were just normal girls doing their job; when not on the clock, these women led altogether different lives. They wore clothes, not just evening gowns or bathing suits. They had hobbies, read books, and some even had families. In one feature, headlined "Some Form! And Re-form in Films," side-by-side photos showed actress Ida Lupino in a yachting costume described as "charmingly revealing" and in slacks, shirt, and cardigan sweater, with the caption "All dressed-up in non-exposure garb, going in for wholesome ex-ercise."[34] In the *Five Star Weekly*, a Saturday supplemental that briefly appeared in the *Pendleton East Oregonian* in 1936, the Hollywood section carried a running propaganda campaign. The following excerpt is one example of the tone of the ar-ticles: "Famous ones of Hollywood are human, 'Even as you and I' . . . the stars are just the same as girls and boys at the typewriters, or men and women reading the evening paper on the front porch—they're grand folk! REAL—that's it. . . . To be true, intelligent stars don't go about intentionally wreck-ing their own glamour, but beneath the professional manner and poise of most of them lurks a yen to have normal fun like normal folks."[35] The phrase "in private life" appeared in order to distinguish private, real-life activities of the stars from work-related activities created to promote a public image: photo shoots, glamour shots, and promotional tours. The *Pendleton East Oregonian* first used the phrase "in private life" when describing the activities of the Heppner, Oregon, rodeo queen.[36] Within a few years contrasting the dual nature of Round-Up queens—active and glamorous rodeo promoters and regular, down-to-earth members of the community—became a standard format for Round-Up royalty.

The glamorous aspect of the rodeo queen phenomena went hand in hand with the new forms of public media, radio, which created a mechanism for queens to become media stars in their own right. When the 1933 Round-Up queen, Jean Frazier, traveled to Portland on a booster trip, she gave two public addresses, one of which involved a radio interview.[37] Although the *Pendleton East Oregonian* did not usually cover the queen's promotional appearances, one article followed 1935 Round-Up queen, Helen Hansell, for a day and detailed her schedule: Pendleton Gun Club at 9 a.m. for photo-op shooting clay targets (she hit twenty-three out of twenty-five), then to the Pilot Rock Gun Club for a cameo appearance during their skeet-shooting tournament. Next stop, the rim rocks near Wild Horse Creek to pose shooting an arrow with Luke Cowapoo, a well-known member of the Umatilla Reservation, (with an artfully posed buffalo in the background), before heading to the Round-Up fair grounds for another photo session, this time on her horse. The last stop of the day was the Pendleton natatorium, where the queen smiled for the cameras yet again, standing on the diving board.[38]

In 1936 the announcement that Mary Robison would rule as queen of the Pendleton Round-Up came under the headline "A Very Busy Young Lady." The article noted, "Mary will be hustling aplenty from now until September 10, the day the big show opens. Every week she's called upon to pose for pictures and appear at celebrations."[39] One of Queen Mary II's promotional activities involved a trip to Portland, Oregon.[40] The photograph that accompanied the article showed Robison, wearing her Pendleton whites, with one foot on the running board of the Lincoln Zephyr, the Round-Up insignia on the door like a royal crest, and the USS *Houston* in the background. Her trip was orchestrated and reported like a movie star's promotional tour. Robison flew into Portland courtesy of United Air Lines, enjoyed a personal tour of the ship with an admiral, flirted with the crew, and had her photo taken with the deckhands while wearing a souvenir navy cap. She then drove off in the elegant Zephyr to participate in a "full schedule of social activities" arranged for her after her meeting with the admiral.[41] And yet in private life, she was still just plain Mary Robison.

The emphasis on distinguishing between a queen's royal duties and her "real" life increased significantly in 1940, when the Pendleton paper gave its readers a peek into the private life of their new queen, Marion Hughes. A full-page spread showed Hughes in a variety of settings and manners of dress, similar to the work/home articles on Hollywood stars at that time. One photo showed Hughes in a formal evening gown, standing next to her piano at home. In another, she worked a needlepoint project, the caption reading, "The hands of Queen Marion are as skilled with the needle as with the reins." Still another showed Marion in front of a picket fence she built: "Actual carpentering, including the use of saw, hammer and nails is one of Queen Marion's hobbies." It was minor carpentry, to be sure, no structural work involved, but the stories and photos, all under the headline "Grit, Good Sportsmanship, Beauty All There," countered the idea that Pendleton Round-Up queens were just flashy packaging.[42]

The 1941 queen, Maxine McCurdy, was the last queen to reign until 1944—the Round-Up went on hold during those war years. McCurdy, like Hughes, was shown in the papers in both her royal capacity and her "private life." One photo featured her in an evening gown: "The queen, who wears white buckskin for an official engagements, is here shown in formal dress—a black velvet evening wrap with ermine hood—a fur that traditionally could only be worn by members of royalty—worn over a gown of yellow flowered taffeta." Another photo showed her on campus "in her student togs and the smile that makes her one of the most popular of them all." And in another, under the heading "Queen Maxine Rides the Skyways Also," she is shown wearing her white buckskins with one foot in the stirrup, preparing to climb into the saddle.[43] Behind the queen and her horse sits a twin-engine airplane. As the *Pendleton East Oregonian* noted, the fact that she knew how to pilot a plane seemed "particularly fitting to the Round-Up city this year—newly made home of Pendleton Field, U.S. Army Air Corps base."[44]

In Pendleton, the number of promotional activities, cameo appearances, and social functions increased, and the Round-Up queens, functioning in the capacity of community representatives, met high-ranking government dignitaries, rodeo stars, movie stars, governors, and occasionally even presidents.[45] Prominently featured in papers across their region, these young women were removed from their ordinary, "private" lives and cast into the heady world of celebrity. And yet as their glamorous activities increased, newspaper discourse continued to emphasize the "real life" activities of the queens, grounding them in the values of the community.

An increase in public responsibility and exposure was one of the many changes that occurred during the 1930s; what the rodeo queens wore when out and about was another. The decade opened with Queen Lois I, sitting for her studio portrait, wearing the traditional Round-Up queen costume—a fringed leather skirt and vest, black tie, and black Stetson hat. Lois also wore English riding boots. Mildred Hansell, a princess on Lois's court, remembers, "Everybody rode with English boots. English was the correct style of riding for a lady. You wore polished boots and jodhpurs, even in a western saddle."[46] Though this statement seems to invite a discussion on costume and class, it is more likely a reflection on the fact that in 1930 there was no standardized western style of dress for women. As late as 1935, the remaining cowgirl athletes at the Pendleton Round-Up still dressed in an eclectic manner. A photo of eight cowgirl athletes appeared in the *Pendleton East Oregonian*'s souvenir edition, and with the exception of Reba Perry, who wore a western-style shirt, kerchief, and boot-cut pants, all the riders wore jodhpurs and sailor shirts, the type of clothing preferred by cowgirl athletes in the 1910s and 1920s.[47] Women's western wear had not yet developed its own distinctive style.

The movies undoubtedly played a large role in directing and standardizing the concept of "real" women's western style, where costumes for western heroines "reflected contemporary fashion rather than re-create authentic western fashions."[48] However, the style described for movie cowgirls, "provocatively tight and unbuttoned shirts and blouses, [and] equally undersized men's trousers," was a sexier version of the style of clothing worn by sponsor girls who had competed at the Stamford Texas Cowboy Reunion since 1931—a fitted shirt, riding pants, the obligatory kerchief, and western boots.[49] Hollywood took the regional style found in Texas, Oklahoma, and New Mexico, glamorized it, and popularized the style through numerous western movies.[50]

In Pendleton, the popularity of women's western costume became apparent in 1940, when the townswomen registered their interest in dressing like cowgirls during the Round-Up. When the Round-Up began in 1910, Pendleton's merchants started the tradition of dressing in western "togs" three weeks prior to the Round-Up to help advertise the event.[51] Over the years, the tradition extended to include all male Pendletonians. Thirty years later, it was "suggested that the ladies wear western costume also."[52] Round-Up directors encouraged Pendleton women to dress like the women they saw at other celebrations, with "loud shirts" and riding pants or jodhpurs. "Such outfits," the paper noted, "are much worn on dude ranches and are especially popular at Sun Valley [Idaho]."[53] To promote the idea the 1940 queen, Marion Hughes, graced the front page and women's section of the *Pendleton East Oregonian*, modeling appropriate, albeit conservative, western wear. In one photo, Hughes posed like one of the fashion models that appeared on the women's page; in the other she adopted a "cheesecake" pose, provocatively bent over a wall to show the embroidered detailing on the back pockets of her riding skirt.[54]

One might expect that the movies, with their emphasis on shiny costumes and revealing clothing lines, would influence the queens' costumes as it had popular women's western wear. But it did not, at least not in Pendleton during this era. Just as it was understood that community-sponsored rodeo queens were not really royalty, neither were they really movie stars. The stigma of theater and spectacle had been breached but only to a point. Professional actresses, models, and entertainers could publicly display themselves in revealing, form-fitting outfits, but young daughters of small-town, middle-class families did not. Their position as glamorous royalty was only temporary, and as such more risqué behavior would not have been appropriate. This attitude toward young townswomen did not limit itself to rodeo queens. In the spring of 1941, film star Jean Arthur's new movie, *The Devil and Miss Jones*, appeared in Pendleton's theater. The *Pendleton East Oregonian* announced that several of Pendleton's merchants would hold a fashion show between the first and second showing of the movie, and to spark more interest in the fashion show there would be a contest. Each of the participating merchants would have as its model a young woman whose height, weight, and measurements matched as closely as possible to those of Jean Arthur. The young women's measurements would be published, and during the fashion show the audience would decide who had a figure closest to the actress and award her the title Miss Jones of Pendleton. Apparently the contest crossed a line of propriety between the world of movie stars and real life; several days after the first mention of the contest, the rules changed. The young women's measurements, the paper announced, would not be made public, and "popular ballot instead of comparisons of measurements with 'Miss Jones' will determine the winner."[55]

In an article on the 1940 Round-Up queen, Marion Hughes, the *Pendleton East Oregonian* noted, "Skiing (and queening) run in the Hughes family."[56] This reference to "queening" marks the first time the word "queen" modified from a noun to a verb appeared in the Pendleton paper. Rodeo queens now had their own word, one that past rodeo queen Betsy Rose Rice defines as "the act of being a queen, actively participating in queen contests, or the culture of rodeo queens."[57] Queening would appear to be a logical development, based on the queen selection practices seen in Pendleton and in the Texas Cowboy Reunion's sponsor contest.

In Pendleton, the idea that a young woman could be queen more than once was not new. The first set of rodeo queens, from 1910 to 1917, created a formidable lineage by repeatedly swapping the crown among themselves. Muriel Saling expanded her queendom to include the Portland Rose Festival and the Astoria Regatta. But in the 1930s it became increasingly common for young women to reign both at their own hometown rodeo and at nearby community rodeos as well. For the most part, rodeo queens were appointed to their position, which illustrates the continuation of reciprocal boosterism to encourage goodwill and trade between towns.[58] As the daughters of small-town elites repeatedly appeared in the papers, as members of various rodeo courts, the idea that one could be queen multiple times became increasingly widespread.

While the papers had mentioned Round-Up royalty appointed to other rodeo courts since 1925, the mentions were very brief: "Miss Agnes McMurray, of Portland . . . and Miss Doris Churchill, queen of the Ellensburg fair this year, have been chosen as attendants for Miss Mildred Rogers, queen of the Round-Up."[59] The description of 1941 Round-Up queen Maxine McCurdy's royal career shows how much that had changed: "Her Majesty, 20, striking brunette with flashing smile, is no stranger to the kingdom of cowboys and cowgirls, for at the age of 14 she was a princess a the Heppner Rodeo; was its queen in 1938, and in 1939 was a Round-Up princess in the court of Barbara Kirkpatrick."[60] Not only did the article pay more attention to McCurdy's starlike attributes, or appearance, but it also highlighted the fact that she enjoyed the opportunity to engage in queening, having served on three previous rodeo courts.

Pendleton's concept of community—extended to anyone involved in the production of the Round-Up—encouraged queening. With so many people from the surrounding area involved with the Round-Up, young women from outside Pendleton commonly found themselves elected to the court as either queens or princesses. The 1936 Round-Up court carried this idea further than most, with only one young woman representing the town of Pendleton. The people outside Pendleton who worked on the Round-Up were often part of the larger rodeo community and participated in their own hometown rodeos. Therefore, queens and princesses on the Round-Up court often held multiple titles.

The amount of attention the queens received, and the glamour so recently attached to the position, encouraged local town boosters to modify the way they used the queen's role to promote their own rodeos. Beginning in 1933 rodeo royalty was featured in the papers as cowgirl athletes had been in earlier times, as teasers to keep the rodeo in the public eye. Appointments to queen and princess positions, announced over a period of time, piqued readers interest to see who would be selected next, where the girl was from, and if she had served as royalty elsewhere. Not only did it help advertise the rodeo, the increased press coverage of the queens, combined with the glamour of the position, encouraged the idea among young women in the region that perhaps they too could someday hold this coveted position.

The Stamford sponsor contest held at the Texas Cowboy Reunion also contributed to the development of queening by turning the royal selection process into a contest—an actual rodeo event where queen hopefuls competed against one another for the crown. In that contest, the queen was a twice-winnowed winner—first selected by her hometown or ranch to compete in the contest, then competing against other sponsor girls. An important feature of sponsor contests was that the young women freely entered into the competition. During the 1930s the number of sponsor contests proliferated, and young women had increased opportunities to enter contests. Rules on sponsorship relaxed too so that by the early 1950s, if no other source was available, friends would "sponsor" each other so they could compete in contests together.[61]

Cooney has described the general character of America in the 1930s as "a complex cultural mosaic under continuing construction." His description applies to the changing rodeo queen role as well.[62] The questions the *Pendleton East Oregonian* posed to potential queens in effect captured the cultural shifts "under construction": "Can you ride? Are you young? Attractive? Do you know how to smile? Do you like crowds? Are you gracious and charming to everyone you meet? Oh yes, AND CAN YOU RIDE?" Pendleton's community-sponsored rodeo queens embodied all of these requirements: royalty, glamour, riding ability, and promotional appeal. And the degree of importance assigned to each of the requirements was influenced, in some way, by the economic and political conditions of the 1930s.

When movies emerged in the 1930s and began to dominate American mass culture, their impact, as Cooney notes, "did not remain confined to the screen . . . but reached outward to blur the lines between entertainment and news, fantasy and reality, public relations and public values."[63] Pendleton Round-Up directors used the glamour image as they had the image of royalty: as a guideline for how to present the young representatives of their town, not as an absolute. While Pendleton boosters imitated the kind of publicity seen with movie stars and the Round-Up queens became actively involved in new forms of media promotion and celebrity-type promotional activities, they remained, in the end, hometown girls.

5. "We Like It Western!"

Redefining Rodeo Queens

In the spring of 1938 Ed McCarty of Chugwater, Wyoming, received a telegram from Pendleton Round-Up director George Strand. The telegram, in typical, breathless, Western Union form, read: "Board unanimous in choice of gene [sic] for 1938 queen congratulations send pictures for publicity purposes please do not release this your newspapers as we wish to make first story here letter follows. . . . Geo Strand."[1] Jean McCarty, a sophomore at the University of Wyoming, was home at the Chugwater Ranch, forty miles north of Cheyenne, when the telegram arrived. She recalls, "I was so excited! I had no idea they were considering me."[2] There was no reason why she should have expected to be named queen. McCarty had visited Pendleton with her parents several times and had even participated in the Happy Canyon horse quadrille, but neither she nor any member of her family was from Pendleton, and no one in her family had served on the Round-Up board.[3]

Prior to 1938 Pendleton had crowned only four queens who were not Pendleton residents.[4] The Round-Up derived so much of its success from the support of the local community that, at first glance, it seems rather odd that the directors would look all the way to Chugwater to find their new queen. But while rodeos tend to be viewed as isolated local events, in reality, a successful show required the participation of diverse groups of people that transcended specific geographical boundaries. The number of people involved in producing rodeos included not only the local boosters and rodeo boards but also cowboy and cowgirl athletes, rodeo association members, announcers, clowns, and stock contractors—the people who specialized in providing the bucking horses, calves, steers, and bulls for rodeo events.

Reflecting back on being told she was the 1938 queen of the Pendleton Round-Up, McCarty recalls, "I think my daddy had an inkling about it, but I certainly did not. I had no idea."[5] Ed McCarty, a well-known stock contractor, actively involved in the Cheyenne Frontier Days rodeo, and very much a part of this larger rodeo community, would have been privy to the fact that Pendleton directors were considering his daughter for the queen position. McCarty's selection as queen of the Pendleton Round-Up introduced a new meaning to the term "community-sponsored rodeo queen": She represented the people directly involved in producing rodeos, a position that exemplifies the dynamics of the rodeo community, transcending state and even regional boundaries. This community took great interest in noting what was new, different, or unusual at the other rodeos. For example, Pendleton Round-Up and Cheyenne Frontier Days rodeo directors borrowed ideas from one another in order to improve their local celebrations. But the story of Queen Jean McCarty gets even more interesting. That same year, 1938, her sister, Helen, reigned as the queen of the Cheyenne Frontier Days, which invites a comparison of two of the largest rodeos in the West and the ways in which Cheyenne Frontier Days adapted the rodeo queen idea to suit the particular characteristics of its town and celebration.

During the era of westward expansion towns sprang up throughout the West with amazing speed. The boosters for these new towns attempted to foster a sense of community by organizing festive events to encourage volunteerism and civic participation. If the event was well organized, a large portion of the local citizens would support it, if not actually participate: the greater the support, the greater the chance the event would be a success. Pendleton and Cheyenne are just two examples of towns in which the local elites, to use Eric J. Hobsbawm's phrase, "invented traditions" to benefit the community and create a sense of civic unity.[6] The town leaders' efforts to find a "useable past" served many purposes: it created a common interest among citizens with diverse backgrounds, interests, and class standing; it created a sense of continuity with the past; and it had the potential to generate income for the local economy. Both Pendleton and Cheyenne invented the tradition of a rodeo for their towns. As these communities looked to their ranching pasts to create new civic traditions, each drew from its own unique local history, traditions, and values. The results were two distinctively different celebrations and, ultimately, two distinctively different types of rodeo queens.

The town of Cheyenne was founded earlier than Pendleton, starting "as one of the 'hell on wheels' tent cities that followed General Grenville Dodge as he pushed the nation's first Trans-Continental Railroad westward in 1867."[7] Cheyenne evolved into a more permanent settlement when the Union Pacific Railroad established a winter settlement there and replaced the tents with rough wooden buildings. The town gained an even more permanent foothold when the U.S. Cavalry established a fort nearby. As this brief history suggests, Cheyenne did not start as a family oriented farming community. Rather, it drew young single men who followed the West's wage-workers' frontier, finding employment in transportation jobs, mining, and the military.[8]

The idea for a frontier days celebration in Cheyenne did not come from within the community, as it did in Pendleton, but from a Union Pacific Railroad employee, Frederick Angier, in 1897. Don Snoddy at the Union Pacific Museum notes that Angier's idea was "purely a mercenary effort" to boost train ticket sales, since "the men who worked with the locals were passenger traffic agents. Their job was to increase passenger traffic on Union Pacific. Regional celebrations, or national in the case of Cheyenne, meant that to reach the destination you had to travel by train. Maybe it meant the chance to haul a circus or at least the rodeo animals."[9] Cheyenne residents also found the idea of hosting an event that would bring visitors and cash very appealing. A slumping national economy affected the major economic markets in the state—mining, lumber, and transportation. The agricultural market suffered as well. Ten years earlier, the winters of 1886 and 1887 had devastated the cattle industry, and it had still not recovered. Shortly after the idea for a rodeo was proposed, a new tradition, Cheyenne Frontier Days, was born.

Thirteen years later, in 1910, when Pendleton town leaders decided to hold a rodeo, they looked to the nationally renowned Cheyenne Frontier Days as a model for establishing their own town celebration.[10] Almost immediately Cheyenne Frontier Days organizers returned the favor by traveling to Pendleton and scrutinizing its successful celebration. Over time, three of the precedents set at the Pendleton Round-Up—an orderly parade, a night show, and rodeo royalty—appeared at the Cheyenne Frontier Days. Since the very first Round-Up, Pendleton staged its Westward Ho! parade, a historic re-creation of civilization marching across the West. Cheyenne had also held a parade each year, beginning with its first Frontier Days celebration, but it was hardly orderly or educational. In keeping with its "hell on wheels" reputation, Cheyenne's parade could only be described as "pandemonium": young men galloping through the streets, some bareback on their cow-ponies, while "unruly cowboys lassoed pretty girls along the way and fired shots at upper story windows."[11] This exuberant display, which Clifford P. Westermeier observes as a "laxity [in] the standard of conduct among other people" of the region, reinforced the frontier, wage-worker character of the town. The local cowboys used the parade not so much to let off a little steam as to reassert their right, or place, within the community.[12] Several attempts were made to "tame the chaos" and hold orderly, theme-oriented parades along the lines of Pendleton's Westward Ho! parade. It was not until 1927 that middle-class sensibilities triumphed over the "sportin' crowd," permanently replacing the rowdy parades of the past.[13]

In 1927 Cheyenne also followed a precedent set by Pendleton when it began holding an organized night show for Frontier Days visitors.[14] Pendleton established their evening show, Happy Canyon, in 1914 to provide entertainment for the thousands of visitors who remained in town after the daytime rodeo was over. The show gave a historic overview of the area—from Native American life before the settlers arrived through the "winning of the West."[15] The Happy Canyon show proved popular with visitors and financially successful as well.

In September of 1926, a delegation from Cheyenne paid a visit to Pendleton. The *Pendleton East Oregonian* reported that the Cheyenne visitors were in town to watch the Round-Up and "to further cement the rapidly growing friendship between the two greatest shows of them all."[16] But the delegation had other motives as well. As the paper reported, "The Cheyenne delegation is particularly interested in Happy Canyon, as Frontier Days has no organized form of night entertainment for its crowd, and Pendleton's methods on the Happy Canyon attraction will be carefully surveyed and studied, with a possible view to establish some form of night entertainment at the Wyoming metropolis."[17]

Cheyenne visitors took notes on the Pendleton evening show

but adapted their idea of what constituted good entertainment to fit their Frontier Days crowd. Rather than follow Pendleton's format of a scripted play, Cheyenne organizers looked to the entertainment world and brought in big name performers—bands, singers, and actors.[18] In 1934 the fan dancer Sally Rand entertained Cheyenne with her "nude and naughty" fan dance act. Rand tantalized viewers with possibilities—never fully revealed to the crowd—and while her risqué performances bordered on the scandalous, they were considered "typical of the entertainment of the old West."[19] Cheyenne Frontier Days directors found a formula that worked: entertainers who were often rowdy, sometimes shocking but in touch with Cheyenne's "hell on wheels" history rather than Pendleton's educational and sanitized historical pageant.

The exchange of ideas among this rodeo community went beyond boosters' concerns for improving the entertainment value of their rodeos. In the late 1920s it included the role of cowgirl athletes in the arena. Cheyenne had been the first rodeo to allow women bronc riders to perform when Bertha Kaepernick gave an exhibit of women's bronc riding there in 1904.[20] Cheyenne also prided itself on holding a rodeo in which most of the events for cowboy and cowgirl athletes were competitive, rather than contract, or exhibition, events. The Cheyenne rodeo experienced a banner year for competitive events in 1927, as the *Wyoming Eagle* reported:

> Cheyenne Frontier Days, Daddy of them all, is known far and wide as a contest show. . . . This means that the events—riding, roping, and bulldogging—are all on a competitive basis with prizes for winners. Some of the Wild West shows do not attract their performers by the contest and the purses but by contracts and such shows are known as contract shows. In such cases top hands and famous cowboys and cowgirls do their riding, roping, and bulldogging daily for a certain specified sum, determined be-

tween the performer and committee in advance. Occasionally the Cheyenne show has had one or two contact exhibitions but this year all events are in the contest class.[21]

However, 1927 was the last year for women to ride in open rough-stock competition in Cheyenne. In 1928, a year before Bonnie McCarroll's death at the 1929 Pendleton Round-Up, Robert Hanesworth, Cheyenne Frontier Days committee secretary from 1926 to 1951, suggested the change, asserting that it was too difficult to determine a winner for women's bronc riding.[22] Women usually rode with the stirrups "hobbled," that is, with the stirrups tied under the horse's belly to keep them from flapping when the horse bucked. With stirrups hobbled, the argument went, it was easier for women to ride out the clock, thus the winner would be determined by the judge's decision. The problem, Hanesworth explained, was that "there were often-time arguments by the husbands of the riders who contended that the judges were partial and that the committee deliberately selected an inferior animal for their lady."[23] As soon as women's events were relegated to contract status, the importance of individual performers diminished. Cheyenne's move from competitive to contract events was one example of the concerns over women's roles in rodeo, which were being debated throughout the entire rodeo community.

The third significant exchange of ideas among the rodeo community focused on the concept of a rodeo queen. Cheyenne began its rodeo, as noted earlier, in 1897, thirteen years before the Pendleton Round-Up, but the directors did not considered the promotional advantages of having a rodeo queen until the Depression. When the Frontier Days committee did decide to have a queen, the selection process and role the young woman played relied heavily on the precedents set in Pendleton.[24] Rodeo organizers were deeply concerned that the poor economy would spell disaster for the Frontier Days celebration. As in

Pendleton, Cheyenne selected its first queens by holding ticket-selling contests, with the dollar amount of ticket sales contributing to the total number of votes. The Cheyenne directors, however, held tighter control over the contestants than did the organizers of the original Pendleton contest. Rather than allowing any young woman in the community to compete, civic groups, such as the Cheyenne Post of the American Legion, selected a young woman as their representative in the contest. It was considered an honor to represent a civic group in the queen race, and it could be exciting and lucrative as well: local merchants donated prizes, ranging from free chicken dinners to evening gowns to engraved calling cards and jewelry, that would appeal to the young, middle-class women who participated in the contest.[25]

Cheyenne's first queen's contest was a cliff-hanger. Six girls entered the competition, and until the very last minute, Patricia Keefe held a substantial lead. The evening before the ticket sales closed the *Wyoming Eagle* was so sure of the outcome it announced, "Patricia Keefe to be Queen."[26] But a flurry of ticket sales upset the outcome. As the next day's paper reported, "The event was decided in the last minutes Friday, when both girls and their sponsoring organizations took to the field in one of the most exciting races ever to accompany such a contest in Cheyenne."[27] Jean Nimmo came from behind to win with a total of 183,000 votes to Keefe's 146,050. Although a role had never been mentioned for a second-place winner during the competition, the directors awarded Keefe with the title, lady-in-waiting, perhaps as consolation for her stunning defeat. The lady-in-waiting role disappeared for the next few years, eventually returning to become a unique characteristic of Cheyenne royalty.

Familiarity with how Pendleton incorporated its royalty into their booster strategy meant Frontier Days organizers did not have to "reinvent the wheel." The first Cheyenne queen was

13. Jean Nimmo and Midnight graced the cover of the 1931 Cheyenne
Frontier Days Rodeo program. From the Collection of the Cheyenne
Frontier Days Old West Museum, Cheyenne, Wyoming.

put right into the spotlight. Within days after winning the title, Nimmo and Keefe traveled to Colorado as part of the annual booster trip, where the *Wyoming Eagle* reported, "The offices of Miss Frontier and her Lady in Waiting were recognized as of great importance in the success of the trip."[28] Nimmo received her crown—a ten-gallon hat—in front of the spectators during the opening night of the show, and her photo featured prominently in the rodeo program, where, casually attired in a short-sleeved shirt, riding jodhpurs, and chaps, she held the halter of and Ed McCarty's most famous bucking horse, Midnight.

The 1932 and 1933 Frontier Days queens were also selected by ticket-selling competitions, but the directors began to realize that a community-wide popularity contest was not perhaps the best way to select a rodeo queen. As Nimmo recalls, "Some of the girls couldn't ride, and were even afraid of horses."[29] In 1934 the directors settled on a format for selecting a queen that had proven successful in Pendleton: Cheyenne Frontier Days directors selected the girl themselves. As Jean McCarty recalls, the new selection process was a better fit for the rodeo community. "The popular vote," she says, "did not go well. Because, you can understand what the committee was interested in was the *history*, and they wanted the *people* who had contributed and lived in the community for a long time and were part of the developing Cheyenne Frontier Days."[30]

The Pendleton Round-Up provided the initial inspiration for Cheyenne's own rodeo queens. But within a very short time Cheyenne developed its own unique queen and court traditions, ones that reflected the distinctive characteristics of its town. Similarities between Pendleton and Cheyenne queens existed, of course, such as the class status of the queens and even the secretive selection process. As in Pendleton, Cheyenne Frontier Days directors discussed and settled on their choice for queen and informed the young woman's parents of their decision to make sure the parents did not have any objections.

Only then did the directors formally ask the young woman if she would accept the position. When the Cheyenne Frontier Days board considered nominating Jean McCarty for the 1939 lady-in-waiting position, her father, a board member at the time, decided to discuss the idea with her. Despite the honor of the nomination, she told him it was not a good idea: "I say, the only reason I felt that way was because Helen had just been queen, and there had been a lot of publicity about me being queen at Pendleton. I said [to my father], 'They'll just think that we've got the queen business corralled!'"[31] And so she declined the nomination.

As in Pendleton, all of the Cheyenne queens were from middle-class families. Cheyenne directors adhered to a rigid selection standard—all the young women selected for the queen position had to be enrolled in college.[32] The Cheyenne directors were also concerned with awarding the queen position to a local woman with strong ties to the history of the area and to Frontier Days. Pendleton directors worked to include young women from Portland or surrounding towns, even if the towns were in Washington or Idaho. Cheyenne directors limited their search to young women from Laramie County. The directors also stipulated that the queens must be descendants of pioneers. Past Frontier Days queens noted that not all pioneer families were in ranching—some were involved in local businesses—however, they all came from the county's "first" families.[33] The Cheyenne directors' requirements for Miss Frontier Days, then, highlighted the importance of middle-class values as well as the girl's lineage and the contributions of her family to the development of Laramie County, Wyoming, and the Cheyenne Frontier Days celebration.

One of the significant innovations at the Cheyenne celebration was the creation of the lady-in-waiting position. As mentioned earlier, the first queen contest ended so badly for the leading candidate that a second-place position was apparently created as a consolation prize. In 1934, when the directors took the selection process into their own hands, they reinstated the lady-in-waiting position. Rather than select a queen every year, the Cheyenne committee selected a lady-in-waiting. The resurrected position reflected the increasing responsibilities of the Cheyenne rodeo queen. The young woman who served in this position became, in reality, a queen-in-training. She traveled with the queen to all the booster events, rode with the queen in the parades and grand entries, and generally learned the royal ropes before ascending to the queen's position the following year.

The ascension to the throne, which occurred during the first day of Cheyenne Frontier Days, marked another way in which communities celebrated their queens according to local tastes. In Pendleton, the queen was presented at the Queen's Ball as part of a personal community celebration before the craziness of the Round-Up engulfed the town. In Cheyenne, a movie star or important political figure crowned the queen before thousands of spectators seated in the rodeo stands. The crowning of the queen in Cheyenne was not a personal moment for the community but rather part of the theatrical spectacle of the rodeo.

Whether inventing a significant role for community-sponsored royalty, like the lady-in-waiting position, or adapting existing details to suit their celebration, the Cheyenne Frontier Days organizers took the basic concept of a rodeo queen introduced in Pendleton and tailored it to fit their own local character. This ability to interpret which characteristics they felt were most important—the ones represented in their choice of rodeo queen, the roles she played, the rituals followed, even the design of the regalia inspired by Sally Rand's own cowgirl costume—allowed Cheyenne to emphasize its own history, character, and vision of itself.[34] The sharing, borrowing, and adapting of ideas between Pendleton and Cheyenne was representative of the amount of interaction among members of the rodeo community. But communities, either grounded in place or geographically unbound, are made up of individuals. Ed McCarty, father of two 1938 rodeo queens, Pendleton's Queen Jean and Cheyenne's Queen Helen, played an important role in this rodeo community; because of his involvement, his daughters were selected as queen of the two largest rodeos in the West.

Born in Chugwater, Wyoming, Ed McCarty began as a cowboy athlete, riding the rodeo circuit in 1912. He first made the news at the Pendleton Round-Up in 1913, taking the steer roping titles in 1913 and 1918.[35] McCarty soon turned his attention to supplying bucking horses, steers, and calves to rodeos, and in 1922 he formed a partnership with Vern Elliott from Johnstown, Colorado. McCarty began furnishing bucking horses, Brahma bulls, Mexican steers, and arena saddle horses that same year.[36] It did not take long for McCarty and his partner to develop their business. As a newspaper reported, by the mid-1920s, they had "run a scrawny bronc and a maverick into a string of stock worth a hundred thousand dollars."[37]

Newspapers liked to promote the idea that rodeo cowboys were rough, uncivilized hands, and one article played up what appeared to be the McCarty paradox: "Strangest part of Ed's early days is the fact that he actually graduated from Cheyenne High School. That hardly sounds like a cowhand."[38] Indeed, the reality suggested that Ed McCarty and his family were firmly situated as middle-class Wyoming ranchers. The family had evolved from pioneer ranchers in the 1860s to successful stock raisers and adhered to middle-class norms concerning education, appearance, and respectability.[39]

Ed McCarty became involved with rodeo participants at all levels of the sport. He and his partner owned some of the most famous bucking horses in the country: Midnight, Five Minutes to Midnight, Carioco, Reservation, Broken Box, and Headlight. These horses were legendary on the rodeo circuit, and to attract spectators town boosters advertised the horses with the same enthusiasm as they did the cowboys who tried to ride them.[40] McCarty and his stock traveled extensively: Madison Square Garden in New York City; Chicago; Los Angles; Denver; Omaha; Baton Rouge, Louisiana; Deadwood, South Dakota; London; San Antonio, Texas; and, of course, Pendleton, Oregon. McCarty and his family traveled by train, which was the common mode of transportation in the 1920s and 1930s for riders and stock on the rodeo circuit. Jean also remembers the emphasis on manners in her family, on appropriate ladylike behavior and dressing appropriately: "You wouldn't get on the train without being properly done."[41]

Although McCarty was probably best known for his rodeo stock, he also owned a stable of racehorses. As Jean McCarty recalls, "You couldn't have a rodeo without a relay race."[42] Cowboy and cowgirl relay races were popular events at rodeos, recalling the old days of the cowboy frontier when cowboys prided themselves on the speed of their horses. McCarty hired well-known cowgirl riders, such as Ruth Roach and Tad Lucas, to ride his horses in the rodeo relay races. Mabel Strickland also rode relay and flat races for Ed McCarty and was a frequent visitor to the McCarty ranch. "She was Aunt Mabel to me," Jean McCarty recalls.[43] Strickland, who had been Round-Up queen eleven years earlier, sent Jean a letter of encouragement during her reign in Pendleton:

> Darling Jean,
>
> I hope you are not completely worn out yet and are still having a grand time. Your dad invited me to see the parade with them from their hotel room window, so believe I'll try and make it Friday morning. We have a phone now. Would have called but that I might not find anyone in. Be seeing you.
>
> > Always,
> > Your adoring Aunt Mabel[44]

Working together and traveling together helped foster sense of community—if not a sense of family—among the rodeo crowd.

Despite her obvious ties to the rodeo community, the question why Round-Up directors selected Jean McCarty of Chugwater, Wyoming, to reign over their show still lingers. There were several reasons why they might have selected McCarty as the 1938 monarch—none of them mutually exclusive. The directors knew that Helen McCarty was queen of the Cheyenne Frontier Days and took advantage of having sister queens to boost their rodeo's publicity. It was also quite likely that selecting Jean was a show of appreciation to Ed McCarty and his excellent rodeo stock for continuing to make the Pendleton Round-Up a success. But it is also possible that an element of politics in the rodeo community contributed to Jean's selection.

Unrest permeated the rodeo community in 1937 and 1938. Basic human imperatives such as wanting to be in a group, wanting to keep others out, trying to keep the group together, or trying to stay in control—these are relevant concerns for all communities, and the rodeo community was no exception.[45] But concern over gaining and keeping control was an especially serious issue during these two years.

The Rodeo Association of America (RAA), organized in 1929, consisted of various people involved in organizing and staging a rodeo—rodeo board members, stockholders, and stock suppliers. The mission of the RAA was, "to standardize rodeo events, maintain a calendar so dates of major rodeos would not be in conflict, and to set a method of determining world championships."[46] Cowboys, excluded from the RAA, formed their own organization. In November 1936 the United Cowboys Turtle Association emerged, designed to protect rodeo competitors from what they considered unfair management practices of the RAA. They argued against mandatory standardized bronc-rid-

14. Jean and Helen McCarty. Photo taken on the McCarty ranch, Chugwater, Wyoming, 1938. Note that Helen, on the right, is wearing the Miss Frontier Days costume. Courtesy of Jean McCarty Dearinger, private collection, Laramie, Wyoming.

ing saddles, against those whom they considered unqualified judges, and against RAA decisions over which contestants could participate in their rodeos.[47] In what reads like any one of a number of labor/management conflicts that rocked the United States during the 1930s, the Turtles threatened to strike rodeos throughout the West—Pendleton included—that did not meet their demands for change.[48]

If carried out, the strikes would have led to financial disaster. The Pendleton Round-Up directors decided to take an offensive position, posting a sign at the registration office, "No Turtles Need Apply," then actively encouraging local, non-professional cowboy athletes to compete at the Round-Up.[49] McCarty, who had "won his spurs" in the rodeo arena as a cowboy, kept on good terms with many professional rodeo athletes. In fact,

McCarty's ability to get along with both groups allowed him to convince the Turtles to drop their demands and participate in the 1939 Round-Up.[50] Throughout the Turtle controversy McCarty continued to supply stock to the Round-Up, representing a show of solidarity among the management level of the rodeo community—the people in charge of putting on the rodeo—as well as an effort to bring the two groups together.

Jean McCarty's selection as queen in Pendleton, at the height of the RAA-Turtle battle indicates that rodeo managers, producers, and suppliers—the upper-echelons of the rodeo community—were unified. Politics aside, as queen of the Pendleton Round-Up, Jean had a full slate of promotional duties to attend. The role of queen had indeed expanded since Bertha Anger first waved to the crowds from her float in 1910. Although promotional obligations declined from 1929 until the worst of the Depression had lifted, by 1938 better economic times, combined with the fact that cowgirl athletes had been relegated to a limited number of contract events, opened the way for community-sponsored rodeo queens to be more visible and take a more active role in the rodeo.

For young Jean McCarty, reigning over the Round-Up proved a wonderful experience: "They just treated you like a queen. They gave you your outfit and my lovely shirts—I always had flowers in my hotel room. They [gave] lovely parties, and the people in Pendleton are so *gracious* and they did *lots* of nice things. And—it was an *honor*."[51]

Prior to the Round-Up celebration, Jean McCarty stayed at Herb Thompson's ranch, just outside of Pendleton (both his daughter Thelma and niece Helen had been frequent members of Round-Up royalty in the 1920s).[52] As Jean recalls, "I went out in the first part of August . . . because you had to be there early . . . you went around the community, like up to Ellensburg, Washington, for a rodeo, and La Grande—and I can't remember, other places. To luncheons, and dinner, and to Portland

15. Jean McCarty, striking the fashionable rodeo pose of the day for the Round-Up publicity photographer. Photo taken on the McCarty ranch, Chugwater, Wyoming, 1938. Courtesy of Jean McCarty Dearinger, private collection, Laramie Wyoming.

to the Rose Festival, and . . . that's what your job was, really. It was to promote the Round-Up."[53] At the Pendleton Round-Up, the queen was no longer just a pretty girl walking her horse into the arena; rodeo queens had replaced cowgirl athletes as the star female attraction in the arena. And these daughters of the West—like the cowgirl athletes they supplanted—would be expected to prove their riding abilities.

When the Pendleton Round-Up directors sent a photographer to the McCarty ranch to shoot publicity photos, they had a particular pose in mind. Following the trend that emerged in 1930, they wanted a photo of Jean on a rearing horse when they announced her as the 1938 queen. Jean thought the whole idea was ridiculous. She had a well-trained horse, one not inclined to rear. In fact, she recalls, he had never reared before, did not want to rear—it took over an hour of hard work to get him to perform the stunt—and once Jean did figure out how to get him to rear, he never did it again.[54]

Each rodeo had its own method for showcasing the riding abilities of its queens. When Jean McCarty traveled to the Ellensburg, Washington, rodeo to promote the Round-Up, all queens—home court as well as visitors—were expected to show their riding abilities as they were introduced to the crowd. For Jean, it proved to be a disconcerting experience:

> I didn't have a horse with me [and a] . . . cowboy gave me this horse to ride. And he said, "Now," he said, "this is a cold-jawed old horse. If he ever starts to run with you, you'll never get him stopped." But I was expected to jump him into the arena and jump him out and then ride him around the track, and then stop before the grandstand, and somebody was supposed to take the horse and [we'd] go up in the grandstand. Well, I got him jumped in, and jumped out, and onto the track—and he took off. And I could not [stop him]. I had his head clear around in my lap and I could not stop him. And, well, I'll never forget it. There were

about four guys came across the track the other way, not *one* of them tried to stop this horse. And I finally ran him clear around, got him off the track, and ran him into the side of a barn to get him to stop. It hurt my pride more than anything else, I guess. . . . And George Strand . . . bless his heart, he came and got the horse, and got me off of him, and we went up in the judges stand. And, as I say, I was so embarrassed I thought I'd die. And George said, "Oh, we liked it! We like it western!"[55]

McCarty was fortunate. An experienced rider, she knew the standard technique for stopping a runaway horse—turning the horse in ever-smaller circles until it could be brought to a halt. Although the horse kept running, she stayed in the saddle and considered her options (the most reasonable, under the circumstances, was to stop the horse by facing it with a barn wall). Her experience indicated a significant change in expectations for rodeo queens. It was assumed queens would be able to ride whatever horse was available, to keep their composure under the most trying circumstances, and to show the gracious girt and can-do attitude of a real western woman.

The response to McCarty's runaway horse from the four cowboy athletes—or rather, the lack of response—brings up the class division within the rodeo community again: working-class contestants and middle-class management. With minor exception, by the late 1930s rodeo queens like McCarty belonged to the upper echelons of the rodeo community. These queens did not have the same relationship with the contestants that cowgirl athletes had enjoyed. Mary Lou LeCompte notes that there were still a few cowgirl athletes participating in rodeo, predominantly in relay races, but by 1938 their numbers were few indeed.[56] The cowboy athletes looked upon the cowgirl athletes' genteel replacements as outsiders. While Jean and her sister Helen had a wealth of experience in riding, roping, and other skills associated with their chores back on the

Chugwater Ranch, there was never a question about whether the young women would compete in the rodeo arena. As Jean recalls, "My father would not allow us to do that."[57] There was, of course, a father's concern over the dangers of riding in rodeo, dangers he had witnessed firsthand. But there was also the concern over ladylike behavior and the potential harm that might come about from freely associating with men. McCarty recalls a family friend who encouraged his daughters to participate in rodeo events, exposing his daughters "to just any— all—men that were around, cowboys or whatever. My father was adamant about that sort of thing, you know."[58]

The weeks Jean stayed in Pendleton for the Round-Up gave her a chance to meet people from Pendleton and become familiar with the community. Her position as an imported queen allowed her to compare Pendleton and Cheyenne attitudes toward their respective celebrations. One of the most striking differences she noticed involved how each of these communities included Native Americans in their celebrations. Unlike Pendleton, Cheyenne is not situated near an Indian reservation. In order to have Indians participate in Cheyenne Frontier Days and to travel with the booster caravans, the directors usually hired thirty Indians from several reservations.[59] A select group of Native Americans brought in for the show was quite a contrast to the number of Indians who freely participated at the Round-Up. McCarty was surprised when she saw the number of Indians at the Round-Up, recalling, "But in *Pendleton*—I think there must have been 500 tipis on the grounds when I was there. And they were all different tribes from all over the Northwest, and they had such *beautiful* costumes. And they— Sioux—had too, but there were just so many of them [in Pendleton] and they participated more in races and things."[60]

Not only were fewer Indians involved in the celebration in Cheyenne, but there was a noticeable difference in the newspaper discourse of Cheyenne and Pendleton papers describing the Indians. In her book on newspaper portrayals of Native Americans in the twentieth century, Mary Ann Weston writes that in general, journalistic practices, traditions, and story organization reinforced stereotypes of Indians rather than challenged them.[61] Weston does not explicitly discuss Indians in celebrations like the Pendleton Round-Up and Cheyenne Frontier Days other than to say, "There were stories that evoked images of Indians as exotic tourist attractions who dressed in colorful costumes and engaged in picturesque ceremonies while boosting the local economies."[62] This is certainly evident in both towns, but this description obscures an important difference between how Pendleton and Cheyenne portrayed Native Americans in their respective towns.

Weston argues that the tone and language used to describe Indians in the news was due to the distance between the Indian community and the paper reporting the news. In local papers where Indians were part of the "community fabric," stories tended to report Indian activities "as people with many-faceted lives, not unlike their white neighbors."[63] The greater the distance the publication was from the story, "the more likely was the story to engage in sweeping generalizations that amounted to stereotyping."[64] The issue of distance is apparent in the news stories in communities who hosted Indian events but did not have day-to-day ties with Native Americans. In Cheyenne the Indians were not part of the community but were "show Indians," brought in as part of the spectacle to highlight Cheyenne's exotic western past. The tone of the language describing the Native Americans was, not surprisingly, highly stereotypical. One example seen in the *Wyoming Eagle* newspaper announced, "The Indians are here! Sixty hideously painted and gaudily garbed redskins, members of the Burnt Thigh tribe, arrived in Cheyenne late this week. . . . Included in the party were 40 bucks, 15 squaws, and 5 children."[65] Cheyenne's paper, distant from the Indians hired for the show, emphasized the "bloodthirsty Indian" image to provide exotic, "Old West" appeal for the Frontier Days celebration, the pejorative descriptions implicitly suggesting savagery, inferiority, social separation, and "a highly stereotypical history of Indian-white relations."[66]

Pendleton was not immune to reaching into the past lexicon to describe the Native Americans who participated in the Round-Up. However, their emphasis was not on the barbarity of the Indians but on the inherent good of their natural, Native qualities.[67] The proximity of the reservation to towns and the connection between communities that developed—or did not develop, in Cheyenne's case—can also explain the rodeo directors attitudes toward Indian women as royalty. When Cheyenne held its Frontier Days celebration in July of 1932, Pendleton's 1933 queen had not yet been selected, so the second Native American queen, Melissa Parr, continued her role and accompanied the Round-Up delegation to Cheyenne. During the Frontier Days celebration, it must have occurred to one of the directors that Cheyenne and Pendleton had shared ideas before, and perhaps they could share another idea—an Indian queen to advertise their rodeo.

The Cheyenne Frontier Days directors most likely did not have any qualms about asking Melissa to be their representative. After all, they had a long tradition of hiring Indians to perform as exotic representatives of Wyoming's frontier era. Their businesslike approach to hiring attractions to draw in spectators—from movie stars to Native Americans—explains why Cheyenne officials could be so bold as to ask a Pendleton queen to reign over their rodeo. It also helps explain Parr's refusal.[68] For Parr, the title queen of the Round-Up meant something personal, and she was willing to represent both her tribe and the Round-Up as queen. However, she had no interest in being put on display as part of Cheyenne's show.

When Jean McCarty, from Chugwater, Wyoming, reigned over

the Pendleton Round-Up in 1938, she represented not just a local, or geographically bound community but a regional rodeo community. Like all communities, this one consisted of a complex group of individuals, complete with celebrities, hierarchies, and conflicts. Members of this rodeo community—especially the directors, who transferred ideas from other rodeos to their own, hoping to attract more spectators and improve the overall quality of their shows—took great interest in each other's rodeos. Unbeknownst to McCarty, she represented all levels of the rodeo community when she served as the Pendleton queen—from the "swipes" (stable hands) to the rodeo presidents—and introduced a new meaning to the term "community-sponsored" rodeo queen.

McCarty's reign allows for a comparison between the position of rodeo queens in Pendleton and Cheyenne. Cheyenne Frontier Days organizers studied the Pendleton role, then adapted it to suit their celebration, which emphasized a wilder, bawdier, Old West interpretation of the West than Pendleton's celebration did. Their lady-in-waiting position, which first appeared in 1931 and returned in 1934, became a unique Cheyenne innovation, while keeping the main characteristics of the role of the rodeo queen intact. As new rodeos sprang up across the West during the post–World War II years, ideas transferred among members of this rapidly expanding rodeo community as they had between Pendleton and Cheyenne and encouraged a shift in the role of community-sponsored rodeo queens.

6. "It Was Great Being Queen"

The Postwar Era, 1944–1955

There was no Round-Up in 1942 or 1943; World War II caused the Round-Up directors to cancel the event for those two years. The directors and city council members worried that large crowds gathered so close to the Pendleton Air Base might pose an inviting target for enemy aircraft. But the directors were also keenly aware of the mood in town; with so many local and professional cowboys off fighting the war Pendleton did not have its heart in staging the big Round-Up celebration. And so in 1942—for the first time since it began in 1910—the show did not go on. As the local newspaper headline explained, "Western Classic Steps Aside for Greater Round-Up of the Axis."[1]

When the Pendleton show resumed in 1944 changes in the queen's role became immediately apparent. Trends that had emerged in the 1930 to 1941 era—queens fulfilling the role of cowgirl and the influence of glamour—became more pronounced. These developments, combined with a neo-Victorian emphasis on femininity and traditional gender roles, laid the groundwork for a new era in rodeo queen history, albeit one that coexisted with an alternative undercurrent that defied conformity. As new rodeos cropped up during this postwar era rodeo queens became ubiquitous feature throughout the West, and hundreds of young women vied for the chance to represent their community and enjoy time in the public spotlight.

Historian Kristine Fredriksson writes that despite Pendleton's decision to cancel the Round-Up in 1942 and 1943, World War II actually encouraged the growth of rodeo.[2] It seems counter-intuitive that rodeo would thrive with travel restrictions, gas and tire rationing, rodeo cancellations, and the draft—as Fredriksson points out, the sport of rodeo required healthy young men, just the sort the draft board found so appealing. But the two major rodeo associations, the Cowboy Turtle Association and the Rodeo Association of America (RAA) worked to overcome these war-related obstacles.[3] To compensate for travel difficulties, the two associations encouraged the development of new, smaller rodeos that could draw on their local populations for support. To encourage spectators to support the new rodeos, both the RAA and the Turtles encouraged rodeo directors to personalize their events, to capitalize on local interests and local riders, and to make the most of the patriotic fervor by associating the sport of rodeo with patriotism.

The RAA began to encourage the development of local rodeos as early as 1941. Fredriksson notes that by then rodeo had found its niche, and RAA directors did not want to loose their spectator base. The cancellation of major western rodeos, like the Pendleton Round-Up, provided an opportunity to develop new contests in communities where none had existed.[4] The new rodeos included sanctioned rodeos—those who followed RAA rules and included the required events—as well as small, non-sanctioned rodeos that existed for perhaps only a few years. The *Pendleton East Oregonian* reported on some of the new rodeos in the area; whereas the Round-Up drew in forty to sixty thousand spectators over a three-day period, shows like the George Attebury Rodeo, first held in 1941, attracted much smaller audiences. Held at the Attebury ranch outside the town of Stanfield, Oregon, and about twenty-five miles from Pendleton, the George Attebury Rodeo attracted only about six hundred spectators.[5] Mildred Hansell, a 1930 Round-Up princess, recalls that before the war, "there weren't many rodeos. Pendleton was one of the few in the country." During the war, however, "anybody who had a corral and a few friends [could] have a rodeo."[6]

Fredriksson notes that travel restrictions imposed by the war led the RAA to advise local rodeos to concentrate on the spectators in their own communities and to make the shows more interesting, not only to those who would normally attend but also to those who had never attended a hometown rodeo.[7] Freedom from RAA requirements opened the door for small rodeos to add or delete events depending on local interests and availability of stock and riders, including amateur women riders. In order to have enough competitors for these new rodeos, members of the Cowboys Turtle Association allowed non-members to participate.[8]

Tailoring small rodeos to the interests of local residents was one way to keep rodeo alive during the war, but patriotism became a major mechanism for gaining attention. The Pendleton Round-Up had actually featured a flag and the national anthem at the start of the show since its origins in 1910.[9] However, Fredriksson notes that rodeo became synonymous with patriotism during the war in a way it never had before.[10] During the war, President Roosevelt specifically instructed Major League Baseball to continue as a morale builder, and the RAA promoted rodeo as a morale builder as well. Some animals were given patriotic names, like Four Freedoms, the champion bucking horse at the 1945 Round-Up.[11] However, Fredriksson writes, "In a curious sense, the competing cowboys represented, to people at home, the fighting men overseas, and parallels were drawn between fighting the enemy and conquering the animal in the arena."[12] Many rodeo directors began to incorporate patriotic themes; for example, in 1941 at the Cheyenne Frontier Days, the crowds cheered "with patriotic spirit" the second annual Parade of Flags in the grand entry.[13] And in Denver, Colorado, at the National Western Rodeo held in 1942, "For the first time in the rodeo's twelve year history, each of the fifteen performances opened with a grand entry, in which 150 mounted cowboys and cowgirls participated. The color and the patriotism displayed in such a parade heightened the desired social consciousness."[14]

Pendleton directors did not wait until the war officially ended to reinstate their rodeo. William O'Neill writes, "By 1944 everyone smelled victory and saw no need to keep their noses to the grindstone."[15] In Pendleton, townspeople and visitors alike showed enthusiasm for Round-Up entertainment. The Dress-Up parade, which formally signaled the beginning of the Round-Up season, set two records in 1944: the largest crowd ever gathered to watch the parade and largest number of mounted entries in the parade's history.[16]

Reinstating the Round-Up in 1944 was indeed a grand event, one that required a queen worthy of the honor. The directors selected Janet Thompson to bear the crown. The Thompson family had a long and active history with the Round-Up, and Janet Thompson descended from an impressive Round-Up royalty lineage: Edna Thompson was a princess on Bertha Anger's court in 1910; Helen Thompson reigned as queen in 1921, Thelma Thompson in 1922, and Shirley Thompson in 1934. Numerous other young Thompsons appeared on royal courts as princesses. In fact, this was not Janet's first stint as queen—in 1935 she co-ruled as Pendleton's first and only junior Round-Up queen.

In their decision to select Thompson as queen, the directors followed the tradition of honoring members of the Pendleton

16. Janet Thompson, 1944 Round-Up queen. When Pendleton resumed its show toward the end of World War II, the queen and court appeared in new riding costumes. The traditional split-buckskin skirts and vests had been replaced by parade suits-matching western style pants and shirts. Courtesy of Howdyshell Photography, Pendleton, Oregon.

community who supported and produced the Round-Up. Family position was not the sole basis for ascension to the coveted position—since 1930 queens also had had to prove they could ride. And it was no longer adequate to simply ride well—a queen needed to show she was a "ranch hand," someone familiar with western skills. The *Pendleton East Oregonian* noted Thompson's reputation "as one of the best girl riders in the Pacific Northwest" and claimed that "from childhood she has been a real ranch hand."[17] But Thompson also fulfilled middle-class expectations. She attended the University of Oregon and enjoyed appropriately genteel leisure activities—golf, tennis, skiing, swimming, and angling (fly fishing).[18] During the war Thompson had participated in the Food for Victory campaign and during pea harvest had worked long hours driving a truck and working a pea loader. In their search for a special young woman to reign over the Round-Up, the directors found in Thompson someone who embodied the values and attitudes of contemporary western womanhood—pioneer lineage, middle-class status, ranch hand skills, and civic responsibility—which made her a solid choice. Leah Conner, 1952 Round-Up queen, recalls, "This girl was really a queen. . . . She was just robust and full of energy and very much a western queen."[19]

Thompson had stepped in to do what was considered "distinctly a man's job" during the war, driving truck and helping with the harvest.[20] In this respect she exemplified the many women who filled the traditionally male positions that were vacated by the men called to war. For the most part women returned to the domestic sphere as soon as the war ended. Maureen Honey argues that while women took over male jobs during the war, the war did not change ideas about women's proper roles.[21] While arguments appeared in the *Pendleton East Oregonian* about the necessity for women to have the skills and training to support themselves should the need arise there was none of the tug-of-war over women's place in society as there had been during the 1920s; rather, during the postwar era the "ideal of family served as a national unifier, becoming a symbol of what the American system was all about."[22] The war era created a yearning for family stability, in which, as Elaine Taylor May notes, "the powerful ideology of domesticity was imprinted on everyday life" and where "traditional gender roles became a central feature of the 'modern' middle class home."[23] The term "neo-Victorian," describes this general cultural movement to move women back into the domestic sphere to create a sense of stability and normalcy. Ironically, the "new" Victorianism did not recreate the gendered domains of a previous era; rather, it was a new creation based on old ideas. Jessica Weiss, describing the domestic ideals of the postwar era writes, "Contrary to the nostalgic image of fifties marriage, this was not traditional terrain; rather it was terrain never before traversed, and it involved struggle, conflict, and extreme gender strain."[24] The emphasis on early marriage and domesticity informed the cultural milieu of 1940s and 1950s era of rodeo queens, and yet as queens discovered, the opportunities of the position gave them the confidence and exposure to move beyond these narrow bounds, if they chose.

World War II finally ended in August 1945, less than a month before the September Round-Up, and Pendletonians prepared to celebrate the war's end with a "Victory" Round-Up. The *Pendleton East Oregonian* reported, "No question about it, with gasoline rationing off, other restrictions removed and the war now a thing of past history, the 1945 show will be jam-packed with guests."[25] The Round-Up directors selected Donne Boylen of Pendleton to reign over the show. Boylen considered her appointment "a dream come true." A *Pendleton East Oregonian* article reported, "Ever since she has been old enough to know what it's all about, she's wanted to be queen of the big show. 'It's a dream I've always had,' said Her Highness, 'and last year, when I was a princess, I thought it was pretty swell, but to be QUEEN! Whew! I'm a lucky gal.'"[26] Media coverage on the queen and her court followed the format developed during the 1930s, with the *Pendleton East Oregonian* announcing the queen for the upcoming Round-Up in June, running another feature article on her one month before the Round-Up, then once a week for the next four weeks printing an article and photo introducing the court princesses.

In 1945, however, the Pendleton paper introduced something new—a queen's section in the souvenir edition, featuring two full pages of photos and text. The articles and photo captions on Boylen covered the usual family history and connections to the Round-Up and her college and ranch-hand accomplishments. The five large photos of Boylen and the accompanying captions reinforced the qualities important for a postwar community-sponsored rodeo queen. One photo showed her astride her horse, wearing her Round-Up costume, signifying her riding ability. In another, she posed wearing a western shirt and riding pants while fixing a bridle—a necessary skill for a "ranch hand" as opposed to a dilettante "cowgirl." And in a third, she appeared in formal attire. The fourth pose, reflecting contemporary expectations for young women, showed the queen in the kitchen, wearing a feminine peasant blouse and skirt and mixing a cake. The article noted, "Donne is a sure-nuf cook, and she is, she can whip up an entire meal from meat courses to dessert" (the paper included her favorite recipe for chocolate cake). The most novel pose, however, showed Boylen in a bathing suit. Compared to the prewar photos of movie stars in swimsuits, hers is a rather modest pose, seated by the edge of a pool. Apparently her "interest in swimming," meant it was fair game to print this chaste-yet-seductive photo of her in a bathing suit.[27]

Taken together, the five photos offer an updated version of true western womanhood. The nineteenth-century pioneer version, according to Elizabeth Jameson, "reflected the cardinal virtues of . . . piety, purity, domesticity, and submissiveness to male authority."[28] During the postwar resurgence of middle-class Victorian standards, community-sponsored rodeo queens exemplified the new generation of gentle tamers in a modern West: capable ranch hands who encouraged family values and morality from the domestic sphere and who enjoyed a few moments of glamour in the community spotlight before settling down to the grown-up task of starting a family.

These chaste-yet-seductive images set a precedent that would continue throughout this era and fit in the neo-Victorian postwar culture.[29] May notes that female sexuality was seen as a healthy defense against the "perverse and immoral" threat of communism. Strong, heterosexual relationships would thwart dangerous communist characteristics—homosexuality and rampant sexual activity—by encouraging early marriage and family values.[30] The demure sexuality of a rodeo queen posed in a bathing suit did not come close to the steamy sensuality of movie star "cheesecake" images, but it did acknowledge the public nature of sexuality, a part of the dating culture that encouraged fulfilling, youthful marriages.[31]

It is interesting to note that "cheesecake" photos of women had nearly disappeared from the *Pendleton East Oregonian* once America entered the war and that the image of actresses changed from arbitrators of fashion taste and scantily clad pin-ups to role models on how to help with the war effort. The few "cheesecake" images that did appear usually featured actresses who had won polls conducted among servicemen, such as "the girl we'd most like to tie the knot with," or "the girl sailors would most like to pinch."[32] However, once the war ended the influence of glamour that had developed prior to America's entry into the war resurfaced even more profoundly. The influence of movie stars and media—especially in terms of exposing the feminine form, "cheesecake"—returned with remarkable rapidity, manifesting itself in mainstream culture in unexpected ways, like rodeo queens in bathing suits.

In 1948 Virginia Wilkinson, from the Umatilla Reservation, reigned as Pendleton's Round-Up queen. Round-Up directors did not keep records as to why they selected all-Indian courts when they did (or any queen and court, for that matter). Most likely their decision rested on a combination of factors. The most obvious is recognition of Native American patriotism—honoring those who helped secure victory for the United States during the war, either by enlisting or by purchasing war bonds.[33] Of course, the directors had a longstanding tradition of making queen and court appointments to honor members of the Round-Up community, of which Umatilla Reservation members were an important part. As a reporter for the *Pendleton East Oregonian* wrote, "Since its inception, the Round-Up has welcomed the Indian as a real part of the great western epic; it's his festival and that of his family, and all have done much to further the success of the Round-Up through the 37 years of performances."[34] The paper noted that Wilkinson "and her family have long been prominent in the Round-Up."[35]

In a larger context, Queen Virginia's selection represents changing views of Native Americans in the United States. The first Native American queen was selected in 1926 at a time when discontent with industrialization created an anti-modern backlash.[36] Native Americans seemed so natural, so removed from the ills of modern society, so at peace with nature that, as Mary Ann Weston writes, "In the 1920s the good Indian might be depicted as someone who possessed serenity, tranquility, and oneness with the natural world that was envied by materialistic whites."[37] In the 1930s Americans embraced ethnic diversity as a way of positioning American culture against Nazi racism. In the immediate postwar era, as Americans positioned themselves against the Soviet Union in the Cold War, it became important once again to demonstrate that Americans were not racist. To counter Soviet claims of racism, it became important to prove that in America all non-Anglo groups were welcome members of society.[38] An American Indian court not only showed the larger society's appreciation for Native American patriotism, it also gave tangible expression to the ideal of cultural pluralism and inclusiveness. The media highlighted the unique role American Indians played in the development of the American way of life and promoted the idea (rather optimistically) that they enjoyed full access and participation in a culturally diverse American society.

As queen of the Round-Up, Wilkinson continued her family's tradition of supporting the celebration with an active publicity schedule. Myrna Williams, a princess on Queen Virginia's court, remembers that they "visited all the local rodeos in the towns around Pendleton; met all visiting dignitaries including presidential candidates; attended the Portland Rose Festival [and participated in] the Rose Parade and all festivities, dinners, dances and tours; [and in] radio interviews, attended all four days of the rodeo and presented awards and prizes to rodeo contestants." In their capacity as the official greeting committee, the queen and court had a police escort, "with siren blasting when we were traveling by car in Pendleton during Round-Up week."[39]

The role of Native American royalty was an odd juxtaposition of Euro-American middle-class standards and maintaining Indianness. Queen Virginia did not have the "private life" photo essay that had appeared four years earlier to show off queens in a variety of "at home" poses. The queen and her court wore their traditional regalia in all the photos, and when the *Pendleton East Oregonian* reported on Wilkinson and her princesses' careers and interests, the story began with allusions to Longfellow's "Laughing Water," and other representations of Indian maidens in literature.[40] Rayna Green writes that Euro-Americans have always had difficulty figuring out how to understand Native Americans—and especially Native American women—in society. For the most part the "Pocahon tas Perplex," the concept of a young Native woman helping whites, served "as a model for national understanding of Indian women . . . a potential cult waits to be resurrected when our anxiety about who we are makes us recall her from her woodland retreat."[41] As Native Americans interacted more often in non-Indian society, and as they sought to join the ranks of the middle class, anxieties among whites increased. Native American royalty highlights the concern of wanting to include non-whites and the uncertainty of how to deal with longstanding biases. While Pendleton was pleased to show Round-Up visitors how the young women on the court had entered the middle-class mainstream, they countered contemporary accomplishments with allusions to a mythic past. "As long as Indian women keep their exotic distance," Green writes, "they are permitted to remain on the positive side of the image."[42]

For spectators at the Round-Up, images of a beautiful Indian queen and her court, dressed in their tribal regalia, helped recreate the image of a Wild West. Robert G. Athearn writes that Americans' search for the West, real and imagined, stood "for a historical experience that has touched every acre of this nation. The myth's appeal goes far beyond that, however. After all, each year carries us farther from that frontier heritage, yet the myth survives."[43] For Williams, dressing in regalia had less to do with recreating a bygone era than with celebrating her own culture, which continued to be very much alive. "Riding in the parade with our horse trappings and Indian Regalia," she recalls, "I felt a great deal of pride to represent our tribe [Cayuse]. I still get a great increased flush when watching the Round-Up parade now."[44]

The emphasis on movie star–like glamour, which abated during Queen Virginia's reign, reached its peak with the 1949 Round-Up queen, Joan Barnett. During the Round-Up the *Pendleton East Oregonian*'s feature story on Queen Joan took the idea of glamour to an extraordinary level. The traditional

17. The combination increased rodeo promotion responsibilities and movie star–like glamour culminated in this "cheesecake" shot of the 1949 round-up queen, Joan Barnett. Courtesy of Howdyshell Photography, Pendleton, Oregon.

family and personal information and by now standard poses did not differ from past coverage. The image of Barnett in a bathing suit, however, was quite unlike any other. No demure pose here. Barnett, wearing high-heeled shoes with her bathing suit and smiling confidently while sitting in a director's chair, struck a pose remarkably similar to the movie-star "cheesecake" images that frequently appeared in the local paper.[45]

Barnett and her court also took promoting the Round-Up to a new level. In addition to the usual local and regional promotional tours, Barnett and her court traveled to Calgary, Alberta, Canada, as visiting royalty at the Calgary Stampede, making public appearances and attending social functions in their honor. But, "most important of all," the *Pendleton East Oregonian* reported, "the girls talked over CBS in a coast to coast hook-up and encouraged everyone to attend the Round-Up."[46] Round-Up royalty now promoted the show locally, regionally, nationally, and even internationally, setting a precedent for other queens to follow.

From the end of the war until 1949, the images of rodeo queens reflected both the characteristics Round-Up directors had found important for their queens to have since the 1920s—riding ability, lineage, and middle-class values—and a growing trend to show the queens in a glamorous, movie star–like manner. Then, beginning with the 1950 Round-Up queen, Kathryn Lazinka, the *Pendleton East Oregonian*'s portrayal of rodeo queens took an abruptly conservative turn. The paper focused almost exclusively on the queen's family lineage and riding, or "ranch hand" abilities, while descriptions of personal appearance almost completely disappeared. The only mention of Queen Kathryn's appearance was to note her red hair.[47] Depictions of her court princesses too were surprisingly short of the complimentary adjectives found only a year earlier; the depiction of Princess Francine Hisler reads more like a wanted criminal poster than a description of Pendleton's royal court.[48] The turn away from glamour for the 1950 queen could represent a backlash against the over-the-top photo essay of Barnett the year earlier. But the outbreak of the Korean War in 1950 also encouraged a second wave of cultural conservatism. In a return to the style of the 1940 and 1941 queen reports, Lazinka is shown doing practical things—roping and branding a calf and at her job as a bookkeeper.[49] Beginning with Queen Kathryn Lazinka's reign, homemaking skills nudged glamour out of the spotlight.

The shift to conservatism was even more pronounced during the reign of Julie King, the 1951 queen of the Pendleton Round-Up. Since 1915 the *Pendleton East Oregonian* had always announced the name of the upcoming Round-Up queen and court on the front page of the paper, but in 1951 the queen and court were conspicuously absent. No large photo essay graced the back page, and the queen's section in the Round-Up souvenir edition did not appear, either. Information on the Round-Up royalty appeared only in the Women's Activities section of the paper. The move from front-page news to the women's section took the court out of the general spotlight and placed it within the confines of domestic environment. Just as corsets and "foundation wear" came back into fashion in the 1950s to mold female figures into an ideal form, rodeo queens were being confined firmly within the realm of women's domestic interests—social and club news, fashions, and homemaking tips.[50] The decision to relegate queen coverage to the women's section did not last long—the next year the queen was right back on the front page, promoting the Round-Up as she always had. However, stories on the queen's more private social activities appeared in the women's section. Moving the coverage of a Round-Up queen and court from the front-page spotlight to the women's section, then continuing to highlight social events there, reinforced the conservative cultural assumption that even western queens found their greatest satisfaction within their appropriate domestic sphere, playing a supporting role outside the arena.

An article, "Queen Julie Sets Sights High for Real American Girl of Today," is indicative of the cultural tone of the early 1950s, reporting that King "is only 18 and looks like a carefree kid, but she has her serious side as well."[51] Despite her youth, the article reported she had "very definite, grown-up ideas of what a real American girl should be. 'I think every girl should know something about business; be taught to earn her own living, if necessary, and above all she should learn to be a good homemaker,' said Her Highness." And the young queen practiced what she preached, cooking for harvest crews, helping keep house, sewing her own clothing, and helping her father run his grain elevator and keep books.

The article emphasizes several important characteristics of the Cold War era. The queen's statement on homemaking reflects the emphasis on sustaining traditional gender roles and also the importance of young women "knowing something about business" in order to "earn her own living, if necessary." The argument that young women needed to be trained for the uncertainties of life often appeared in newspaper essays, such as Ruth Millett's syndicated column We, the Women. In one essay, Millett discourages the idea of "feminizing" high school education for women, arguing, "It seems to make sense until you stop to realize that girls are going to live in a man's world, too. . . . The woman who is prepared for nothing but homemaking today faces a mighty insecure future. It was enough for Grandma, but it isn't enough for Granddaughter."[52] The era in which Queen Julie reigned was more culturally rigid than when cowgirl queen Mabel Strickland ruled. In the "golden era of the cowgirl" the proper role of women was still being debated, and women capitalized on that state of flux. Yet despite the enormous pressure to conform to a feminine ideal in the 1940s and 1950s, these women too were thinking beyond the confinements of the domestic sphere.

In her essay on women and employment in the postwar era, Susan M. Hartman writes, "The celebration of domesticity notwithstanding, by the mid-1950s rates of women's employment matched the artificially high levels attained during World War II."[53] Working outside the home before marriage, like Queen Julie, or after marriage but before childbearing, became a social reality, and the "incongruence between dominant values and norms and the reality of women's lives" persisted. But work outside the home was considered of secondary importance compared to creating a positive domestic environment, a message reinforced by movies, women's magazines, television shows, and literature of the time and reflected in the photo essay that accompanied the queen's interview.[54]

In 1952 and 1953 Native American queens again reigned over the Pendleton Round-Up. Leah Conner, the 1952 queen, remembers that in 1952 everything seemed to be changing at the Round-Up and suggests, "The public needed something at the time, and we were a change from the usual."[55] Directors of the 1952 Round-Up were indeed looking for changes; ticket sales were in a slump. In 1944, the year the Round-Up resumed, approximately forty thousand spectators traveled to Pendleton for the show; in 1946 the number increased to over sixty thousand.[56] These numbers are truly remarkable considering the 1940 U.S. census listed the population of Pendleton at 8,847.[57] By 1950, however, the declining number of spectators traveling to Pendleton created serious concerns for the directors. In 1951 they "sent out questionnaires to regular patrons seeking ways to add more color and snap to the performance."[58]

Conner and, in 1953, Dianna McKay were selected as part of Round-Up booster strategy to encourage interest in the show. All-Indian courts were unique, and they brought attention to one of the most distinctive features of the Round-Up:

18. Leah Conner, queen of the 1952 Pendleton All-Indian Court. The first Native American queen to be featured in an "at home" photo essay in the *Pendleton East Oregonian*, she was shown wearing both traditional regalia and modern clothing. Courtesy of Howdyshell Photography, Pendleton, Oregon.

the participation of the Confederated Umatilla Tribes, as well as visiting tribal members from throughout the West. The sheer number of Native Americans gathered in one place, which for many years numbered over one thousand, was a distinct characteristic of the Pendleton Round-Up. Visitors to the Round-Up saw the large teepee encampments, tribal dances, Indian horse races, and exhibitions of traditional Native American handiwork. Every issue of the *Pendleton East Oregonian*'s souvenir edition featured articles on leading members of the Umatilla Reservation, regional Indian history, and photos of tribal members dressed in their regalia. The *Pendleton East Oregonian* announced, "When the Pendleton Round-Up board named Queen Leah of the Umatilla tribe as queen of the 1952 Round-Up, they chose wisely and well. . . . [Their] choice gives recognition to all Indians as a great and enduring people, and particularly to those of our area who have been loyal in support of the Round-Up."[59]

Native American queens, like all Round-Up queens, exemplified the directors' concept of western womanhood. The focus on family lineage, though, had additional significance for members of the all-Indian courts, representing as it did "America's attachment to a romantic past and a far distant nobility."[60] While the Indian queens were members of families who actively participated in the Round-Up, it was also important for an Indian queen or princess to be related to a famous chief. There was little doubt of Conner's claim to royal lineage. She recalls, "My grandmother was a niece of Chief Joseph. . . . She was the only living descendent of Ollicut his brother. So I am—or we are, my family is—the only descendants of Chief Joseph."[61] Round-Up boosters were quick to remind *Pendleton East Oregonian* readers that the Native American queens were descendants of the only American royalty that had ever existed.

Conner became the first Native American queen to be featured in an "at home" photo essay in the *Pendleton East Oregonian*. For Conner, and again for McKay the following year, the images in the newspaper showed the queen both in traditional regalia and in modern clothing. The essay accompanying the photos read, "In the center picture she is shown in her priceless beaded costume. At left, the queen is in riding costume [western-style shirt and pants]. She has ridden and won in Indian horse races at the Round-Up and is a skilled horsewoman. . . . Below, the queen at the home of her parents, Mr. and Mrs. Gilbert Conner, makes a huckleberry dumpling. Yes, those are real huckleberries and the queen picked them herself. She is an accomplished cook. . . . She will be a junior at Willamette University this fall." In other photos Conner posed "taking a few stitches in the beading of her native costume," in an evening gown, and with her tennis racquet; predictably, the article noted, "She also swims and dances, plays the piano and tenor sax."[62]

Reflecting on the images in that photo essay, Conner laughed and said, "They were all wrong! My mother had done all the cooking and picking huckleberries. My family laughed because I am not the greatest huckleberry picker."[63] The images were not *all* wrong—Conner was an excellent rider, she played tennis, and she did sew. But the images were carefully constructed to exemplify Pendleton's feminine ideal in 1952, one based on national precedent: a young woman who was beautiful, athletic, educated, and well-versed in domestic skills, regardless of ethnic heritage, all of which reflected middle-class attributes.

During the 1940s Pendletonians wanted to show they were culturally inclusive, but "the 1950s good Indian was someone who fit in."[64] The images of Conner and McKay, quite different than Virginia Wilkinson's just a few years earlier, showed Native American young women as part of the cultural mainstream, promoting "an American way of life, a unified society that shared values, beliefs, aspirations, and lifestyles—in other words, conformity."[65] It is a misconception that, to use L. G. Moses's words, "Indians cease to be Indians if they learned to live as whites did. American Indians, just as other humans, changed from one generation to another."[66] In large part, gathering for rodeos or powwows encouraged continuation and adaptation of Indian identity, not its erasure.[67]

Describing the Native Americans who participated in Wild West shows at the turn of the century, Moses writes, "In the very act of dressing up, the participation signaled a kinship with a ritualized cultural memory."[68] Through their participation in the Round-Up celebration, including the Happy Canyon show, Native Americans from the Umatilla Reservation likewise celebrated their cultures. Conner recalls her most memorable experiences as Round-Up queen was "knowing I was the queen and the audience knew I was the queen." Riding into the arena, wearing her family regalia, and knowing she represented her people as a true all-American queen "was mind-bursting," she says.[69]

In 1953 Dianna McKay reigned as the last all-Indian court queen. The Round-Up and Happy Canyon combined their offices after 1953, and Happy Canyon started selecting a princess to represent their pageant.[70] This marked the beginning of a separate-but-equal track for Round-Up royalty: Native American young women ruled over the night show as Happy Canyon princesses, while rodeo queens reigned over the daytime rodeo. In the late 1970s the Round-Up directors changed the queen selection process from an appointed position to an application and interview process. No distinction was made between Indian and non-Indian applicants.[71]

After the two final Native American courts, in 1954, Joan Pearson, or Queen Joan II, ruled as the Round-Up queen.[72] The coverage of Pearson once again highlights the paradoxical image of western womanhood: competent cowhand and genteel young woman. In her official public appearances—during the booster trip to Portland, making a cameo appearance at the local football game, or presenting awards at the show—the paper featured her on the front page, dressed in her Round-Up costume.[73] But in 1954 the *Pendleton East Oregonian* increased its coverage of the queen at private, social functions, placing those articles and photos in the women's Social and Club News section.[74] In one photo, taken the day after the rodeo ended, Pearson wore a dress and pearls while looking over her Round-Up scrapbook.[75] An example of true western womanhood, Pearson could be tough enough to ride on an eight-day cattle drive and reign like a queen from atop her horse but know when it was time to hang up her spurs and dress again in pearls.

The 1955 queen, Kathryn Wyss, had served as a princess on the previous year's court. As the *Pendleton East Oregonian* noted, Wyss, a top ranch hand herself, had accompanied her good friend Queen Joan II on numerous cattle drives.[76] Wyss's newspaper coverage traverses familiar terrain—where she attended college, her pioneer heritage, and her family's involvement with the Round-Up. Yet Wyss showed a different side of western womanhood, indicating that the old debate over who should rule the rodeo arena—cowgirl athletes or community-sponsored rodeo queens—had resurfaced. Despite the rhetoric about domestic aspirations, some young women wanted to participate in rodeo as contestants. The photo essay on Queen Kathryn, especially when compared with the previous year's queen, is remarkable. There are no images of Wyss in an evening gown, cooking, or holding a tennis racquet. Instead, a series of photos show her roping a calf, wrestling it to the ground, then branding it. The accompanying text reads, "During the Round-Up she will, at the earnest request of the Round-Up management, not demonstrate her roping and cow-riding, but is entered in the relay races, team of four, riding with three cowboys."[77]

The fact that Wyss roped or rode in relay races in a competition was not so remarkable (although cow-riding was). Riding clubs like Pendleton's Mustang Club hosted amateur competitions, and men and women competed against one another in roping. The 1950 Round-Up queen, Kathryn Lazinka, also roped and branded a calf for her photo essay, and Lazinka's younger sister, Jean, a 1951 Round-Up princess, competed in amateur events, some against men. The *Pendleton East Oregonian* went so far as to report, "Jean won prizes not only for racing, but for roping and other rodeo events, and could be a professional performer, if she so desires, but prefers to remain in the amateur class." A wise choice, since the opportunities for women to earn a living in professional rodeo in 1951 were slim indeed.[78]

The *Pendleton East Oregonian* reported that Wyss, "despite her accomplishments as a cowgirl . . . has no wish for a rodeo career, though she loves rodeo sports."[79] Referring to Wyss as a cowgirl signaled an important shift in the use of the word, back to the definition used up to describe cowgirl athletes during the early years of rodeo. In the mid-1930s the term "cowgirl" shifted in meaning, becoming associated with dilettante riders, whereas "ranch hand" entered the vernacular meaning someone with competent ranching expertise. In the early 1950s, however, "cowgirl" reverted to its previous definition, signaling the acceptability, albeit on a limited basis, of young women competing in the rodeo arena again. By the mid-1950s women were beginning to compete in rodeo again. Most, like Wyss, engaged in the sport as amateurs, but an important door had been opened during the war. As women began to enter the arena the question arose once more, Who deserves to wear the queen's crown?—Someone who competed as a rodeo contestant? Or a non-rodeo contestant who rode well? The number of rodeos grew dramatically in the war and postwar years; with the increased number of rodeos came a corresponding rise in opportunities for western women to hold a rodeo queen title, and the question continued to present itself.

The increase in local rodeos played an enormous role in expanding the rodeo queen phenomena. Each new rodeo required a queen, and the number of queen positions that became available encouraged a more diverse pool of applicants. As part of an expanding rodeo community, directors faced with the decision of how to select their queen could look to the two models circulating in the rodeo community: the Pendleton model, where Round-Up directors appointed the queen, and the Stamford model, which used a competition to determine its queen. The competition process, whether based on ticket selling, riding ability, or any other number of criteria, was a more democratic method of queen selection than rodeo director appointment. Any young woman who met the specified criteria, which usually required being single, living in a specific town or county, and having access to a horse, could enter the rodeo queen contests and take her chances. The advertisement in the *Grant County (WA) Journal* is fairly typical: "Want to be queen of the Columbia Basin Rodeo and Grant County Fair at Moses Lake this summer? If you're a girl between 17 and 24, unmarried, can ride a horse and have poise and good looks, you have a chance."[80]

The increased visibility of rodeo queens that began in the mid-1930s, and the often movie star–like publicity they received in local and regional newspapers, played a large role in popularizing the image of the glamorous "cowgirl" rodeo. Western movies too helped disseminate the genteel cowgirl image: Female stars like Dale Evans presented the image of a western woman, a "cowgirl," both glamorous and firmly adhering to postwar middle-class standards. The image of daring young women on horseback, exhibiting what Shelley Armitage calls "behavior thought to be unusual for women" yet still within bounds of middle-class behavior, became increasingly available—and desirable—through the role of rodeo queen.[81]

Across the West an increasing number of young women took advantage of rodeo queen contests to make things happen for themselves. The proliferation of rodeos and the popularity of rodeo queen contest opened the possibility for any young women, not just the social elite, to be a rodeo queen. The rodeo queen contest also encouraged "queening"—competing for the rodeo queen title either more than once or at more than one rodeo. Young women who hoped to become queen no longer had to wait for a rodeo board to appoint them—they could go out and try to win the crown on their own.

The phenomenon of the community-sponsored rodeo queen truly came into its own during the postwar era, as thousands of young women actively sought to win a crown. The queens shared many similar experiences, honors, and rewards that the position offered. Despite the culture of conformity that dominated the country, queens found the role an opportunity to participate in the public sphere that would not have otherwise been available to them. Three local rodeos—in Soap Lake, Washington; Burwell, Nebraska; and Nampa, Idaho—provide examples of new queen contests based on the Stamford model, a competition. And like the three major rodeos—Pendleton Round-Up, Stamford Texas Cowboy Reunion, and Cheyenne Frontier Days—each town focused on unique local characteristics to attract spectators, just as they created their queen's role according to local interests and community values.

The origins of rodeo in the small town of Soap Lake in eastern Washington State is fairly typical of new rodeos that sprang up during the war years. In 1942 the town celebrated the Fourth of July with its traditional celebration on the beach, complete with a queen contest.[82] The next year, Soap Lake boosters replaced the July Fourth townwide beach party with a rodeo. The *Grant County Journal,* one of the local papers, announced that along with the "world famous performers"

19. Nancy Neumann, 1951 Soap Lake Rodeo Queen, Soap Lake,
Washington. Courtesy of Nancy Neumann Martini,
private collection, Seattle, Washington.

slated to ride in the show, there would be added attractions: "a
special feature will be a bareback riding contest for servicemen
only," which would hopefully attract contestants and their
friends from the Larson Air Force Base, located fifteen miles
up the road.[83] "The cowgirls will not be forgotten," the paper

reported, "$10.00 in defense stamps will be the prize for the best costumed cowgirl." In 1943 professional cowgirl athletes were only considered a minor draw for spectators, lumped in with other novelty performers, as the notice toward the end of the article indicates: "Added attractions at the rodeo will be Miss Shirley Mitchell, well known in rodeo circles for her wild bronc riding; [also appearing] a clown and his trick horse."

Soap Lake did not hold a rodeo the next year, but in 1945 the rodeo returned as an annual event and included a community rodeo queen competition. Several years later, in 1951, Nancy Neumann responded to an advertisement in the local paper inviting all young, unmarried girls in the town to compete for the Soap Lake rodeo queen title. She recalls there were eight girls competing, and "we were all asked to sell rodeo tickets. We sold in town, and we were driven to the surrounding towns to sell to merchants and ask the merchants in the shops to sell for us." Once ticket sales ended, "the three that sold the most were the final contestants. We each gave a speech in front of the judges and from that talk the judges made their decision [for queen and princesses]. I assume the decision was made from a number of things—how we presented ourselves, looked, and spoke and dressed."[84]

For Ruby Dearmont, 1949 queen of the Nebraska Big Rodeo in Burwell, Nebraska, the selection process was very different. The Burwell rodeo began in 1921, during the time Garfield County reached its peak population of 3,496.[85] Influenced by the growing popularity of rodeo queens, the Burwell rodeo crowned its first queen, Madelon Butts, in 1947. In a published history of the Burwell rodeo, Butts states that for the first queen contest, "We were judged on poise, personality, and appearance; not on horsemanship. In fact, I wore a dress in the contest when I was crowned." Apparently, Butts had no riding experience, and she recalls, "The next year they decided they had better pick a queen who knew a little about horses,

20. Jeanette Clancy, 1957 Snake River Stampede Rodeo queen.
Courtesy of Jeanette Clancy Rutledge, private collection,
Nampa, Idaho.

so they added horsemanship to the points in judging."[86] Dearmont recalls that when she competed for the queen's title two years later, all the young women—"and there were a bunch of us, maybe ten"—rode into the arena. They dismounted in front of the judges, mounted back up, then "took off as fast as the horse could go."[87] The best rider won the title of queen for the next year's rodeo. Staging rodeo queen contests was a learn-as-you-go experience, and in the early years especially, rodeo directors made adjustments to the judging criteria to help select a queen that would best represent their community and rodeo, whether that meant a top rider or someone who could handle heavy publicity demands.

The Snake River Stampede, held in Nampa, Idaho, also established a queen's contest well after the rodeo began in 1911. Jeanette Clancy Rutledge, who competed in the rodeo queen contest in 1956, and won the title in 1957, recalls that horsemanship had always been important. However, Rutledge remembers, "The year I was queen was the first year they put poise and personality into it [the competition]. Because the year before that, the girl couldn't say one word when they gave her a mike."[88] Community-sponsored rodeo queens, whether they reigned over new rodeos or established ones or were appointed or competed for their crown, consistently remarked on the thrill of being involved in the biggest, most exciting event in their community. Ann Dinneen Smith, Cheyenne Frontier Days queen in 1947 recalls, "I can't imagine any girl in those days not doing it. It was a pretty big deal to the girl and her family."[89] Another Cheyenne Frontier Days queen, Norma Bell, who reigned in 1949, "dreamed of being Miss Frontiers since I was five. Lois Crane was asked to be Lady-in-Waiting when I was five, and that year I had her for my kindergarten teacher."[90] For others, like Neumann, the rodeo and parade were the highlights of an otherwise humdrum summer in "a dusty little cow town."[91] Neumann and her friends competed in the Soap Lake rodeo queen contest together for several years, trading queen and princess positions amongst themselves. And Rutledge, from the Snake River Stampede recalls, "Well, actually here in the [Nampa] Valley there . . . wasn't really anything else going on in your life. But, you know, in the summertime it was horses, horses, horses. And, well, this was *the* big thing in the summer. Every June they had this big queen contest. You just looked forward to going to it. I mean, I guess it was because it was the biggest event there was. And then the more I watched it the more I wanted to be it."[92] Then of course, there was the glamour of the position, with photos and features articles in the newspapers, riding in the parade and grand entry, traveling to promote the rodeo, and meeting famous personalities—even at the small shows, rodeo queens hobnobbed with politicians, local boosters, and visiting celebrities.

The young women interested in reigning as queen at big and small rodeos alike were usually active in their communities, whether they lived on a ranch, in town, on the edge of town, or in a rural community. However, like a number of the past queens, Smith recalls that her queen experiences "brought me into another plateau, so important at the stage of life. . . . I met people, it opened doors, and boosted my confidence."[93] Myrna Williams, a Pendleton Round-Up princess in 1948, remembers that the experience "did help me to speak to people I did not know—because later I graduated from a nursing program and became a registered nurse."[94] Neumann was very enthusiastic about her experiences as rodeo queen. The daughter of German immigrants, she was firmly convinced that her role as queen opened up opportunities for her to participate in the community that, without the title, would have been impossible.[95] And Conner recalls, "My family was quite active in the community and my father was active in tribal politics, as had been my grandfather. . . . [However] the publicity of being a Queen gave me more awareness of the larger society."[96]

For Pendleton Round-Up queens, the 1941 to 1955 era continued with the earlier characteristics of the role, with its attributes of royalty, western womanhood, celebrity status, and increasing visibility in the media. With the addition of the neo-

Victorian concepts of femininity that emerged after the war years, the role of community-sponsored rodeo queens entered a new and enduring phase, emphasizing riding ability, glamour, and traditional views of femininity. Outside of Pendleton the expansion of new rodeos and the corresponding rise in the number of new rodeo queen positions encouraged more women—and a wider cross-section of young women—to join the ranks of rodeo queens. It was during this era, then, that the phenomena of the community-sponsored rodeo queen truly came into its own. Later, as the number of past rodeo queens grew, these women developed their own community, to celebrate their accomplishments, to support their local rodeos, and to ensure that the tradition of rodeo queens continued.

It would seem that, with the proliferation of new rodeos and rodeo queens, the perennial dispute over who should rule the rodeo—cowgirl athletes or community queens—should end. But it did not. The bourgeoning number of rodeo queens and women rodeo competitors actually kept the issue alive by bringing up the question: Were rodeo queens true examples of western womanhood? Answering these questions is tricky because it requires first identifying who is asking the questions, then deciding whether or not to accept their definitions of western womanhood. In the late 1940s, women with ranch-hand skills who wanted to participate in traditional rodeo events were the most vocal critics of rodeo queens. As discussed in the next chapter, a small group of these women from West Texas took the initiative and created rodeos and rodeo queens according to their own definition. Then, beginning in the 1970s, feminist writers began challenging the qualifications of community-sponsored rodeo queens as they compared them to the early-nineteenth-century cowgirl athletes.[97]

In her photo essay on 1950s rodeo queens, Joan Burbick— one of the few writers to approach the subject—accurately notes that during this era women were increasingly presented as "decorative in their roles in both film, TV, and the rodeo grounds."[98] In one photo, showing a queen and her court galloping across an arena, Burbick writes, "The thrill of the ride, the felling of power and assertion rides out of the photograph defying the use of queen as masthead, symbol, figurine."[99] Burbick failed to understand a key point: a rodeo queen *was* the symbol of her rodeo. The most important part of her role *was* to be a highly visible spokesperson and promote the show. None of the community-sponsored rodeo queens interviewed for this study would have wanted to defy their position as "masthead" or "symbol" (although there might be some discussion on the term "figurine"). They did not consider themselves victimized by a male-dominated rodeo patriarchy.[100] Instead, the women interviewed spoke of their time as queen as an opportunity to expand into the wider world, and for some, it gave them the confidence to move into a career outside the home. Reflecting on the criticism that rodeo queens were primarily pawns in the world of rodeo, Smith says, "You young women today just don't get it. It was great being queen."[101]

7. All-Girl Rodeos

Challenging the Definition of Rodeo Queen

In 1950, when the *Pendleton East Oregonian* featured Round-Up queen Kathryn Lazinka in a photo essay, the headline read, "At Home on the Range." There was no metaphor here: seated easily in the saddle, Lazinka was shown on her horse looking over a heard of cattle, selecting a calf, roping it, branding it, then watching it return to the herd. Emphasizing the "top hand" aspect of the Round-Up queens had become common. But the article also included an unexpected piece of information: In 1948 Lazinka had won the senior championship title for the Mustangers, Pendleton's saddle club. In that competition she had bested seasoned men riders in roping, racing, musical ropes, and other events. In 1949 Lazinka lost the title by just one point.[1]

Lazinka competed in rodeo as an amateur contestant. Her non-professional status aside, Pendleton directors had not selected a queen who competed in rodeo events since 1927, the year cowgirl athlete Mabel Strickland reigned over the Round-Up. A shift had occurred in the rodeo world: women were starting to reappear in the arena. Lazinka's presence in the arena was possible because of changes that occurred during World War II. During the war, the Rodeo Association of America encourage new rodeos that catered to local riders and riders' interests. In doing so, the RAA unintentionally created opportunities for women to compete in the traditional rodeo events.

Lazinka represented women who entered rodeo contests on an ad-hoc basis. But in West Texas, a community of women worked together to bring back professional cowgirl athletes. Here the concept of community is explored again, this time narrowing to focus on a specific group of individuals from the southwest region who came together to reestablish women's presence as competitors in rodeo. Despite the fact that since the late-1920s venues for women to compete had decreased dramatically, the idea of cowgirls competing in rodeo had not disappeared entirely. Sponsor contests, which originated in 1931 at the Texas Cowboy Reunion, combined the tradition of cowgirls competing in the arena with the boosterism potential of rodeo queens. These contests were a mechanism that helped galvanize a cowgirl athlete community in the 1940s. Under the banner of patriotism during World War II, cowgirl athletes re-established their presence and skills in the arena by holding all-girl rodeos. In 1947 two cowgirl athletes and former sponsor girl queens, Nancy Binford and Thena Mae Farr, took the idea of an all-girl rodeo a step further. In direct contradiction to the trend that regarded queens as society belles and allowed women only cameo appearances in the rodeo arena, they set about to reinstate the definition of rodeo queen as champion rider.

Revisiting an earlier definition of rodeo queen, one based on championship status, required only a short look back in time. In 1927 when the directors of the Pendleton Round-Up selected Mabel Strickland as queen of the rodeo, she was the epitome of a rodeo queen. The Pendleton newspaper described

Strickland as a rare example of womanly beauty and talent.[2] She easily met the current standards of femininity; the papers touted her beauty and grace, noting, "There is nothing masculine in her appearance and she does not wear mannish clothes. She dresses with excellent taste, whether in the arena or on the street."[3] The papers praised her status as world champion relay and trick rider and her position as the only women steer roper. Strickland was also renowned for her bronc riding and "her skills as a horsewoman and her talent for showmanship made her a popular rider."[4] Strickland struck a delicate balance between a New Woman's search for a career outside the home, and a traditional woman's commitment to femininity and family, making her a natural to "rule" the 1927 Round-Up.

By 1928 opportunities for cowgirl athletes had reached their height; nearly one-third of rodeos included contests for women.[5] After 1928, however, the number of contests open to women declined rapidly, and by the early 1940s, only a few contests remained open for women competitors. Three factors led to the decline of cowgirl athletes: an intensifying debate over the propriety of women competing in rough-stock events in rodeo, the formation of the Rodeo Association of America, and the Great Crash, a harbinger of the Depression. These three factors converged in 1929, making it a fateful year for professional cowgirl athletes.

A not-so-subtle change in newspaper discourse indicates these larger, national trends had local support. The *Pendleton East Oregonian* changed from enthusiastically supporting cowgirl athletes in the early 1920s, featuring them in stories and photos, to ignoring them by the end of the same decade. Indeed, in 1929 the future of women competing in events faced serious challenges, not only in Pendleton but from rodeo boards as general public support waned throughout the West. In Cheyenne, Wyoming, the Frontier Days board eliminated women competitors in bronc events in 1928: Newspaper articles in

Cheyenne indicate that popular support from the women riders declined considerably from just a year earlier.[6]

Bonnie McCarroll's death at the 1929 Pendleton Round-Up provided the proverbial straw that broke the camel's back, uniting the growing opposition to women riding broncs in open competition. McCarroll, a well-known rider in the rodeo community, was thrown from her mount during the saddle bronc event. Her foot hung up on a stirrup, and the crowd watched in horror as the horse dragged her around the arena until it could be brought to a stop. When she died several days later at the Pendleton hospital, newspapers from around the country discussed the tragedy—and the propriety of women competing in rough-stock events. An article in the *Yakima (WA) Republic* reflected prevailing attitudes, stating, "Bonnie McCarroll, rodeo queen, is dead. . . . Here is an instance of human injuries and death that impels the question of whether such a show is worth such a sacrifice."[7] McCarroll's death spelled the end for women competing in rough-stock events at Pendleton and, increasingly, in rodeos across the West. Prior to McCarroll's death, cowgirl athletes were rarely criticized for participating in dangerous events. As Mary Lou LeCompte points out, cowgirl athletes were "praised for their courage and tenacity."[8] Two years earlier, when Mabel Strickland injured her hand in Pendleton during a roping event, the newspapers cheered her plucky attitude, writing that she had continued "with the steer until the job was finished, then she waved a bloodstained hand at the audience and went to the hospital tent."[9] But publicity from McCarroll's death became a strong argument against women performing in the bronc riding event, and as one of the three largest rodeos in the country, Pendleton's decision to immediately end women's bronc riding became a precedent other rodeos followed.

Also in 1929, the Rodeo Association of America made its debut. The rodeo community had grown to the point where it needed to create guidelines to standardize "events, rules, regulations, judging, refereeing, timing, and arena conditions."[10] An important part of the standardization process included deciding which events would be included in all RAA-sanctioned rodeos. When the list came out, it did not include women's bronc riding as one of the four events required for RAA-approved rodeos. The RAA did not prohibit women's bronc riding; local rodeo committees had the freedom to decide if they wanted to feature the event and, if so, whether it would be competitive or exhibition. But when the RAA later increased the number of required events from four to eight, many rodeos included the new events, "usually at the expense of locally popular contests and events for women."[11] Women's bronc riding did not disappear entirely. The RAA rules encouraged rodeo boards to showcase the event as an exhibition by hiring well-known cowgirl athletes to perform for the crowds rather than offer it as a competitive event.

Lastly, economic hardships caused the number of professional rodeo cowgirls to decline, beginning with the stock market crash in 1929 and continuing through the Great Depression. While established rodeos like the Pendleton Round-Up and Cheyenne Frontier Days managed to stay solvent during the Depression, smaller rodeos and rodeos that were only marginally successful were unable to continue. The result was that while top women riders could still find work at the major rodeos as exhibition riders, the number of overall opportunities for cowgirl athletes, particularly the lesser-known cowgirls, was severely reduced.[12]

A common thread that tied together the death of a famous rodeo queen, the decision of the RAA not to require women's bronc riding, and limited opportunities for women to compete during the Depression concerned the proper role for women in American society. In one way or another, they each addressed the question, Where do women belong? As noted earlier, during the 1880s middle-class women had begun to challenge the idea that their sex limited their activities exclusively to the domestic sphere.[13] From the 1880s well into the 1920s, debates raged as men and women, traditionalists and modernists, argued over the proper role for women. An analysis of newspaper discourse, however, suggests that by 1927 the traditionalist view had gained a slight edge.[14] The economic crisis in the late 1920s further encouraged this movement toward a resurgence of traditional gender roles.

The introduction of the sponsor contest in 1931 at the Texas Cowboy Reunion in Stamford exemplified this shift away from serious athletic competition and into more "suitably feminine" roles. The sponsor contest was widely copied throughout Texas and into Oklahoma. Embracing the larger cultural movement toward cultural conservatism, the contest played a key role in redirecting the image of a cowgirl queen from one who could compete in contests that focused on usable cowhand skills to that of a beautiful socialite who competed for the title of queen in areas only marginally associated with ranching skills, such as riding a horse around barrels or flagpoles.

The sponsor girl contests dealt a serious blow to cowgirl athletes, whether they cared for bronc riding or not. The contests were a way of allowing women to compete in the arena as they had in the past; however, the emphasis on regalia, poise, conducting themselves with grace at social events held in their honor, and working with the press shifted women's role in rodeo, in effect, elevating the women from the position of working professionals competing in the arena to the management level by helping local boosters. Although the Texas Cowboy Reunion always insisted that the sponsor girls were top-notch riders, and a number of later contestants like Nancy Binford and Thena Mae Farr did compete in rodeos in the late 1940s, descriptions of riding skills were not given top billing and were often left out entirely. Instead, the changing newspaper dis-

VOTE FOR
Isora DeRacy
(THE REAL COWGIRL)

Vote For
A Girl
Who Can
Really
Ride
and
Rope

Mrs. DeRacey
is a
True Daughter
of the
West

Mrs. Isora De-Racey, whose picture appears here has been entered in the race for Rodeo Queen by her friends. She is a real cowgirl, and can rope and tie a calf in 30 seconds. The picture recently appeared in the Ft. Worth Star - Telegram.

FOR RODEO QUEEN

(This Circular is paid for by friends of Mrs. DeRacey and was printed without her knowledge).

21. "Vote for Isora DeRacy" poster emphasizing the skills some thought should be required of a rodeo queen. Courtesy of the National Cowgirl Museum and Hall of Fame, Fort Worth, Texas. Isora DeRacy File.

course emphasized the girls' social position, reinforcing the importance of their amateur status as contestants and adherence to community standards of appropriate, middle-class feminine behavior.[15]

This shift in rodeo queen criteria did not sit well with women the community of women who struggled to continue competing in rodeo. Isora DeRacy, reared on a ranch near Pecos, Texas, was one of the few women who both competed in rodeos during the 1930s and served as a rodeo queen. DeRacy competed in calf roping, a relatively new event in rodeo. Pressure from humane societies led most states to replace steers, the traditional choice in roping events, with calves. The switch from steer to calf roping was haphazard, and as individual rodeos made the change, the rules on whether or not to allow women to compete in calf roping events lacked consistency as well.[16] Women found the opportunity to compete, usually against cowboys, at small, non-RAA rodeos. Organized rodeos—that is, rodeos affiliated with the RAA—did not sanction women's calf roping. However, if a particular rodeo offered special "challenge" or "jackpot" roping events outside the purview of RAA events, women could participate. In Texas women who lived on ranches and worked cattle as part of their regular ranch chores had the opportunity to compete in these challenge events, and DeRacy gained a reputation as a top roper around Pecos.[17]

A "Vote for Isora DeRacy" poster provides an example of the community of riders who felt that rodeo queen status should be based solely on ranch-related skills. DeRacy is pictured astride her horse, rope clearly visible; the text alerts the public to her accomplishments, noting, "She is a real cowgirl and can rope and tie a calf in 30 seconds."[18] The anonymous friends who printed and circulated the poster encouraged voters to honor "a girl who can really ride and rope" with the rodeo queen title and, by implication, vote against a woman who had social standing, good looks, or could sit a horse tolerably well but lacked the real ranch hand skills that would place her squarely within the western tradition.[19] Despite efforts like those of DeRacy's anonymous friends, it was not until the early 1940s, during World War II, that opportunities emerged for women to return to rodeo and reclaim the earlier definition of rodeo queen.

In a very real sense World War II both devastated and created a renaissance for cowgirl athletes. On the one hand it sounded the death knell for the few professional women riders who remained in the sport, mostly as exhibition riders. As Theresa Jordan notes, professional opportunities for these women became "a casualty of the war," as rodeo producers, finding it hard to continue the tradition of two strings of broncs—one for the cowboys and one for the cowgirls—cut the women's events.[20] On the other hand, the shortage of professional riders created a vacancy that amateur riders would step in to fill.

During World War II the RAA encouraged the development of new rodeos to keep interest in rodeo alive. Suspending RAA regulations, the new rodeos promoted events that focused on local riders' abilities and interests. This allowed women to enter rodeo contests on an ad-hoc basis. The women competed in limited number of traditional rodeo events, such as calf roping and cutting.[21] The RAA strategy for allowing women to participate in rodeo followed a similar logic to the creation of women's ball clubs, where women's leagues were set up as a temporary expediency to keep interest in the game alive and stadiums occupied until the men returned from the war.[22] World War II, then, did not end the tradition of women competing in the sport; rather, it changed the dynamics by replacing the few remaining professional riders with a growing number of amateurs.

Women who participated in rodeo during the war years were, as always, independent contestants. They did not have to belong to a team to enter rodeo events and had to freedom to compete without the restrictions faced by women hired into corporate team sports like baseball. Cowgirl athletes did not have to undergo mandatory charm lessons, make-up courses, or off-hours chaperoning. Although the cowgirls did not enjoy the financial benefit of corporate backers to keep them in the arena, there was no one to prevent them from joining in local rodeos or holding casual all-girl competitions when and where they could.[23]

The war encouraged women to return to competition in another way: under the banner of patriotism. During the war the connection between rodeo and patriotism became firmly established. While many rodeo cowboys left to fight the war, women could do their part by staging a rodeo to provide entertainment for their communities at home. In 1942 when local communities throughout the West were calling off their rodeo celebrations, the first organized all-girl rodeos appeared in Texas. The rodeos strongly emphasized patriotism and morale boosting. Despite the title, "all-girl" or "all-cowgirl," these were not youth rodeos. They included older, and often married, athletes like Vaughn Kreig and Tad Lucas, who had performed during the heyday of women's rodeo in the 1920s, as well as young, amateur riders.

Fay Kirkwood produced the first widely publicized all-cowgirl rodeo at the Fannin County Fairgrounds in Bonham, Texas. The headline in the *Bonham Daily Favorite*, "World's First All-Girl Rodeo to Begin Friday," was placed under the top two headlines, which read, "2 Axis Drives Stemmed Momentarily" and "42 Billion Dollar Bill for Army Reaches House," and was surrounded on all sides by news about London, German paratroopers, and the need for more planes.[24] In keeping with the rodeo's patriotic theme, the newspaper announced a special event to pay tribute to the war effort: "The program for the rodeo itself will consist of the cowgirls' drill and 'V for Victory' formation."[25]

The article indicated that opening day would feature, among other events, "sponsor girls from every town in North Texas" and a "special contest for the sponsor girls and amateur riders."[26] The language indicated a subtle but important distinction being made between sponsor girls—the young women selected by their towns who could ride a horse tolerably well and for whom this might be the only foray into sponsor contests and "amateur riders"—the young women who competed regularly in sponsor events throughout the region, or perhaps, as in Pendleton, in private riding clubs.

Since the Bonham rodeo had the distinction of being the first all-girl rodeo, perhaps it is not too surprising that it was not as "all-girl" as the Tri-State All-Girl rodeo organized by Nancy Binford and Thena Mae Farr five years later. At Kirkwood's show fifteen women riders entertained the crowned, yet half of the rodeo committee was made up of men, and event number 13 was listed as "Presenting as Special Guest—The Only Cowboy to Take Part in the All Girl Rodeo."[27] The rodeo also conformed more closely to how 1940s rodeo defined women's participation in the sport by featuring exhibition events rather than having open competition as the men did. Of the seventeen events, which included everything from the grand entry to the finale, the "V for Victory" formation, only bulldogging and the sponsor contest were not advertised as exhibition events. Nevertheless, the success of this rodeo encouraged Kirkwood to hold two others during that summer of 1942.

No information remains on Kirkwood's second all-girl rodeo, but for her third and final rodeo, produced for the servicemen stationed in Wichita Falls, Texas, Kirkwood increased the number of competitive events. In her study on professional women rodeo performers, LeCompte writes that while planning the Bonham rodeo, Kirkwood learned that local cowgirls wanted to compete in professional contests, such as bronc riding, bull riding, and roping events. In her last rodeo, Kirk-

22. Nancy Binford (right) and Thena Mae Farr, posing for publicity photographs for the Tri-State All-Girl Rodeo. Courtesy of the National Cowgirl Hall of Fame, Fort Worth, Texas.

wood included more contests and opened them to anyone who wanted to participate.[28]

Mary Ellen "Dude" Barton was one of the amateur riders who took advantage of the increased number of competitive events at the Wichita Falls rodeo. Reared on the sprawling

Matador Ranch in West Texas, Barton learned to ride and rope at an early age and had participated in numerous sponsor girl events in the region. When she returned from the Wichita Falls competition, Barton's hometown paper announced, "No one in this section familiar with Miss Barton's rope and saddle ability was surprised when she returned home with about everything Wichita Falls had on its prize list."[29] The paper made a rather pointed distinction between women with ranch-hand skills, like Barton, and sponsor girls, saying, "to match her with the average satin and gabardine riding girl left the outcome a 'forgone conclusion.'"[30]

In 1942 Vaughn Kreig, arena director for Kirkwood's rodeo, also produced an all-girl rodeo. Kreig's program was more forcefully patriotic than Kirkwood's. The front page of the official program read, "The All-Cowgirl Rodeo is formed with the idea of entertainment for our fighting forces. With women taking part in all branches of war work, to the front came the cowgirls riding to the strains of martial music, the American flag held high, and the show is on! The cowgirl's dream a reality. Keep 'Em Flying! Keep 'Em Rolling! Buy War Bonds and Stamps! And On to VICTORY!!"[31] It is interesting to note the sentence "The cowgirl's dream a reality" sandwiched in among the patriotic rhetoric. If her dream was to compete with other women in rodeo again, Kreig had plenty of company: Twenty women participated in the show, half of whom had ridden in Kirkwood's rodeos. Kreig, who competed as a professional rider in the late 1920s and early 1930s before retiring in 1937, competed in four events at her rodeo: calf roping, bronc riding, bulldogging, and steer riding. These were traditional rodeo events performed by women, and eight out of the nineteen listed events were contests.

Although Kreig advertised her rodeo as entertainment for the military troops, it was also clearly organized as a vehicle for women to compete in rodeo events. In a promotional flyer for her show Kreig wrote, "This show was organized because the cowgirls riding events have been discontinued in the present day rodeos, and as the girls love the rodeo as a sport, love their horses, and have the rodeo spirit, their thought was to form their own rodeo, where they could demonstrate their ability and skill in riding and roping, as well as the other rodeo events such as Bronc Riding, Bulldogging, Calf Roping, Brahma Bull Riding, Trick Riding, Etc."[32] Keeping with local customs, the Flying V Rodeo included a sponsor contest. However, the producers made a point of stating that the horsemanship element—a flag race—would be a timed event, an important break from the tradition of subjectively judging sponsor contests.[33]

In 1944, one year before the end of World War II, rodeos around the country came back and enjoyed greater popularity than ever. If cowgirl athletes expected to be welcomed back into the arena as professionals, however, they were in for a disappointment. The mood of the country had taken a decidedly conservative turn. While public support for the all-girl rodeos suggested the possibility of expanding, or at least maintaining, inroads made during the war, women competitors found themselves excluded from professional rodeo once again. The RAA reverted to prewar policies and made no concession to women interested in competing in professional rodeo.

LeCompte writes that screen star Gene Autry compounded the problems women riders faced in trying to reestablish their position in professional rodeo. Autry established his Flying A Rodeo Company in 1942 and began producing a series of large rodeos. He soon dominated the East Coast rodeo circuit as well as major rodeos in Houston, Los Angles, Shreveport, and Toronto.[34] Although Autry's rodeos followed RAA wartime guidelines for keeping major rodeos in close proximity to one another, he did not provide opportunities for women to compete, as smaller, local rodeos did. As LeCompte notes, "All of Autry's rodeos were very much alike, and . . . none included contests for cowgirls."[35] Instead, Autry hired beautiful young women to perform non-competitive riding stunts for the spectators. LeCompte argues that Autry's Flying A Rodeo became the standard for rodeos across the country, ultimately spelling the "final doom" for cowgirl competitors in major rodeos.[36] But taking a larger view, the role of women in Autry's rodeos—and the public's acceptance of that role—illustrates the culmination of traditionalist pressures against women competitors that began in 1929.

In 1947 sponsor contests and the occasional "jack pot" calf roping contest were the only opportunities open for women to compete in rodeo. It was in this climate that the third major all-girl rodeo made its debut, when two West Texas cowgirls, twenty-five-year-old Nancy Binford and nineteen-year-old Thena Mae Farr decided to hold a rodeo. When they created the Tri-State All-Girl rodeo Binford and Farr set about to re-shape the meaning of the term "rodeo queen" into one that was representative of their cowgirl community but still acceptable to the conservative social norms of mainstream American society. As Binford announced to the press, "This is going to be a rodeo, not a social event."[37]

In an ironic twist, the sponsor contests that originated at the Texas Cowboy Reunion provided the springboard for amateur cowgirl athletes to get back into the ring as serious competitors. The importance of the sponsor contests relied on its duality as both beauty and riding contest. And, as noted earlier, the emphasis on which aspect to stress was up for personal interpretation. For a number of young women reared on West Texas ranches, the horsemanship element mattered most. The sponsor contests had given women seriously interested in competing a chance to get together, encouraging the development of a community of amateur riders who wanted to compete in rodeo. Fay Kirkwood, who staged the first all-girl rodeo in 1942, had competed at the Texas Cowboy Reunion in 1933 and 1934.[38]

In the immediate postwar years, between 1945 and 1947, the sponsor contest at the TCR saw the largest number of women sponsored by ranches in its history as one quarter of all contestants came from ranches.[39] The number may, in fact, have been slightly higher, since small towns in the area quite likely sponsored young women who lived on nearby ranches.[40]

Competing at various sponsor contests throughout the region gave the amateur cowgirl athletes a chance to discuss the relative merits of such contests. A common complaint, as one newspaper, noted, was "Some of the cowgirls denounced as 'crooked' many sponsor contest where judging is done on riding, girl's appearance, etc."[41] It is unlikely that Binford and Farr had any complaints about the middle-class element of their sponsor contest or about the fact that it attracted beautiful contestants. Both women were attractive. Farr had won the Miss Seymour, Texas, beauty pageant four times. Binford served as the Sweetheart of the Amarillo Riders for a number of years and had served as the queen of the Fort Worth stock show earlier that year.[42] Moreover, both were college educated and came from wealthy ranching families. Sponsor contests, then, brought together women who liked to use their ranch-hand skills and compete, encouraging a community of amateur riders who, with the memory of competing in rodeos during the war still fresh in their memory, wanted to compete in real events again. The sponsor contests also gave women like Binford and Farr experience in public relations, something that would be useful as they worked to promote their all-girl rodeo.

With the memory of wartime all-girl rodeos still fresh and the possibility of competing in organized rodeo in anything other than the occasional "jackpot" event unlikely, Binford and Farr began planning their rodeo. Binford recalls approaching the Chamber of Commerce about holding an all-girl rodeo: "They said if we thought it was possible, that they would let us put on an all-girl rodeo and see if it would be successful during

23. In another publicity photo, Nancy Binford and Thena Mae Farr show that being expert horsewomen has not prevented them from developing domestic skills. Courtesy of the National Cowgirl Hall of Fame, Fort Worth, Texas.

their state fair."[43] Once they had the Chamber's approval, Binford and Farr began contacting riders. When asked in a 1985 interview if she was worried that there would not be enough women to compete in the events, Binford replied, "Oh no— we had asked many girls just to be sure that we would have enough to produce the rodeo. We had eight ropers out the first day and some of them had never thrown a rope in an arena, and there wasn't a calf missed. They were real excited about it, and it turned out real well."[44]

Getting support from their cowgirl community was one thing, promoting the rodeo to the public was another. In order to be a success, this rodeo, like all rodeos, needed paying spectators. It was important to both Binford and Farr that the rodeo encourage their community of riders with traditional rodeo events but without alienating the general public with fears of mannish, or unwomanly, behavior. The renaissance of traditional gender roles that emerged after World War II emphasized appropriate masculine and feminine behaviors. These behaviors, usually defined in opposition to one another, depicted men as strong and aggressive, women as weak and passive. As Beth Bailey notes, "despite the powerful ideology of the happy homemaker women continued to encroach into the male sphere"; social critics were concerned that women were robbing men of their masculinity by adopting masculine roles.[45] This issue was of particular concern for women seeking to reestablish their presence in the rodeo arena. As one newspaper reported, "The rodeo will feature all of the 'rough and ready' events familiar to rodeo fans, except girls will be in the saddle."[46]

Photos, interviews, and newspaper articles depicted the cowgirl athletes as western women in the truest sense—they roped calves, they rode bucking broncs, some even rode bulls. But according to the reports, they accomplished these feats looking like ladies. The papers not only described the appearance of the women but also reported on the personal lives of Binford, Farr, and other cowgirl athletes, describing their after-rodeo hobbies, interests, and family. One paper reported that "after a day in the arena, [cowgirls] went home to cook dinner for the family, work a little needlepoint, or maybe on a Friday night, get dressed up for a night on the town [with their husbands]."[47]

24. By creating a venue for women to compete on their own terms, Binford and Farr helped reinstate the champion rider as rodeo queen. Above, Maurine Harlan rides a bronc at the Tri-State All-Girl Rodeo. Courtesy of the National Cowgirl Hall of Fame, Fort Worth, Texas.

Binford, apparently aware of the perceived contradiction between womanly behavior—concern with feminine appearance, domesticity, and motherhood—and rodeo, explained in one of her many interviews, "Look at little Jeanette Campbell. She got married, and now has a baby boy. She'll be here for this show. There are others, too."[48] Reporters also alerted readers as to which of the cowgirls were still in the marriage market, not-ing as one interview did, that Binford was not only an accom-plished rider, but "by the way—she is good-lookin' and single, guys."[49] This emphasis on femininity and domesticity quite likely helped to reassure readers that traditional gender distinc-tions and heterosexuality remained intact even as the women competed in the traditionally male sport of rodeo.[50] This was especially important for a sport that advertised women would participate in "all the events that made up the best of male ro-deos."[51] By showing that the cowgirl athletes conformed to the most important feminine behaviors, Binford assured the public that the cowgirl athletes were, indeed, feminine women.

While designed to allow women to compete in real rodeo events, the Tri-State All-Girl rodeo maintained the tradition of the sponsor contest. Using their position as producers, Binford and Farr changed a few of the rules, eliminating the cowgirl costume portion of the contest and ending the practice of hav-ing a panel of male judges subjectively evaluate how the women rode around the barrels. Instead, the contest was objectively evaluated—it was timed—and the woman who competed the pattern with the fastest time won.

The Tri-State All-Girl Rodeo matched the definition of all-girl rodeo more completely than any other had. With the exception of the announcer, all involved—contestants, judges, promot-ers, and staff supporters—were women.[52] And the rodeo was a huge success. Standing room only crowds cheered cowgirls as they competed in bareback riding, calf roping, the sponsor con-test, cutting, team tying, saddle bronc riding, steer riding, and an exhibition bulldogging performance. Perhaps most gratify-ing was the fact that Binford and Farr were able to redefine the term "rodeo queen": above a photo of women contestants for the all-girl rodeo, the title read, "Rodeo Queens." At this rodeo, like the cowgirls a generation earlier, to wear the title of "queen" required champion rider status. At the Tri-State All-

Girl Rodeo there were no teas, luncheons, or formal dances. As Binford had promised, it was a rodeo, not a social event.

Encouraged by the success of the rodeo, twenty-three of the cowgirl contestants met immediately afterward and organized the Girls Rodeo Association, or GRA. As the newspapers reported, "The main purpose is to standardize rodeo rules applying to girl contestants, and to eliminate unfair practices."[53] A singularly important decision concerned sponsor contests; the association stated that it "intended to bar cowgirl sponsor contests from Rodeo Cowboy Association and Girls Rodeo Association–approved rodeos except where it is made a timed event."[54] In 1942 Vaughn Kreig's Flying V rodeo had taken a rather lonely stand against the subjectivity of the sponsor contest by insisting on timing the event. The GRA would enforce the practice, turning the sponsor contest into a strictly athletic contest. This change was crucial for women to spring back into serious rodeo competition. By discarding the subjective elements and focusing on an objective evaluation of the horsemanship component, the sponsor contest became what is known today as barrel racing, a highly competitive, lucrative, and popular event in professional rodeo.

The GRA also dropped the costume judging portion of sponsor contests. Recognizing the importance of maintaining a feminine image, however, the new bylaws stated that participants in GRA-sanctioned contests "had to ride in the opening parades and always be dressed in colorful attire when they appear in the arena."[55] The concern with image extended to include concepts of correct feminine behavior as well, and the 1949 rule book stipulated that sanctions would be applied to members who swore in the arena, drank publicly on the rodeo grounds, or behaved in an otherwise unladylike manner.[56] During the early years of the GRA, the community of cowgirl athletes worked hard reinstate the image of queen as champion rider and to maintain their ability to compete. LeCompte notes, "The camaraderie and friendship with the group were much stronger than the competition between individuals, since all wanted this sport to succeed."[57]

Binford and Farr accomplished their goal: the Tri-State All-Girl Rodeo brought their community of amateur cowgirl athletes together to compete in traditional rodeo events, and they reinstated the concept of rodeo queen as champion rider. Yet this redefined image of rodeo queen did not take hold in the general public. Despite their efforts to prove to audiences that the cowgirls were regular women just using their homegrown skills to compete in the arena, they rode beyond the pale of acceptable feminine behavior for the conservative postwar era. Press reports, while generally positive, revealed concerns over "invading," as one paper put it, "one of the last strongholds of a man's world." A *Quarter Horse Journal* article, reporting on preparations for Binford's and Farr's second all-girl rodeo in Amarillo, Texas, wrote, "The female frolic had its inception in Amarillo last fall when a group of girls, most of them reared on ranches in New Mexico, Texas, and Oklahoma and had learned as youngsters the real ups and downs of the cattle business, decided to sponsor a rodeo of their own for a little fun and diversion."[58] Apparently the women's return to riding in traditional rodeo events appeared acceptable only as long as it remained "a diversion," as an amateur show, and separate from men in the all-girl format.

Still, the importance of Binford's and Farr's efforts to change the definition of rodeo queen cannot be overlooked. They created a venue for women to compete in rodeo on their own terms and outside of wartime exigencies. By creating an opportunity for women to participate in all-girl rodeos and assuring spectators they were still feminine, they emphasized the fact they were not social oddities but women who could participate in society as wives, mothers, and daughters, as well as compete in rodeo and paved the way for women to re-enter the professional world of rodeo. And beginning in the 1950s, the number of community-sponsored rodeo queens who competed in rodeo slowly grew.

When Kathryn Lazinka represented the Pendleton Round-Up as its queen in 1950, she was riding the wave of newfound opportunities for women to compete in rodeo events. Not since Mabel Strickland had a rodeo contestant been elected as queen. Despite the fact that both women "rodeoed" and served as queen, the two women exemplify the changes in women's involvement in rodeo and the changing expectations of normative female behavior. When Lazinka reigned as queen the paper reported that her friends urged her to ask Round-Up president John Hales and arena director E. N. Boylen if she could perform an exhibition calf roping at the Round-Up. "'The answer is NO,' they said firmly." Although the directors, "explained to the disappointed monarch that the queen of the Round-Up will have enough to do . . . without appearing on the show program," in 1950 it was not yet acceptable for young women to perform in a professional rodeo venue.[59]

But that would change. Binford's and Farr's efforts to change the definition of rodeo queen, by encouraging women to participate in rodeo and assuring spectators that they were still feminine, had a slow-growing but important impact on the rodeo queen phenomenon. Beginning in 1950, the number of community-sponsored rodeo queens who competed in rodeo slowly began to grow. In 1954 Cheyenne Frontier Days queen Margaret Hirsig participated in amateur rodeo, as did 1955 Pendleton queen Kathryn Wyss. Cowgirl athletes did not displace the community-sponsored rodeo queen; rather, the image of cowgirl athlete and community-sponsored queen, held in dynamic opposition for forty years, was slowly being reconciled. Before too long it would be commonplace for rodeo queens to represent middle-class values as well as compete in rodeo events, proving that "beauty and rodeo can be mixed."[60]

8. From Local Community to National

Miss Rodeo America

In November 1959 the *Pendleton East Oregonian* announced, "Pendleton's Vickie Pearson Takes 'Miss Rodeo of America Title.'"[1] Pearson, the 1959 Round-Up queen, competed in and won the Miss Oregon Rodeo competition, held in Pendleton during the Round-Up. Winning the state rodeo queen title was a necessary step for competing at the national level for the Miss Rodeo America title, which Pearson won as well. Fifty years after Pendleton invented the community-sponsored rodeo queen phenomenon, one of their own would represent the entire rodeo community as the 1960 Miss Rodeo America. The rodeo queen role that began simply enough as a modified goddess of liberty parade queen in 1910 had changed significantly by Pearson's time. It had become more visible and glamorous. The debate in mainstream society over appropriate gender behavior—exemplified in the rodeo community by rodeo queens and cowgirl athletes—reached a tentative equilibrium in the early 1950s when rodeo queens began competing in rodeo events again, an equilibrium not seen since the mid-1920s. In her role as Miss Rodeo America, Pearson represented a new generation of community-sponsored rodeo queens: women who not only competed for rodeo queen crowns but as competitors in the rodeo arena as well.

The Miss Rodeo America contest, which began in 1956, is discussed here as the last major manifestation of the rodeo queen phenomenon. It serves as the focal point from which to examine the interwoven themes that shaped the evolution of role, especially the discourse surrounding rodeo queens, cowgirls, and definitions of western womanhood. From the very beginning, the importance of a community-sponsored rodeo queen resided in her relationship to her community and to the sport of rodeo. The connection between queens and their communities expanded between 1910 and 1956, from local to regional to specific groups within larger communities and finally to an overarching national rodeo community.

Whatever the community, though, the queen remained its symbolic representative. Even at the national level, Miss Rodeo America represented a commitment to community. The official Miss Rodeo America mission statement reads, "Miss Rodeo America symbolizes the youth of our nation who wish to further promote the sport of professional rodeo, and in so doing, promote the great western way of life. She is the ideal western type girl, and is the person who will represent professional rodeo as she travels the length and breadth of our country."[2] This one short paragraph describes the essential characteristics of a good rodeo queen—at any level. The young woman acts as an ambassador for the rodeo, promotes the sport, and is qualified for the position because she exemplifies the "ideal western type girl." The introduction of Miss Rodeo America elevated the rodeo queen's sense of community to a new level, beyond geographical parameters, while preserving the essential characteristics of the local community rodeo queen.

The move from rodeo queens sponsored by a local community to representing the sport at the national level came about in large part as a result of changes in the organizational structure of rodeo in the 1940s. Rodeo evolved from its origin as a casual gathering of cowhands to a spectator sport, and as it did the sport grew into a business for rodeo producers and a livelihood for the cowboy and early cowgirl athletes. As discussed earlier the Rodeo Association of America, representing rodeos in the Northwest and California, formed in 1929 to encourage standardizing rodeo rules and regulations and to increase the profitability of the sport for rodeo producers. The National Rodeo Association (originally known as the Southwest Rodeo Association) originated in 1938 for the same reasons and oversaw rodeos predominantly in Oklahoma, Texas, and New Mexico.[3] In order to protect riders' interests from rodeo management, the Cowboy Turtles Association organized in 1936.[4] These organizations reflected the growing interest in rodeo as a spectator sport, and profitability for producers and competitors alike.

In 1946 the Rodeo Association of America merged with the National Rodeo Association and formed the International Rodeo Association (IRA). Clifford P. Westermeier writes that this was a significant move, "for it shows the trend toward uniting of similar organizations."[5] The most significant change for rodeo dealt with standardizing eligibility, agreeing on who could or could not compete: "Rodeo contests shall be 'OPEN' to all contestants who wish to enter, whether they are members of the R.C.A. [Rodeo Cowboy Association, known previously as the Turtles] or not, with the understanding that anyone who is on the R.C.A. blacklist or who are undesirable to managements, shall not be permitted to participate."[6] Since Pendleton held the distinction as one of the largest rodeos in the country, it is not surprising that a Pendleton Round-Up director, E. N. Boylen, became the "new rodeo czar" for the IRA in 1946, coming to the new role with instructions to "put the rodeo sport on the highest plane possible."[7] While communities throughout the West still hosted their own rodeos and kept their own local orientations, for the benefit of the sport they now adhered to national rodeo standards.

One of the advantages of the new IRA was that it included a unified marketing strategy to promote all rodeos associated with it. Each town still promoted its own show, but boosters could now rely on the benefit of the larger umbrella organization to help spotlight the show. The IRA created the position of Miss Rodeo America as an ambassador for the entire sport, to travel around the country appearing on television and radio and making public appearances to promote local rodeos.[8] In a very real sense the relationship between the International Rodeo Association and Miss Rodeo America remained similar to the traditional one between local town boosters and their community-sponsored rodeo queen, but on a much larger scale. In this expanded role, the influence of glamour and the ability to interact with the celebrities and media became important for the young women who served as Miss Rodeo America. Young women interested in competing for the title recognized they would need a polished appearance and public speaking skills. For Vickie Pearson, the possibility of becoming a national representative for the sport of rodeo encouraged her to seek advice on creating a more professional image. As the *Pendleton East Oregonian* noted, "Preparations have been under way several days for the appearance of Miss Pearson. She has been coached on walking, posture, make-up and stage presence by Morgan Hicks at the request of her parents. Hicks has worked as a stage manager in New York."[9]

The professional image of Miss Rodeo America represented but one of the changes in the sport of rodeo. By the 1930s the professional rodeo cowboy had emerged. With the new organizational structure and pay increases, a cowboy could make a decent living "riding the circuit," which meant competing in an average of thirty rodeos a season.[10] As rodeoing became a profession, rodeo schools opened up to help riders hone their skills; junior schools developed for young contestants enjoying the sport at the amateur level or hoping to make a career in the sport in the future. To accommodate the increasing diversity of people interested in competing, a vertical hierarchy of rodeos also developed, based on specific age groups: college rodeo, high school rodeo, and later, junior rodeo, which encouraged increased participation in the sport as well.

Rodeo expanded horizontally too, as minority participants—blacks, Hispanics, and women—sought to create their own rodeos outside of the predominantly white, mostly male venue. In his work on the rejection of cultural conformity, so much a part of American culture during the Cold War era, Todd Gitlin writes, "There are pleasures and addictions and evanescent communities galore to be found under the big tent of popular culture, but what there is not is a sense of common citizenship. Instead, people seek solidarity among those who resemble themselves."[11] Groups that felt excluded by traditional rodeo or wanted to hold a rodeo to celebrate rodeo tradition within their own unique community began to do just that.

As the sport of rodeo expanded, so too did the role of rodeo queens, as each of these new rodeos selected queens who best represented its own community. This trend began in earnest during the 1947 Tri-State All-Girl Rodeo. Although earlier all-girl rodeos had celebrated the return of women competitors, at Binford's and Farr's rodeo, each contestant was considered a cowgirl queen in her own right. Later, all-Indian and all-black rodeos appeared, highlighting the skills of two under-recognized cowboy groups in the West. Less traditional communities also organized their own rodeos. For example, the gay community organized its first rodeo in 1979 and by 1983 had developed a four-state circuit. To fit the unique characteristics of the gay community, three queens are selected for each rodeo.[12]

Changes in the national rodeo organization encouraged the

25. Vicki Pearson won the title of 1959 Pendleton Round-Up queen and Miss Oregon Rodeo and continued on to win the 1960 Miss Rodeo America pageant. Courtesy of Howdyshell Photography, Pendleton, Oregon.

development of the Miss Rodeo America figure. At the same time, these changes influenced rodeo queen competitions as well, helping to establish the progression of titles necessary to win the national honor. By 1955, the year the IRA formulated the idea for the Miss Rodeo America role, queening had become a common phenomenon throughout the rodeo community. The development of new rodeos in the early 1940s, combined with the growing popularity of queen contests, encouraged the phenomenon. Then too, as a rodeo hierarchy developed with college, high school, and junior rodeos, an expansion in queen contests followed. Dallas Hunt George, Miss Rodeo America in 1957, recalled that she won her first title, 1955 High School Rodeo Queen, in the national competition held in Harrison, Nebraska. She won the Burwell, Nebraska, Big Rodeo title in 1956, as well as the Ak Sar Ben rodeo queen title in Grand Island, Nebraska—a necessary step to compete as Miss Rodeo Nebraska in the national contest.[13]

Beginning with the first Miss Rodeo America competition, then, all the contestants held at least one other rodeo queen title; by 1959 Miss Rodeo America hopefuls needed to win local and state titles in order to become eligible for the national crown. Susan M. Stauffer, Miss Rodeo America 1959, explains, "The competitions are a progression—first local, then state and finally national. Each is more difficult as your responsibilities broaden. You always are celebrated by your home communities as you move through the progression. The national is a tremendous responsibility as you are viewed as an important role model."[14]

During her reign as the 1959 Round-Up queen, Vickie Pearson's personal and family attributes that made her worthy of holding the title were touted by the *Pendleton East Oregonian*: "She has been riding since she was a child and has worked as a cowhand on her father's ranch since she could ride. Beauty, brains, and ability—what more could you ask in royalty?"[15]

With the advent of the Miss Rodeo America title, one could ask that their rodeo queen also competed in rodeo events. The princesses on Pearson's court showed how far this trend had developed: The young women on her court both competed in rodeo and served on various rodeo courts—more so than previous Round-Up courts. Sylvia Harvey "participated in Mustanger rodeos and finds the pole bending event particularly enjoyable." Princess Lynda Ferris, the *Pendleton East Oregonian* noted, "won many ribbon, trophies and buckles in competition at various rodeos and horse shows. . . . She received trophies three times for pole bending, twice for barrel racing, and once for stake racing. She also received the Texas barrel racing trophy for Oregon last year." Princess Ruth Tibbets, also with an impressive listing of trophies, was Miss Fort Dalles Rider and queen of the 1958 Arlington, Oregon, rodeo.[16]

Pearson, like all the young women who competed for the title of Miss Rodeo America, participated as a rodeo contestant. Miss Rodeo America titleholders from 1956 to 2001 participated in a variety of events, from barrel racing to bull riding; 88 percent of the women competed in barrel racing, and 56 percent competed in the next two most common events, goat tying and pole bending.[17] The chance to compete, based on opportunities that opened up for amateurs during World War II and with the emergence of women's rodeo, was paralleled by women's eligibility to enter sports across the country. Susan Cahn notes that women in the 1950s, "accepted the basic premise of natural gender distinctions to which, in principle, men and women should conform. Yet they also rejected the equation of athleticism with masculinity, employing an elastic definition of femininity based on personal reputation and on compliance with the often more flexible gender standards of local neighborhoods, rural communities, and peer groups."[18] Since rodeo events were often extensions of ranch chores young women performed at home, rural attitudes about competing in this sport were more accommodating in the 1940s and 1950s than attitudes about competing in other sports. Young women who wanted to participate in sports such as track and field events, considered the most masculine of activities, often faced stiff resistance by parents, peers, and school officials.[19]

During this era, the fact that young women participated in rodeo as queens, rodeo competitors, or both did not seem to encourage divisions among the women participating in rodeo in different capacities. Elsa Neumann Jensen, 1958 Soap Lake Rodeo queen and later a member of the Washington Women's Barrel Racing Association, recalls that the young women in rodeo at the time did not think one way or the other about rodeo queens, cowgirls, and cowgirl queens. They participated because they enjoyed riding and rodeo.[20]

Miss Rodeo America presides over the sport of rodeo, but she also reigns over a community of rodeo queens—the women who compete for titles at all levels. Beginning in the 1940s, a queening culture emerged in rodeo, one that developed from a sense of camaraderie through shared experience, symbolism, language, and memories.[21] Although rodeo queens, like members of any large community, "will never know most of their fellow-members, meet them, or even hear of them, yet in the minds of each lives the image of their communion."[22] One of the concerns within the community of rodeo queens revolved around maintaining a queenlike image: gracious, charming, knowledgeable in rodeo history, and capable in riding skills—the type of monarch appropriate for presiding over her rodeo community. Fascination with European royalty—a major component in the early development in the community-sponsored rodeo queen phenomenon—faded from the popular press after World War II.[23] The connection between rodeo and a young female "queen," however, remained firmly fixed.

The growing number of young women who engaged in "queening" in the early 1940s, might suggest the possibility for professional rodeo queens, like the professional rodeo athletes. Indeed, just as rodeo athletes began attending rodeo clinics and schools to hone their riding skills, rodeo queen clinics developed to help young women with their riding, appearance, dress, and interview skills. But the establishment a professional rodeo queen persona did not happen. Serving as royalty in a democratic society, while considered an honor, continued to be recognized as a temporary position: At the end of her reign, a queen gracefully steps aside for the next young woman to take her place. As the 1981 Pendleton Round-Up queen, Susan Talbot, remarked, "Once Saturday Round-Up rolls around, we always say, 'You're now a has-been!'"[24] Most willingly step down from the post to resume their lives; however, for the few who have difficulty turning in the scepter, one member of the queen community gave stern advice: "IT IS NOT FOR LIFE, you are not Queen Elizabeth. . . . Get over it!"[25]

Vickie Pearson, celebrated in her hometown for winning the Miss Rodeo America pageant in 1959, does not appear in the list of past Miss Rodeo Americas. The *Pendleton East Oregonian* discretely ignored her resignation; an article at the Miss Rodeo America archives, however, noted "Martha Lehmann, who was queen of the 1959 Fiesta de los Vaqueros, will take over as the Rodeo Queen of America [*sic*] next week at the North Platte, Nebraska, rodeo. She took over the spot when Vickie Pearson, of Pendleton, Oregon, became ineligible to continue her role when she got married last month."[26] For Miss Rodeo America hopefuls, the idea of stepping down from such a coveted position might sound truly remarkable. But it was still 1959, and as Brett Harvey writes, "A young woman approaching adulthood after the war was surrounded by powerful inducements to marry."[27] Many women in the 1950s turned their backs to professional or career-advancing opportunities to pursue marriage. In her decision to step down from the Miss Rodeo America position, Pearson represented the prevailing

neo-Victorian attitudes that developed after World War II, emphasizing traditional gender roles centered on creating a home
and family.

Although Pearson and her generation had more opportunities to participate in rodeo as a queen, rodeo contestant, or
both, societal pressure to put family above personal goals remained strong. Pearson's choice to step out of the public spotlight and into domesticity is instructive on several levels. As
just mentioned, it highlighted the imperative to marry. But
in the debate over representations of western womanhood, it
also helps explain why cowgirls, not rodeo queens, hold sway
over the image. Cowgirls received more attention than rodeo
queens, especially within the context of modern feminist history, whereas rodeo queens, perceived as never having moved
beyond traditional domestic sphere, received little scholarly attention. Since the role of queen came into its own in the postwar years, thousands of women have enjoyed reigning as a
rodeo queen throughout the West. Yet in the rare cases when
one finds mention of the phenomenon, the tone and language
used to describe community-sponsored rodeo queens remains
dismissive or derogatory.

In her essay on the Cowgirl Hall of Fame, Laura Jane Moore
recalls the early years of women's history in the 1970s. Wom-
en's historians, she writes, focused on "contribution history,"
concerned as they were with discovering "the extent [that] the
West was liberating for white women."[28] Ranch women and
cowgirl rodeo athletes became popular areas of study, women
who seemed liberated from the restrictions of postwar gender
expectations—femininity, domesticity, and willingness to sub-
merge personal aspirations for the family. While outside tending cattle, riding the range, or engaged in any number of necessary ranch chores, these women crossed boundaries between
male and female spheres, enjoying the kind of freedom usually
reserved for men.

It is not too surprising then that historians ignored rodeo queens. At best the rodeo queen pageants recall the sponsor girl contests of the 1930s and 1940s, in which winning depended only in part on riding ability, and reinforced conservative concepts of femininity in order for women to remain in the patriarchal rodeo structure. At their worst, pageants like the Miss Rodeo America, with their criteria for poise, photogenic, and interview skills, dance perilously close to the Miss America pageant, albeit with contestants all wearing western garb, answering questions pertaining to rodeo, and competing in a standardized talent event—horsemanship. The implication was that this sort of performance could hardly be taken seriously. Could this "superficial" display of young women really represent the spirit of the West?

In her study on the 1960s and 1970s generation of women, Susan J. Douglas writes, "According to the prevailing cultural history of our times, the impact of boys was serious, lasting, authentic. . . . The impact of girls was fleeting, superficial, trivial."[29] Laura Jane Moore also notes that the image, or myth of the West, became "personified by the image of the strong, independent, freedom-loving cowboy—[and] is white and masculine at its core." Language used to describe cowgirls included words also associated with cowboys, like "independent," "free spirited," and "adventuresome," while rodeo queens—ranchhand skills, rodeo competition, or commitment to the sport notwithstanding—received descriptions like "mere props or decorations, not legitimate athletes," or "mastheads, symbols, figurines."[30] Richard W. Slatta summarizes the scholarly sentiment of pre-1960s queens: "Like cowboying, rodeo was originally a male province. Women served as window dressing in the roles of rodeo queen and dance partner."[31]

No serious attention had been paid to the role of rodeo queen, and for the most part, the image of these young women first seen in Westermeier's 1948 history of rodeo, continues to persist: "Many contests, especially those of a community na-ture, invariably have, as a feature which is introduced early in the show, a young lady who has been selected as Queen of the Rodeo. Dressed in flashing regalia, suitable for the occasion, she is accompanied by two ladies-in-waiting. It is a sought—for honour by the belles of the town; the chosen ones enjoy this honor and popularity and have much attention showered on them for the duration of the contest."[32]

The position was indeed "sought-for," the young women did have "much attention showered on them." However, the im-plicit message in Westermeier's description is that once women no longer participated as contestants on a more or less (usu-ally less) equal footing with cowboy athletes, they became an updated version of the gentle tamer of the West, sporting a tiara and gold lamé rather than a bonnet and calico. That im-age of the community-sponsored rodeo queens shows little un-derstanding as to why the role existed and little concern as to whom the "belles" might be or why they were considered representative of the town's western heritage.

Candace Savage perpetuates the misperception of rodeo queens in her book *Cowgirls* when she writes, "While cowgirl athletes were being forced out of rodeo, a new group of cow-girl-look-alikes were welcomed with open arms. They were the 'sponsor girls,' young women who were nominated by their local communities to compete in beauty contests. As ranch-country debutantes, their job was to 'add a little charm and glamour' to the testosterone-soaked world of male athleticism. . . . In most cases, a competent working cowgirl who could rope and ride had little or no chance against a pretty young thing with a rich daddy, who could afford to deck herself out in fancy cowgirl clothes."[33] On the page facing this statement is a photo of Nancy Binford and Thena Mae Farr noting their role in starting the Tri-State All-Girl Rodeo. But there is no mention of the fact that Binford and Farr competed successfully—and often—as sponsor girls, that both came from wealthy families, or that together they developed the Tri-State All-Girl Rodeo using their sponsor girl experiences and the help of a community of women riders that developed from competing in sponsor girl events.

Americans hotly debated the important gender characteristics and roles during the era of New Women; the rumblings of a good debate over what makes a western woman is now starting to make itself heard. Susan J. Douglas writes of women historians, "In our haste to deny our own history, to repudiate what we know regard as our preconscious selves, we've lost sight of the fact that those selves weren't quite so preconscious, frivolous, or passive, and that there is an important connection between them and us."[34] There is a growing awareness that earlier feminists, in their efforts to emancipate women from constraining roles by celebrating nontraditional female accomplishments overlooked the more subtle ways in which women negotiated agency. Most rodeo queens were, indeed, more than the "pretty young things with a rich daddy" that Savage dismisses. Instead, the young women took on important roles within their respective communities, symbolizing the connection of the town to its frontier past, helping promote the sport of rodeo for the benefit of the community, and actively participating in an area of their own personal interests and way of life (and besides, not all women wanted to ride broncs).[35] So the question remains, Did wanting to be a rodeo queen disqualify someone from being considered a true western woman, part of America's western heritage?

Patricia Limerick describes the "Myth of the American West," saying, "You can't buy into the cowboy myth if you're a woman because you don't have the right anatomy."[36] But Limerick also notes, "In the long run, the boys are trapped in this tough-guy role." The image of western women, perpetuated by the feminist writers, emphasizes the non-feminine aspect of their lives, and in doing so, runs the risk of becoming trapped in the same "tough-guy" role as the cowboys. In large part, cowgirl athletes like Binford and Farr were able to compete because they were successful in showing that doing "mannish" activities—riding bulls, riding broncs, roping calves, and competing in activities that required physical strength and daring—would not diminish their feminine qualities and turn then into "one of the guys." Binford, Farr, and Pendleton Round-Up queen Kathryn Lazinka are representative of the women who were interested in competing, who, according to Cahn, "did not necessarily accept the wider culture's definition of feminine and masculine traits. Instead, they subtly reinterpreted femininity, expanding its boarders to include the very athletic qualities that many perceived as masculine."[37]

In the contemporary discourse of gender, the question persists, Who best illustrates the image of western women—the rodeo queen or the cowgirl? The question itself, though, is really part of the problem. It reflects the dichotomous worldview of the Victorians and postwar neo-Victorians, who insisted that middle-class, genteel young women who served as rodeo queens and modern cowgirl athletes could not exist in the same person.[38] But they could. And they did. And they continue to do so. And yet the debate continues. When former Miss Rodeo U.S.A. Rebecca Passion won first and second in roping events, one of the other contestants "came up to her and asked if she had won her belt buckle roping, Rebecca said no and tilted the best buckle for her to read. When she read Miss Rodeo U.S.A. 2001 she said, I didn't think you girls knew what you were doing, I guess I was wrong."[39] As the community-sponsored rodeo queens made clear, young woman found equilibrium within the parameters of neo-Victorian decorum, proved a valuable asset on the ranch, and even competed in rodeo events. Rodeo queens did not trade in their femininity for "mannish" qualities; rather, they capitalized on them, "reify[ing] gender stereotypes while simultaneously challenging those roles."[40]

Lisa Eisner's work *Rodeo Cowgirl* comes closest to reconciling the images of "cowgirl" and "rodeo queen" as an example of a western woman. Recollecting the first time she saw a rodeo queen, at age eight, she writes,

> I was a complete tomboy, totally out of touch with my girlie side. Until we rode past the rodeo queens. I'll never forget that vision. I looked at them high up on their big powerful horses. They looked like superheroes with their gold sequined shirts reflecting on their green hats and their tiaras shooting light everywhere. They were like fireworks, a laser show, a disco ball. The bright Western sun hitting all those rhinestones and sequins. It was blinding. They were a cross between Annie Oakley and Liberace—all sparkly! I couldn't even imagine that I was the same species as these women, let alone the same gender. But the second I saw them, I knew. I was ready to ditch the bike and the Converse sneakers. I was ready for a bra and a tiara. I was ready to be a rodeo queen.[41]

Eisner never became a rodeo queen herself, but her fascination with the rodeo queens led her to publish a photographic record of the rodeo girls as she saw them—"sequined icons of feminine strength among the dusty down-n-dirty world of the American West."[42]

Images of royalty, community, boosterism, and rodeo history—all are inextricably interwoven in the history of community-sponsored rodeo queens, and all remain in a constant state of flux. Vickie Pearson, the first Pendleton Round-Up queen to win the Miss Rodeo America crown, exemplified the changes that had occurred with the rodeo queen phenomenon in the fifty years after Bertha Anger's inaugural reign. In that half-century, community-sponsored rodeo queens evolved into an integral part of the western tradition. Communities throughout the West adopted and adapted the rodeo queen phenomenon to suit the characteristics of their own celebrations. However, the main characteristics of the community-sponsored rodeo queen—a symbol of their rodeo and themselves, a self-conscious connection to the frontier West, and a metaphor for western woman—remained.

The debate over women's role in society continues, and the argument over who best represents western womanhood strikes a chord since the western ideal plays such a large role in our national conception of self. Will the dichotomist views of western womanhood ever be reconciled? Will gender relations reach the point where women will be able to enter all the rodeo events that are open to men? If they do, will rodeo queens fade from view? Or perhaps the definition of western womanhood will free itself from the dichotomies that have guided it for so long and broaden to encompass for each woman the opportunity to find fulfillment as she defines it for herself.

Appendix A

Pendleton Round-Up Queens and Princesses, 1910–1959

1910
Queen: Bertha Anger
Princesses: Genevieve Clark
Edna Wissler
Edna Thompson
Iva Hill

1911
Queen: Laura McKee
Princesses: Irma Baer
Iva Hill
Muriel Saling
Norma Alloway

1912
Queen: Muriel Saling
No princesses

1913
Queen: Gladys McDonald
No princesses

1914
Queen: Lula Matlock
No princesses

1915
Queen: Doris Reber
No princesses

1916
Queen: Muriel Saling
No princesses

1917
Queen: Lula Matlock
No princesses

1918–20
No queen

1921
Queen: Helen Thompson
Princesses: Kathryn Thompson
Thelma Thompson
Daphne Gibbs
Elsie Fitzmaurice

1922
Queen: Thelma Thompson
Princesses: Helen Thompson
Jean Skeen
Jessie Drumheller
Adeline Scroggins

1923
Queen: Jessie Drumheller
Princesses: Thelma Thompson
Elizabeth Hailey

1924
Queen: Josie Sedgwick
No princesses

1925
Queen: Mildred Rogers
Princesses: Doris Churchill
Agnes McMurray
Catherine McNary
Mary Clarke

1926
Queen: Esther Motanic
No princesses

1926
Queen: Mabel Strickland
Princesses: Jean Frazier
Mary Bond
Janet LaFountaine
Elizabeth Crommelin

1928
Queen: Mary Duncan
Princesses: Roberta Morrison
Dorothy Barthell
Lois McIntyre
Kathleen McClintock

1929
Queen: Kathleen McClintock
Princesses: Allegra McCormmach
Adelyn McIntyre
Dena Lieuallen
Kathryn Furnish

1930
Queen: Lois McIntyre
Princesses: Mildred Hansell
Virginia Sturgis
Evelyn Cresswell
Annabel Tullock

1931
Queen: Betty Bond
Princesses: Shirley Thompson
Jessie Thompson
Jean Cronin
Barbara Castleman

1932
Queen: Melissa Parr
Princesses: Carrie Sampson
Josephine Sheoships
Rosalie Kanine
Rose Badroads

1933
Queen: Jean Frazier
Princesses: Cathryn Collins
Sally Sigrist
Dorothy Doherty
Anne Kistner
Ruth Porter

1934
Queen: Shirley Thompson
Princesses: Mary Robison
Hazel Barton
Margaret Broznan
Betty Tubbs
Ruth Porter

1935
Queen: Helen Hansell
Princesses: June Thompson
Velma Powell
June Lemons
Helma Carstens
Maxine Conley

1936
Queen: Mary Robison
Princesses: Beverly Simpson
Patricia Ward
Jeanette Potter
Eva Wilcox
Edna Rice

1937
Queen: Cathryn Collins
Princesses: Barbara Kirkpatrick
Alta Bell Troxel
Helen Shafer
Betty Jane Holt
Irene Bannister
Marion Hughes

1938
Queen: Jean McCarty
Princesses: Betty Jean Tippett
Lila Ellen Boone
Betty West
Mary Jane Hawkins
Josephine Brock
Ann Little

1939
Queen: Barbara Kirkpatrick
Princesses: Peg Thompson
Patty Cowan
Jean Richards
Lavern Herndon
Jane Boyer
Maxine McCurdy

1940
Queen: Marion Hughes
Princesses: Wanda Piper
Adarene Fisk
Shirley Brady
Betty Troxel

1941
Queen: Maxine McCurdy
Princesses: Anne Thompson
Helen Proebstel
Mary Hassell
June Kirkpatrick

1942–43
No Round-Up

1944
Queen: Janet Thompson
Princesses: Donne Boylen
Pat Mann
Christine Lieuallen
Susan Sturgis
Marilyn Glenn
Jerry McIntyre

1945
Queen: Donne Boylen
Princesses: Barbara Tippett
Mary Esther Brock
Beverly Barrett
Gloria Gibbs

1946
Queen: Jackie Hales
Princesses: Pauline Lieuallen
Suzanne Lieuallen
Patti Folsom
Marge McKenzie

1947
Queen: Patti Folsom
Princesses: Marion Andrews
Janet Young
Charlotte Montag
Joyce Trowbridge

1948
Queen: Virginia Wilkinson
Princesses: Thelma Parr
Laura McKay
Velva Bill
Gladys Sheoships
Edna Quaempts
Myrna Williams

1949
Queen: Joan Barnett
Princesses: Barbara Raymond
Barbara Owens
Kathryn Lazinka
Marlene Lieuallen

1950
Queen: Kathryn Lazinka
Princesses: Nancy Collins
Francine Hisler
Bette Belle Lieuallen
Shirley Warner

1951
Queen: Julie King
Princesses: Creagh Brennan
Jean Lazinka
Thelma Harvey
Kathleen Folsom

1952
Queen: Leah Conner
Princesses: Dianna McKay
Bernice Ryan
Artina Quaempts
Audrey Blackhawk

1953
Queen: Dianna McKay
Princesses: Doris Scott
Yvonne Scott
Linnea Sampson
Loretta Quaempts

1954
Queen: Joan Pearson
Princesses: Gayle Grilley
Judy Grieves
Ann Kirkpatrick

Kathryn Wyss

1955
Queen: Kathryn Wyss
Princesses: Sandra Curl
Sharon Bryant
Deanna Whitley
Lili Mae Mascal

1956
Queen: Sandra Curl
Princesses: Terry Hill
Tammy Dix
Judy Thompson
Claudette Edwards

1957
Queen: Terry Hill
Princesses: Gayle Austin
Linda Pearson
Susan King
Judy Fischer

1958
Queen: Judy Lazinka
Princesses: Jan Beamer
Kay Smutz
Loretta Anderson
Marcia Bull

1959
Queen: Vicki Pearson
Princesses: Martha Boyer
Silva Harvey
Linda Ferris
Ruth Tibbets

Appendix B

Rodeo Queen Questionnaire Respondents

Pendleton, Oregon, Round-Up Royalty

Kathryn Furnish Ramey	1929 princess
Betty Jane Holt Graybell	1937 princess
Jean McCarty Dearinger	1938 queen
Helen Proebstel Swanson	1941 princess
Myrna Williams Tovey	1948 princess
Leah Conner	1952 queen
Susan Koch Talbot	1981 queen
Tiah Degrofft	2000 queen

Cheyenne, Wyoming, Miss Frontier Days

Marie Duff Nimmo responding for Jean Nimmo (deceased)	1931
Lois Crain Moor	1934
Leona Brunor Gillen	1935
Catharine Schroeder Holmes	1937
Louise Holmes Bartlett	1939
Teddy Ann Storey Varineau	1942
Lois Hofman Deaver	1946
Ann Dinneen Smith	1947
Norma Jean Bell Morris	1949
Joy Vandehei Kilty	1950
Laura M. Bailey	1951
Jane Henderson Uchner	1952
Margaret Hirsig Wilson	1954

Other Rodeos

Odalee Bradee	1950 Reno, Nevada, Rodeo queen
Nancy Neumann Martini	1951 Soap Lake, Washington, Rodeo queen
Sharon Peterson Laegreid	1952 Isanti County, Minnesota, Rodeo queen

Miss Rodeo America

Dallas Hunt George	1957
Susan Cox Valley Stauffer	1959
Martha Robertson	1960
Karen James	1962
Joyce Kernek	1963
Patricia Koren Sanmartin	1965
Carolynn Seay Vietor	1966
Nancy Simmons Brannon	1967
Sherie Vincent Scott	1968
Chris Vincent Williams	1970
Pam Martin Minick	1973
Connie Della Lucia Robinson	1975
Terry Ann Edington McAdams	1977
Almabeth Carroll Kaess	1978
Debbie Johnson Garrison	1979
Diana Putnam	1980
Brenda Bonogofsky Pickett	1983
Sandy Meyer Brazile	1984
Leslie Pattern White	1985
Vickie Vest Woodard	1986
Kellie Dilka Lambert	1988
Chrissy Sparling Neuens	1989
Lisa Poese Jamison	1991
Shelly Williams	1999

Notes

Introduction

1. Rupp, *Let 'Er Buck*, 2.

2. "How the Round-Up Appeals to Me," *Pendleton East Oregonian*, September 22, 1922.

3. Banner, *American Beauty*, 250.

4. Joan Burbick's book *Rodeo Queens and the American Dream* appeared as the first full-length treatment on rodeo queens. Taking a postmodernist/feminist approach to the subject, the work is inadequate as a scholarly history of the rodeo queen phenomenon.

5. For an excellent example of a community study, see Haywood, *The Victorian West*.

6. For examples of community studies, see Vaught, *Cultivating California*, and Murphy, *Mining Cultures*.

7. Banner, *American Beauty*, 250–51. Banner notes that when George Washington traveled from Mount Vernon to New York City to assume the presidency in 1789, "delegations of young women dressed in white strewed palm branches in front of his carriage in the cities along his route."

8. Lavenda, "Family and Corporation," 63.

9. U.S. Census Bureau statistics courtesy of Mary L. Finney, Pendleton Public Library, Pendleton, Oregon, March 14, 2002.

10. "Pendleton Girls Will Ride in Westward Ho!" *Pendleton East Oregonian*, September 16, 1910.

11. Pratt and Manning, *In Search of the Corn Queen*, 17.

12. Kertzer, *Ritual, Politics, and Power*, 17.

13. Kertzer, *Ritual, Politics, and Power*, 61–63.

14. Rupp, *Let 'Er Buck*, 15.

15. The history of rodeo has become increasingly popular. The titles listed here represent some of the best work on the subject. See, for example, M. Allen, *Rodeo Cowboys in the North American Imagination*; Fredriksson, *American Rodeo*; Lawrence, *Rodeo*; LeCompte, "The His-

panic Influence of the History of Rodeo"; Westermeier, *Man, Beast, Dust*; and Wooden and Ehringer, *Rodeo in America*.

16. Schwantes, "Patterns of Radicalism." See also Carlson, *The Cowboy Way*; Allmendinger, *The Cowboy*; and Dary, *Cowboy Culture*.

17. For historiography on cowboys, see, for example, Slatta, *Cowboys of the Americas*; and Hoy, *Cowboys and Kansas*.

18. For historiography on cowgirls, see, for example, Jordan, *Cowgirls: Women of the American West*; Sloan, *Women in Cattle Country*; Roach, *The Cowgirls*; Crandall, *Cowgirls: Early Images and Collectibles*; Wills and Artho, *Cowgirl Legends*; Savage, *Cowgirls*; and Burbick, *Rodeo Queens and the American Dream*.

19. Savage, *Cowgirls*, 28.

20. Cott, *The Grounding of Modern Feminism*, 277.

21. Westermeier, *Man, Beast, Dust*, 83. Mary Lou LeCompte's *Cowgirls of the Rodeo: Pioneer Professional Athletes* remains the leading study on professional cowgirl athletes.

22. McGovern, "The American Woman's Pre–World War I Freedom," 333.

23. Welter, "The Cult of True Womanhood," 44.

24. Cott, *The Grounding of Modern Feminism*, 217. The percentage of women entering the professional sector increased to 14.2 percent of all employed women by 1930.

25. Gilman, "The New Generation of Women."

26. Cott, *The Grounding of Modern Feminism*, 199.

27. McFadden, *The Power and Beauty of Superb Womanhood*, 1–49, especially 10, 30, and 48.

28. For a discussion on women's emancipation by contemporary writers, advertisers, and the popular media, see Cott, *The Grounding of Modern Feminism*, 272.

29. Cahn, *Coming on Strong*, 29–30.

30. Cahn, *Coming on Strong*, 29–30.

31. McGovern, "The American Woman's Pre–World War I Freedom," 318.

32. Fass, *The Damned and the Beautiful*, 15; see also Glenn, *Female Spectacle*, 5.

33. Peiss, *Cheap Amusements*, 4–6.

34. McGovern, "The American Woman's Pre–World War I Freedom," 319.

35. Derry, "Corsets and Broncs," 5.

36. Glenn, *Female Spectacle*, 2.

37. Remley, "From Sidesaddle to Rodeo," 46.

38. McGovern, "The American Woman's Pre–World War I Freedom," 327.

39. Gordon, "Any Desired Length," 24.

40. Behling, *The Masculine Woman in America*, 16.

41. Behling, *The Masculine Woman in America*, 15.

42. Shirley Flynn, personal interview with the author, December 10, 2001.

43. Gordon, "Any Desired Length," 43.

44. Gordon, "Any Desired Length," 43.

45. Ella Granger, "Cowgirls of Eastern Oregon," audio tape HO 820630, *Horizons*, National Public Radio, 1982.

46. Burgess and Valaskakis, *Indian Princesses and Cowgirls*, 79.

47. "How the Round-Up Appeals to Me," *Pendleton East Oregonian*, September 22, 1922.

48. Armitage, "Rawhide Heroines," 175.

49. Haywood, *The Victorian West*, 13.

1. Community-Sponsored Rodeo Queens

1. "Who Was *Really* the First Round-Up Queen?" *Pendleton Eastern Oregonian*, September 14, 1979. Bertha Anger's name was not listed in the 1910 *Pendleton East Oregonian* papers as the first queen of the Round-Up. The 1911 queen, Laura McKee, did make the papers. Because there was no public acknowledgment, some assumed Anger did not fulfill the role as first queen.

2. *Enter into the Past: A Self-Guided Walking Tour of Pendleton's Historic Downtown District* (Pendleton OR: Pendleton Chamber of Commerce, n.d.).

3. Boylen, *Episode of the West*, 1; personal information on Boylen found on book jacket.

4. Searcey, "History of Pendleton Round-Up Association Queens," 3.

5. "Fourth of July." *Pendleton East Oregonian*, June 16, 1887.

6. "Pendleton Will Celebrate: A List of Those Who Have Already Subscribed," *Pendleton East Oregonian*, June 22, 1888.

7. "Fourth of July Celebration," *Pendleton East Oregonian*, June 22, 1888.

8. "Pendleton Will Celebrate," *Pendleton East Oregonian*, June 22, 1888.

9. Abbott, *Boosters and Businessmen*, 4.

10. "The Frontier Celebration," *Pendleton East Oregonian*, July 30, 1910.

11. "Mark Moorehouse Will Take Notes on Cheyenne Show," *Pendleton East Oregonian*, August 22, 1910.

12. "Frontier Show for Pendleton," *Pendleton East Oregonian*, July 29, 1910.

13. "Frontier Show for Pendleton," *Pendleton East Oregonian*, July 29, 1910.

14. "How the Round-Up Grew from Modest Beginning to Show of World Proportions," *Pendleton East Oregonian*, souvenir edition, September 11, 1913.

15. "Indians Ask for Week of Racing," *Pendleton East Oregonian*, August 27, 1910.

16. Westermeier, *Man, Beast, Dust*, 297–98.

17. Westermeier, *Man, Beast, Dust*, 298–99.

18. "Westward Ho! to Be Great Spectacular Frontier Pageant," *Pendleton East Oregonian*, August 20, 1910.

19. "Celebration at Pendleton Pronounced a Big Success," *Pendleton East Oregonian*, July 5, 1907. The parade directors must have been visionaries, considering there were only forty-five states in the Union at the time.

20. "Pendleton Girls Will Ride in Westward Ho!" *Pendleton East Oregonian*, September 16, 1910.

21. Frink, "Pendleton Round-Up Royalty of 1910," 11.

22. "Westward Ho! to Be Great Spectacular Frontier Pageant," *Pendleton East Oregonian*, August 20, 1910.

23. "Italian Royalty on Roller Skates," *Pendleton East Oregonian*, April 25, 1910; "King's Dog Misses Him," *Pendleton East Oregonian*, June 6, 1910; "Tired of Being a Prince, Is Found Playing 'Injun,'" *Pendleton East Oregonian*, March 31, 1910.

24. Searcey, "History of Pendleton Round-Up Association Queens," 3.

25. Frink, "Pendleton Round-Up Royalty of 1910," 11.

26. "Contest Is on for Stanfield's Queen" *Pendleton East Oregonian*, June 24, 1910.

27. The prize would be worth about $1,800 by today's standards.

28. "Contest for Stanfield Queen Grows Exciting," *Pendleton East Oregonian*, June 29, 1910.

29. Higham, "The Reorientation of American Culture in the 1890s," 82.

30. Armitage, "Rawhide Heroines," 179; Welter, "The Cult of True Womanhood," 43–71.

31. See especially Zunz, *Making America Corporate*; Peiss, *Cheap Amusements*; and Banner, *American Beauty*.

32. "Who Was *Really* the First Round-Up Queen?" *Pendleton East Oregonian*, September 14, 1979. No records exist to indicate who the other candidates were.

33. "Westward Ho! Parade Barbaric in Splendor, Witnessed by Thousands," *Pendleton East Oregonian*, September 16, 1911.

34. "Westward Ho! Parade Barbaric in Splendor, Witnessed by Thousands," *Pendleton East Oregonian*, September 16, 1911.; "Westward Ho! Seen by 30,000," *Pendleton East Oregonian*, September 28, 1912.

35. "Boosters Show Spokane What May Be Expected at Round-Up," *Pendleton East Oregonian*, September 16, 1914.

36. "Miss Doris Reber Will Be 'Queen of Round-Up,'" *Pendleton East Oregonian*, September 18, 1915.

37. "Annual Pageant Brings to Mind the Olden Days," *Pendleton East Oregonian*, September 25, 1915.

38. "Muriel to Reign over Regatta and Round-Up," *Pendleton East Oregonian*, August 25, 1916.

39. "Muriel to Reign over Regatta and Round-Up," *Pendleton East Oregonian*, August 25, 1916.

40. "Muriel to Reign over Regatta and Round-Up," *Pendleton East Oregonian*, August 25, 1916.

41. "Queens Who Have Reigned over the Round-Up," *Pendleton East Oregonian*, September 22, 1916.

42. "Queen Lula Rules This Year over Round-Up; Former Queens Married," *Pendleton East Oregonian*, September 18, 1917.

43. "Round-Up Board Opposed to Royalty and Says No Queen," *Pendleton East Oregonian*, September 13, 1918.

44. "Miss Matlock to Be Queen of Round-Up," *Pendleton East Oregonian*, September 18, 1917.

45. Although Pendleton residents considered rodeo an all-American sport, many of its characteristics were based on Hispanic traditions. Cattle herding and the development of large ranches began in Texas after the Civil War; the cowboys hired on the ranches not only adapted vaquero equipment and techniques for working cattle but also the tradition of holding competitive events during a round-up—bronc riding, roping, etc.—that would form the basis for rodeo in America.

46. "Countess among Round-Up Visitors," *Pendleton East Oregonian*, September 13, 1918.

47. Kesey, *Last Go-Round*, 85. Kesey, author of *One Flew Over the Cuckoo's Nest* and *Sometimes a Great Nation*, was originally from Oregon State. *Last Go-Round: A Real Western* was the last book he published before his death.

48. Lula Matlock and Muriel Saling had each served as queen twice. Muriel Saling had also been a princess in 1911. Genevieve Clark was a princess in 1910 and 1911, as was Iva Hill.

49. "Round-Up Board Opposed to Royalty" *Pendleton East Oregonian*, 13 September 13, 1918.

2. "Who Will Reign as Queen?"

1. "Round-Up Board Opposed to Royalty," *Pendleton East Oregonian*, September 13, 1918.

2. "Who Will Reign as Queen of Let 'Er Buck City during Round-Up Is Question Confronting Association Members," *Pendleton East Oregonian*, August 26, 1921.

3. "Queen Helen of the Round-Up and Her Maids," *Pendleton East Oregonian*, September 22, 1921.

4. "New Girl Rider Here for Show," *Pendleton East Oregonian*, September 19, 1912.

5. Glenn, *Female Spectacle*, 15.

6. "Who Will Reign," *Pendleton East Oregonian*, August 26, 1921.

7. Glenn, *Female Spectacle*, 20.

8. "Rudd Will Handle 'Round-Up' Work," *Pendleton East Oregonian*, June 17, 1922.

9. "Many Seek Information Already as to Time of Holding Round-Up Here," *Pendleton East Oregonian*, June 5, 1922.

10. "Thelma Thompson Is Round-Up Queen," *Pendleton East Oregonian*, August 21, 1922; Photo of trick rider, *Pendleton East Oregonian*, June 6, 1922.

11. "Thelma Thompson Is Round-Up Queen," *Pendleton East Oregonian*, August 21, 1922.

12. Queen Thelma's family connection to the Round-Up was unusually poignant, as her grandfather, Umatilla County sheriff and Round-Up president Ti Taylor, had been murdered earlier that year by an escaped convict.

13. "Miss Alladeen Scroggins, Representing La Grande Will Be in Round-Up Parade," *Pendleton East Oregonian*, September 21, 1922.

14. "Pendletonians Invited to Attend Dayton Show," *Pendleton East Oregonian*, June 2, 1922.

15. Bonnie Sager, personal interview with the author, July 30, 2001.

16. Kathryn Furnish Ramey, personal interview with the author, August 1, 2001.

17. For examples of the changing roles of women, see "No Chance for a Knockout," *Pendleton East Oregonian*, June 8, 1922 (women boxing); "Jazz Dance Is Cocaine of Physical Movement Says Theodore Kosloff," *Pendleton East Oregonian*, July 14, 1922 (women and the new, sensual form of jazz dancing); "Man Gives Way in Other Quarter," *Pendleton East Oregonian*, August 28, 1922 (women taking up chess, a game previously thought to be too "deep" for their intellects; "They're Here—'Firewomen!'" *Pendleton East Oregonian*, June 13, 1922 (women in full firefighting attire and driving the fire truck).

18. "Shapeliness of Blond Clerk Blocks Work of Collecting Municipal Taxes," *Pendleton East Oregonian*, August 5, 1922.

19. For example, "Coast Venus," *Pendleton East Oregonian*, June 7, 1922 (photo of a California bathing beauty contest winner); and "Hot Weather Riding Habit," *Pendleton East Oregonian*, August 4, 1923 (photo of a socialite galloping her horse, attired in a bathing suit).

20. Latham, *Posing a Threat*, 65, 69.

21. "She's Champion Trick Rider," *Pendleton East Oregonian*, September 2, 1922.

22. See Bledstein and Johnson, *The Middling Sorts*.

23. *Pendleton East Oregonian*, September 13, 1923.

24. "Round-Up Queen Selected for 1924; Movie Star Chosen," *Pendleton East Oregonian*, September 2, 1924.

25. Clippings collected by Allens Clipping Service, which clipped articles related to a specific topic or subject from newspapers around the country indicate wide-spread interest in the Round-Up (Round-Up Hall of Fame Archives, Pendleton, Oregon).

26. Glenn, *Female Spectacle*, 2.

27. "Round-Up Queen on Her Royal Chair," *Sanger (CA) Herald*, October 9, 1924. The personal attendants were Freddy Gilman and 1923 Pendleton Round-Up steer roping champion Tommy Grimes ("The Round-Up Queen for 1924," *Pendleton East Oregonian*, September 18, 1924).

28. *Pendleton East Oregonian*, September 17, 1925.

29. "Mildred Rogers Is Named Queen of '25 Round-Up," *Pendleton East Oregonian*, August 14, 1925.

30. "Mildred Rogers Is Named Queen," *Pendleton East Oregonian*, August 14, 1925.

31. "Queen's Aids [sic] Named: Miss Agnes McMurray, Miss Churchill Picked," *Pendleton East Oregonian*, September 9, 1925.

32. "Boosters Show Spokane What May Be Expected at Round-Up," *Pendleton East Oregonian*, September 16, 1914.

33. *Pendleton East Oregonian*, September 16, 1922.

34. *Pendleton East Oregonian*, souvenir edition, September 17, 1925.

35. "No More Bobbed Hair for Them!" *Pendleton East Oregonian*, July 25, 1927.

36. "Prairie Rose and Prairie Wolf," *Pendleton East Oregonian*, September 18, 1924.

37. "Bobbed-Hair Is Banned," *Arkansas Record*, October 24, 1924; Rupp, *Let 'Er Buck*, 181.

38. "Real American Beauty Contest Is a Feature of Pendleton's Round-Up," *Pendleton East Oregonian*, souvenir edition, August 29, 1930.

39. Mellis, *Riding Buffaloes and Broncos*, 109; Eliza Cowapoo won Pendleton's first Native American beauty contest in 1923. See Rupp, *Let 'Er Buck*, 181.

40. "She's California's Challenge to Pendleton's Round-Up Queen," *Pendleton East Oregonian*, September 10, 1926.

41. "Princess America Takes Part in Parade Here Saturday Morn," *Pendleton East Oregonian*, September 17, 1926.

42. "Cayuse Girl Is Selected Queen, Is Signal Honor," *Pendleton East Oregonian*, August 17, 1926.

43. "Cayuse Girl Is Selected Queen," *Pendleton East Oregonian*, August 17, 1926.

44. For example, in Oregon, Indian princesses from the Umatilla Reservation reigned with non-Indian princesses and queens at the Chief Joseph Days Rodeo. This practice began in the mid-1940s as part of a strategy by Umatilla tribal elders involved with the rodeo to support the Chief Joseph Days events (Leah Conner [Tamastslikt Cultural Center, Umatilla Reservation], personal correspondence with the author, May 29, 2003).

45. For more information about the women on the mixed (Indian/white) courts, see "These Attractive Girls," *Pendleton East Oregonian*, June 19, 1951; and "Jessie M. James," *Pendleton East Oregonian*, July 16, 1954.

46. Iverson and MacCannell, *Riders of the West*, 4.

47. Tamastslikt Cultural Institute Center exhibits, Umatilla Reservation, Oregon.

48. Mellis, *Riding Buffaloes and Broncos*, 14.

49. "Prowess of Girls Shown in He-Man Sport of Rodeo," *Pendleton East Oregonian*, souvenir edition, September 17, 1925. Women occasionally competed against men at other rodeos, but evidence to date does not indicate that ever happened at Pendleton.

50. The Round-Up directors did allow Strickland, however, to give an exhibition of her steer roping skills during the rodeo.

51. "Prowess of Girls Shown in He-Man Sport of Rodeo," *Pendleton East Oregonian*, souvenir edition, September 17, 1925.

52. "Chivalrous Round-Up Cowboys Decline to Compete against Pretty Girl Who Beats Them," *The Dalles (OR) Optimist*, September 3, 1926.

53. See M. Allen, "The Rise and Decline of the Early Rodeo Cowgirl," 123.

54. M. Allen, "The Rise and Decline of the Early Rodeo Cowgirl," 124.

55. "Prowess of Girls Shown in He-Man Sport of Rodeo," *Pendleton East Oregonian*, souvenir edition, September 17, 1925.

56. "Prowess of Girls Shown in He-Man Sport of Rodeo," *Pendleton East Oregonian*, souvenir edition, September 17, 1925.

57. Riley, "Historical Perspectives on Marriage," 91.

58. "Prowess of Girls Shown in He-Man Sport of Rodeo," *Pendleton East Oregonian*, souvenir edition, September 17, 1925.

59. "Fox Movietone Will Take Round-Up File," *Pendleton East Oregonian*, September 12, 1928.

60. "Aides to Queen Mary Are Selected Today," *Pendleton East Oregonian*, September 5, 1928.

61. "Queen Mary, Attendants to Attend Dance," *Pendleton East Oregonian*, September 14, 1928.

62. "Queen Mary I Arrives to Rule Over Pendleton's Big Annual Round-Up," *Pendleton East Oregonian*, September 4, 1928.

63. "Queen, Attendants Will Be at Dance," and "Queen Fishes," *Pendleton East Oregonian*, September 11, 1928.

64. LeCompte, *Cowgirls of the Rodeo*, 99.

65. "First Day of Round-Up Real Success," *Pendleton East Oregonian*, September 20, 1928.

66. "Books? Great Stuff. But Give Claire Belcher a Buckin' Bronc in the Great Outdoors," *Pendleton East Oregonian*, souvenir edition, September 21, 1928.

67. "Books? Great Stuff," *Pendleton East Oregonian*, souvenir edition, September 21, 1928.

68. LeCompte, *Cowgirls of the Rodeo*, 90.

69. "Books? Great Stuff," *Pendleton East Oregonian*, souvenir edition, September 21, 1928.

70. "Queen Kathleen," *Pendleton East Oregonian*, September 19, 1929.

71. Furnish Ramey, interview.

72. "Royalty Rides," *Pendleton East Oregonian*, September 14, 1929.

73. The Round-Up board helped to defray costs by supplying some of the elements of the costume (Furnish Ramey, interview).

74. Furnish Ramey, interview.

75. See "Round-Up Publicity Man Returning after Covering the West: Five Million People Held to Have Been Affected By Let 'Er Buck Talk," *Pendleton East Oregonian*, September 12, 1924.

3. A New Kind of Community Rodeo Queen

1. Rupp, *Let 'Er Buck*, 45–46.

2. Mildred Hansell Miley, telephone interview with the author, April 29, 2002.

3. Pro-Rodeo Hall of Fame statistics on new rodeos (courtesy of Pat Hildabrand, Pro Rodeo Hall of Fame, Colorado Springs, Colorado).

4. Ware, *Holding Their Own*, xvi.

5. As discussed in the introduction, cowgirl athletes were hired by rodeo promoters to act as queens of rodeos. There was no formal contest between cowgirl athletes for this role.

6. Population statistics courtesy of Matilda Bolin (Stamford Chamber of Commerce), personal correspondence with the author, May 21, 2002.

7. "Beginnings of Cowboy Reunion," *Stamford (TX) Western Observer*, June 19, 1980.

8. "How It Started: Texas Cowboy Reunion Developed from Idea to Big Institution." *Stamford (TX) American*, July 15, 1938.

9. "Program of Stunts Ends Saturday," *Fort Worth (TX) Star-Telegram*, June 25, 1931.

10. Even though Kristine Fredriksson states in her book *American Rodeo* that only working cowboys competed at the Pendleton Round-Up and

the Prescott, Arizona, Frontier Days, her information is inaccurate. Pendleton Hall of Fame president Bonnie Sager noted that while the Round-Up was "proud to have working cowboys compete," they made up only a small part of the contestant list. Prescott Frontier Days started restricting their contestants to working cowhands in 1939—fifty-one years after the Prescott rodeo began (Fredriksson, *American Rodeo*, 5, 16; Bonnie Sager, telephone interview with the author, February 3, 2001).

11. *Stamford (TX) American*, February 14, 1930, qtd. in Hearn, "The Texas Cowboy Reunion,"26. The Southwest Rodeo Association, which functioned in a similar manner to the Rodeo Association of America, did not organize until 1938 (Westermeier, *Man, Beast, Dust*, 339).

12. Hearn, "The Texas Cowboy Reunion," 25–26.

13. Slatta, *Cowboys of the Americas*, 117.

14. Rotunda, *American Manhood*, 178.

15. Kimmel, "The Cult of Masculinity," 241.

16. Kimmel, "The Cult of Masculinity," 241; Rotunda, *American Manhood*, 241.

17. Kimmel, "The Cult of Masculinity," 239.

18. Kimmel, "The Cult of Masculinity," 237.

19. Freedman, "The New Woman," 383.

20. Freedman, "The New Woman," 381.

21. "Eligible for Cowgirl Contest," *Fort Worth (TX) Star Telegram*, June 21, 1932.

22. *Stamford (TX) American*, February 14, 1930, cited in Hearn, "The Texas Cowboy Reunion," 36.

23. Shelton, *Fifty Years a Living Legend*, 94.

24. "Group of Cowgirls Will Head Line of March First Day," *Stamford (TX) American*, June 12, 1931.

25. "Ranch Girls to Represent Various Towns," *Stamford (TX) American*, June 12, 1931.

26. Hearn, "The Texas Cowboy Reunion," 36.

27. "Olympic athletes are packing tuxedos in their bags besides their track suits for word has gone out that a gay round of dances, teas, and parties is being arranged for them by one hundred socially prominent Californians named as hostesses for the world sport carnival at Los An-

gles" ("Here's Olympic Games Hostess," *Pendleton East Oregonian*, July 15, 1932).

28. Shelton, *Fifty Years a Living Legend*, 95.

29. In later years hostesses were photographed on horseback, wearing cowgirl costume.

30. Freedman, "Separatism as Strategy," 515, 518.

31. Shelton, *Fifty Years a Living Legend*, 94.

32. Matilda Bolin, (overseer, Texas Cowboy County Museum, Stamford, Texas), personal interview with the author, November 22, 2000.

33. Britt, "Women in the New South," 419.

34. Shelton, *Fifty Years a Living Legend*, 94.

35. "Cowboy Reunion Sponsors Being Picked by Towns," *Stamford (TX) American*, May 20, 1932.

36. LeCompte, *Cowgirls of the Rodeo*, 118.

37. Information is based on an examination of TCR rodeo programs, which list the names of all registered contestants as well as all the events (program files in the Texas Cowboy Country Museum, Stamford, Texas).

38. Cahn, *Coming on Strong*, 78.

39. Statistics are compiled from the *Abilene (TX) Reporter-News* listing of registered sponsor girls, 1932–49.

40. "Bathing Revue to Select Girls for Graham's Delegates," *Graham (TX) Leader*, June 2, 1938.

41. "Pulchritude in Absentia—City's in a Jam," *Abilene (TX) Reporter News*, June 17, 1938.

42. "Drive Launched to Organize City Delegation to Reunion: Dorothy Comer to Head Caravan Leaving Monday," *Abilene (TX) Reporter-News*, evening edition, June 30, 1938.

43. Lavenda, "'It's Not a Beauty Pageant!'" 31–46.

44. Program files, Texas Cowboy Country Museum, Stamford, Texas.

45. "Stamford Plans Cowboy Reunion," *Santa Anna (TX)*, June 3, 1938. This description is representative of other local newspaper articles published throughout the West Texas region in the months prior to the Texas Cowboy Reunion (Blue Newspaper Scrapbook, Texas Cowboy Country Museum Archive, Stamford, Texas).

46. "Sponsor Contest This Year for First Time Will Compete for Day Money," Texas Cowboy's Reunion program, 1957 (Texas Cowboy Country Museum Archive, Stamford, Texas). The dress code was finally dropped in 1975; however, an incident involving a sponsor girl competing in a tube top—Matilda Bolin recalls, "By the time she crossed the finish line, that tube top was nothing but a belt!"—brought back a modified dress code.

47. Stamford Texas Cowboy Reunion Official Program (program file, Texas Cowboy Country Museum, Stamford, Texas).

48. Mahood, "Cowgirl Sponsors from Various Towns and Cities," 8.

49. "New Registration Brings Stamford Reunion Sponsor List to Forty-Seven," *Fort Worth (TX) Star Telegram*, July 2, 1939.

50. Peiss, *Hope in a Jar*, 6.

51. See in particular Peiss, "Going Public."

52. "Mabel Strickland Held to Be Greatest of Cowgirls," *Pendleton East Oregonian*, September 19, 1925.

53. Peiss, "Making Faces," 144.

54. Manko, "Depression Proof Business Strategy," 145.

55. Peiss, *Hope in a Jar*, 140, 166.

56. "Stamford Seethes as Cattle Country Gathers to Rodeo: Beauties Gathering," *Waco (TX) Tribune Herald*, July 2, 1938.

57. "Sponsors Put through Paces: Preliminary Trials Held at Stamford: 49 Are Entered in Main Contest Today," *Colorado City (TX) Gazette*, n.d.

58. Data was compiled from local newspaper descriptions of the women and their sponsoring communities, 1932–49.

59. Stoeltje, "Females in Rodeo," 46.

60. "City's July Fourth Sponsors Selected," *Sweetwater (TX) Reporter*, June 30, 1938.

61. Of the 45 sponsors from ranches, 14, or 31 percent, were married. Of the town contestants, 113 of the 413 women, or 27 percent, were married. As the community-sponsored rodeo queen contest became more common throughout the West, the requirements changed to allow only unmarried women to participate.

62. The names of women participating in the Texas Cowboy Reunion

Sponsor Contest were published in a number of West Texas newspapers during the rodeo.

63. Mary Ellen "Dude" Barton, telephone interview with the author, May 7, 2001.

64. Webb, *The Great Plains*, 496.

65. Fischer, *Albion's Seed*, 633.

66. Fischer, *Albion's Seed*, 834.

67. Fischer, *Albion's Seed*, 677.

68. Fischer, *Albion's Seed*, 676.

69. See Bull, *Hillbilly Hollywood*; and George-Waren and Freedman, *How the West Was Worn*.

70. Beverly Stoeltje discusses gender among rodeo contestants but focuses on the post-1949 period in her essay "Gender Representations in Performance."

71. Vickie Rutledge Shields and Colleen Caughlin, discuss the theory of hyper-femininity as a vehicle for women to gain access to rodeo in the 1970s and 1980s in their essay "Performing Beauty Queen Culture."

72. Hearn, "The Texas Cowboy Reunion," 33, 44.

73. "Top Hands to Compete in Reunion Rodeo," *Borger (TX) Herald*, June 29, 1938.

74. See, for example, *Hoofs and Horns*, *Western Horseman*, *Ranch Romances*, and the *Saturday Evening Post*.

4. Riding Pretty

1. "Ups and Downs of Rodeo," *Pendleton East Oregonian*, August 8, 1931.

2. May, *Homeward Bound*, 41.

3. Armitage, "Rawhide Heroines," 177.

4. Hansell Miley, interview.

5. Hansell Miley, interview.

6. "Ups and Downs of Rodeo," *Pendleton East Oregonian*, August 8, 1931.

7. "Queen Mary II and Court Charming Rulers of Show," *Pendleton East Oregonian*, souvenir edition, September 10, 11, and 12, 1936.

8. Lavenda, "'It's Not a Beauty Pageant!'", 31.

9. Traced back to its Scottish roots, the word originally meant "grammar." Since grammar—specifically Latin grammar—belonged to the elite membership of clergy, the word became associated with the secretive incantations of the church, a perhaps logical association of erudition with occult practices (*The Oxford English Dictionary*, 2nd ed., vol. 9 [Oxford: Clarendon Press, 1989], s.v. "glamour").

10. Haddow, *Pavilions of Plenty*, 5.

11. J. Allen, *The Romance of Commerce and Culture*, 46–47.

12. See Leach, *Land of Desire*, for the late-nineteenth and early-twentieth-century foundations for the later revolution in packaging products.

13. Cooney, *Balancing Acts*, 6.

14. Cooney, *Balancing Acts*, 24.

15. "Hold That Pose! And She Did," *Pendleton East Oregonian*, March 29, 1941.

16. Banner, *American Beauty*, 264–70. A good example of a photo taken with the camera angle is seen in the *Pendleton East Oregonian*, March 29, 1941.

17. Brumberg, *The Body Project*, 83.

18. See Banner, *American Beauty*, 283.

19. "Unseen for Years," *Pendleton East Oregonian*, May 30, 1939; "Forward Bangs and Forward Pompadours," *Pendleton East Oregonian*, April 1, 1941.

20. "Beauty Lessons Are Taught in the Home," *Pendleton East Oregonian*, March 11, 1939.

21. May, *Homeward Bound*, 19.

22. "It's a Man's Job Done by a Girl," *Pendleton East Oregonian*, August 10, 1931.

23. May, *Homeward Bound*, 19.

24. "Salary Hiked," *Pendleton East Oregonian*, March 1, 1941.

25. "Today's Cinderella," *Pendleton East Oregonian*, August 1, 1935.

26. "While Other Royalty Totters Queens of the Round-Up Retain Their Throne," *Pendleton East Oregonian*, souvenir edition, September 29, 1931.

27. The *Pendleton East Oregonian* ran a photo and story on Princess

Natalie Paley of Russia (half sister of the Grand Duchess Marie of Russia). The royal visitor had secured and acting contract and was en route to Hollywood. "Movie Title," *Pendleton East Oregonian*, July 13, 1935.

28. "Royal Indian Blood Rules over Round-Up," *Pendleton East Oregonian*, August 13, 1932.

29. Cooney, *Balancing Acts*, 108.

30. For example, "Royal Indian Blood Rules over Round-Up," *Pendleton East Oregonian*, souvenir edition, September 8, 9, and 10, 1932.

31. "Queen of the 1932 Round-Up Is Second Indian Princess to Reign at Show," *Pendleton East Oregonian*, souvenir edition, September 8, 9, and 10, 1932.

32. "Real Round-Up Daughter Whose Father Was on the Round-Up Board before She Was Born," *Pendleton East Oregonian*, July 29, 1933.

33. Glenn, *Female Spectacle*.

34. "Some Form! And Reform in Films," *Pendleton East Oregonian*, August 4, 1934.

35. "Five Star Weekly," *Pendleton East Oregonian*, Saturday supplement, June 11, 1936.

36. "Dorothy Doherty Named Queen for Heppner's Rodeo," *Pendleton East Oregonian*, September 4, 1933.

37. The *Pendleton East Oregonian* proudly reported, "Queen Jean has a good speaking voice and this was apparent at the Broadway Theater and in her talk oved [*sic*] KGW" ("Round-Up Group Royally Treated on Portland Trip," August 31, 1933).

38. "Our Good Queen Did Smile Well," *Pendleton East Oregonian*, August 5, 1935.

39. "A Very Busy Young Lady," *Pendleton East Oregonian*, July 27, 1936.

40. "Queen Had Modern Mount," *Pendleton East Oregonian*, August 14, 1936.

41. "Round-Up Queen Visits Admiral," *Pendleton East Oregonian*, August 6, 1936.

42. "Grit, Good Sportsmanship, Beauty All There," *Pendleton East Oregonian*, September 11, 1940.

43. Even though it is necessary to elevate a leg to reach the stirrup, the

pose takes it cue from the movies, particularly the musicals that began to show more leg during the 1930s (Fenin and Everson, *The Western*, 210).

44. "Pendleton to Honor Her," *Pendleton East Oregonian*, September 6, 1941; "After the Round-Up," *Pendleton East Oregonian*, September 12, 1941; "Queen Maxine Rides the Skyways Also," *Pendleton East Oregonian*, September 12, 1941; "Queen Maxine I—She Rules the Round-Up," *Pendleton East Oregonian*, September 12, 1941.

45. Cheyenne's Frontier Days queens experienced the same increase in celebrity status during this period.

46. Hansell Miley, interview.

47. "Meet Some of Pendleton's and Most of the World's Best Known Cowgirls." *Pendleton East Oregonian*, souvenir edition, August 29, 1935. Pictured are Charlotte Tullis, Donna Cowan, Vivial Goad, Helen Delores, Reva Gray, Reba Perry, Mrs. Chuck (Fox) Wilson, Mary Jane Hawkins.

48. Fenin and Everson, *The Western*, 190.

49. Fenin and Everson, *The Western*, 190.

50. See Bull, *Hillbilly Hollywood*; and George-Waren and Freedman, *How the West Was Worn*.

51. "Pendletonians Are to Be Cowboys from Sept. 9 to Sept. 23," *Pendleton East Oregonian*, August 19, 1933.

52. "How About This for Round-Up?," *Pendleton East Oregonian*, August 10, 1940.

53. "Matrons and Maids Alike Would Look Just Right in Western Togs in Pendleton," *Pendleton East Oregonian*, August 10, 1940. Banner notes a vogue for dude ranches in 1930 encouraged the Levi Strauss Company, makers of denim jeans since the 1860s, to begin manufacturing women's jeans (*American Beauty*, 277).

54. "For Well Dressed Cowgirl," *Pendleton East Oregonian*, August 10, 1940.

55. "Lucky Girl Will Get Complete New Outfit," *Pendleton East Oregonian*, April 26, 1941; "Popular Ballot to Determine Winner of 'Miss Jones' Title," *Pendleton East Oregonian*, April 30, 1941.

56. "Grit, Good Sportsmanship, Beauty All There," *Pendleton East Oregonian*, September 11, 1940.

57. Betsy Rose Rice (former rodeo queen), personal correspondence with the author, May 2, 2002.

58. Abbott, *Boosters and Businessmen*; and Abbott, "Boosterism.".

59. "Queen's Aids [*sic*] Named: Miss Agnes McMurray, Miss Churchill Picked," *Pendleton East Oregonian*, September 9, 1925.

60. "Heppner Girl to Reign over Classic," *Pendleton East Oregonian*, July 26, 1941.

61. Stoeltje, "Females in Rodeo," 46.

62. Cooney, *Balancing Acts*, 26.

63. Cooney, *Balancing Acts*, 85.

5. "We Like It Western!"

1. George Strand, telegram to Ed McCarty, 1938, private collection of Jean McCarty Dearinger, Laramie, Wyoming.

2. Jean McCarty Dearinger, personal interview with the author, December 12, 2001.

3. The horse quadrille is a re-enactment of folk dances performed on horseback ("Daughter of the West to Rule Round-Up," *Pendleton East Oregonian*, n.d. [1938 Round-Up Scrapbook, Pendleton Round-Up Hall of Fame Archive, Pendleton, Oregon]).

4. Movie star queens Josie Sedgwick (1924) and Mary Duncan (1928) were from Los Angeles; Mary Robertson (1936) lived in Walla Walla, Washington; and Cathryn Collins's (1937) family had recently moved from Pendleton to Portland, Oregon.

5. McCarty Dearinger, interview.

6. Hobsbawm and Ranger, *The Invention of Tradition*. The essays in *The Invention of Tradition*, which deal with creating a sense of community in emerging nations, are remarkably applicable to smaller polities, such as developing western towns. This is especially noticeable in terms of town leaders looking for a usable past and the small number of elites who were responsible for creating the "new" traditions.

7. Blevins, *Dictionary of the American West*.

8. Schwantes, "The Concept of the Wageworker's Frontier."

9. In 1897 Union Pacific ticket agent Frederick Angier approached the editor of the *Cheyenne (WY) Sun-Leader*, Col. E. A. Slack, with the idea

of staging a one-day rodeo in Cheyenne (Don Snoddy [historian for the Union Pacific Museum, Omaha, Nebraska], personal correspondence with the author, August 31, 2001).

10. "Mark Moorehouse, exhibition manager for the 'Round-Up' left last evening for Cheyenne to attend the frontier celebration to be held in that city this week. He has been especially commissioned by the 'Round-Up' organization to make observations, note defects as well as successful features and also to enlist the services of the best talent to be found at the big Cheyenne celebration. Every effort will be put forth to exceed the Cheyenne show, both in the matter of a performance and that of attendance and for that reason no stone will be left unturned" ("Mark Moorehouse Will Take Notes on Cheyenne Show," *Pendleton East Oregonian*, August 22, 1910).

11. Flynn, *Let's Go! Let's Show! Let's Rodeo!* 83.

12. Westermeier, *Man, Beast, Dust*, 97.

13. Flynn, *Let's Go! Let's Show! Let's Rodeo!* 83. "At least 31 parades had been a feature of that many Frontier Days celebrations, but the pageant of 1927 set a standard that other years can shoot at for a long time. . . . Everything in the development of Wyoming was included in the parade, from the buffalo distinguished as the oldest inhabitants on the Union Pacific to the passenger and freight trains of the present. The spectacle was absolutely complete, and that means quite a lot of territory covered to anyone who is familiar with the romantic history of the West" ("Parade Here Is the Finest West Has Ever Staged," *Wyoming Eagle* [Cheyenne], July 29, 1927).

14. "City Will Have Night Show for Frontier Days," *Wyoming Eagle* (Cheyenne), May 6, 1927.

15. Rupp, *Let 'Er Buck*, 175. The name for the show capitalized on a piece of local history—a settlement near Pendleton, named by its settlers. Roy Raley, one of the men who initiated the Round-Up and who also served as its first president, scripted the Happy Canyon play. The show was performed without a change to the script from 1914 to 2000.

16. "Cheyenne Frontier Days' Officials Are Here for Annual Round-Up; Friendship of Two Great Western Shows Growing," *Pendleton East Oregonian*, September 15, 1926.

17. "Cheyenne Frontier Days' Officials Are Here," *Pendleton East Oregonian*, September 15, 1926.

18. "City Will Have Night Show for Frontier Days," *Wyoming Eagle* (Cheyenne), May 6, 1927.

19. William Fairchild, Cheyenne Night Show committee member, qtd. in Flynn, *Let's Go! Let's Show! Let's Rodeo!* (105).

20. LeCompte, *Cowgirls of the Rodeo*, 40. This was a bronc riding exhibition, not a contest against cowboys.

21. "Everything Frontier Days Is Contest: No Contracts Drawn for Any Performers in Show," *Wyoming Eagle* (Cheyenne), weekend edition, July 23–24, 1927.

22. Golden Age of the Cowgirl, Cheyenne Frontier Days Old West Museum, Cheyenne, Wyoming.

23. Hanesworth, *Daddy of 'Em All*, 146–47. While Cheyenne's first official queen appeared in 1931, there was one earlier instance of a woman who promoted the show. Helen Bonham, a Cheyenne cowgirl athlete was hired to serve as Miss Wyoming and promote the twenty-fifth anniversary of Cheyenne Frontier Days. Celebrated as she was, the Miss Wyoming title was a one-time promotional effort; she was never called Miss Frontier Days.

24. "Three Girls in Race for Queen of Old Frontier," *Wyoming Eagle* (Cheyenne), June 5, 1931.

25. "Look 'Em Over and Take Your Choice," *Wyoming Eagle* (Cheyenne), July 7, 1931.

26. "Patricia Keefe to Be Queen," *Wyoming Eagle* (Cheyenne), July 15, 1931.

27. "Jean Nimmo Elected 'Miss Frontier' as Contest Ends: Patricia Keefe Finishes in Second Place after Leading until Final Hours of Competition," no newspaper identified, July 16, 1931, Jean Nimmo scrapbook, Cheyenne Frontier Days Old West Museum Archive, Cheyenne, Wyoming.

28. "Booster Trip Is Highly Successful," *Wyoming Eagle* (Cheyenne), July 20, 1931.

29. Jean Nimmo Dubois, "Cheyenne Frontier Days—Miss Frontier," interview by Eleanor D. McMilan, December 8, 1992, Cheyenne Pioneer Days Old West Museum Archive, Cheyenne, Wyoming.

30. McCarty Dearinger, interview.

31. McCarty Dearinger, interview.

32. All twelve past Frontier Days queens interviewed for this research were sophomore or juniors in college when they served as queen, and all mentioned that being in college was a requirement for the position.

33. Past Miss Frontier Days queens who responded to a written questionnaire are listed in appendix B.

34. At the Cheyenne Frontier Days, the influence of the entertainment world on queen costumes encouraged a more traditional look. During the first years of their community-sponsored rodeo queens Cheyenne royalty did not have a trademark costume. Frontier Days directors supplied the young women with satin shirts and a hat, but they wore their own riding pants. When the entertainer Sally Rand visited the celebration in 1935, she suggested her cowgirl costume—a white split-leather skirt, with matching leather bolero over a satin shirt—would make a stunning Miss Frontier Days costume. The directors agreed, and in 1936 the queen and her lady-in-waiting wore the new outfits (Flynn, *Let's Go! Let's Show! Let's Rodeo!* 93).

35. Rupp, *Let 'Er Buck*, 197.

36. "Pair of Roamin' Cowpokes: Nation's Top Rodeo Men, Ed McCarty and Vern Elliot, Tell Story of Success with Their Western Bronco Shows," newspaper article, c. 1925, Ed McCarty folder in the People file, Cheyenne Frontier Days Old West Museum Archive, Cheyenne, Wyoming.

37. "Pair of Roamin' Cowpokes," newspaper article.

38. "Pair of Roamin' Cowpokes," newspaper article.

39. "My grandmother moved to Cheyenne, as she had done with my father and his brother, and then her second family, which was an aunt and an uncle of mine. She was an amazing lady. She came when my mother died, and [my grandmother] was in her sixties . . . and my brother was only six weeks old. So, you see, she got us all raised, and when my father remarried—my step-mother had a ten year old and an eight year old—she took them. She put them through school" (McCarty Dearinger, interview).

40. Good bucking horses were hard to find: In 1925 Midnight was

insured for $5,000, (approximately $50,000 by today's standards). Jean McCarty recalls how well the horses were cared for: "We always shipped our stock everyplace by baggage class. Nothing ever went freight, it was always baggage" (McCarty Dearinger, interview).

41. McCarty Dearinger, interview.

42. McCarty Dearinger, interview.

43. McCarty Dearinger, interview.

44. Mabel Strickland to Jean McCarty, September 1938, private collection of Jean McCarty Dearinger.

45. See Anderson, *Imagined Communities*.

46. Flynn, *Let's Go! Let's Show! Let's Rodeo!* 99.

47. Westermeier, *Man, Beast, Dust*, 96–104. According to the First Frontier ProRodeo Circuit Web site, the Turtle name was adopted because the cowboys were slow to organize, and once they did organize, they stuck their neck out to get what they wanted (http://www.firstfrontiercircuit.com).

48. Clifford Westermeier writes that the Turtles, who started out trying to resolve legitimate complaints, evolved into "an organization of [labor] monopolists, strikers and unreliable racketeers" (*Man, Beast, Dust*, 112).

49. Photo of sign, July 9, 1938, *Saturday Evening Post*; Westermeier, *Man, Beast, Dust*, 119.

50. Turtle members wanted to select judges themselves, and they wanted the Round-Up to ban any non-union riders from competing at the rodeo ("Turtles Sign Up Round-Up Entry," *Pendleton East Oregonian*, March 15, 1939).

51. "Turtles Sign Up Round-Up Entry," *Pendleton East Oregonian*, March 15, 1939.

52. Rupp, *Let 'Er Buck*, 195.

53. McCarty Dearinger, interview.

54. McCarty Dearinger, interview.

55. McCarty Dearinger, interview.

56. LeCompte, *Cowgirls of the Rodeo*, 137.

57. McCarty Dearinger, interview.

58. McCarty Dearinger, interview

59. As a full-page advertisement for the Frontier Days celebration read, "Part of the band of Sioux Indians selected from the Indian reservations to participate in the Frontier Days Celebration" ("Greetings to the Entire World from the Frontier Days Committee," *Wyoming Eagle* [Cheyenne], July 15, 1927).

60. McCarty Dearinger, interview.

61. Weston, *Native Americans in the News*, 2.

62. Weston, *Native Americans in the News*, 15.

63. Weston, *Native Americans in the News*, 15.

64. Weston, *Native Americans in the News*, 56.

65. "Indians Will Leave Tonight for Colorado," *Wyoming Eagle* (Cheyenne), July 17, 1931.

66. Weston, *Native Americans in the News*, 59. For a discussion on how Native Americans used such displays to their advantage, to resist assimilation, see Moses, *Wild West Shows*; and Ellis, *A Dancing People*.

67. "Royal Red Man," *Pendleton East Oregonian*, souvenir edition, September 8, 9, and 10, 1932.

68. "Queen Melissa of the '32 Show Is Feted, Cheyenne," *Pendleton East Oregonian*, August 3, 1933.

6. "It Was Great Being Queen"

1. "Action Taken after Council OK's Request: Western Classic Steps aside for Greater 'Round-Up of the Axis,'" *Pendleton East Oregonian*, August 1, 1942.

2. Fredriksson, *American Rodeo*, 67.

3. As noted earlier, the Cowboy Turtle Association was organized by rodeo riders; the Rodeo Association of America was organized by rodeo producers.

4. Fredriksson, *American Rodeo*, 73.

5. "Attebury Rodeo Honors Divided," *Pendleton East Oregonian*, July 6, 1944; "4th Annual Mustanger 'Spring Show' May 21," *Pendleton East Oregonian*, February 23, 1944.

6. Hansell Miley, interview.

7. Fredriksson, *American Rodeo*, 74.

8. Relaxing this rule was not completely altruistic on the Turtles' part:

While they did hope to encourage non-professional riders to participate in the sport and help keep rodeo alive during the war, they also hoped to recruit new members into the sport once the war ended (Fredriksson, *American Rodeo*).

9. Betty Branstetter, personal correspondence with the author, June 2, 2002.

10. Fredriksson, *American Rodeo*, 67.

11. "Mel Stonehouse on Four Freedoms," *Pendleton East Oregonian*, September 13, 1945.

12. Fredriksson, *American Rodeo*, 78.

13. Flynn, *Let's Go! Let's Show! Let's Rodeo!* 110.

14. Fredriksson, *American Rodeo*, 69.

15. O'Neill, *A Democracy at War*, 393.

16. "'44 Round-Up Dress Up Parade Record Breaker, Crowd Huge," *Pendleton East Oregonian*, September 15, 1944.

17. "'44 Round-Up Dress Up Parade," *Pendleton East Oregonian*, September 15, 1944.

18. "'44 Round-Up Dress Up Parade," *Pendleton East Oregonian*, September 15, 1944.

19. Leah Conner, personal interview with the author, July 31, 2001.

20. "Janet Thompson Named as Queen of Round-Up," *Pendleton East Oregonian*, July 1, 1944.

21. Honey, *Creating Rosie the Riveter*, 4.

22. For example, see "We, the Women," a syndicated column that appeared in the *Pendleton East Oregonian* in the mid-1940s advocating the need for women to have the skills necessary to support themselves should the need arise; Honey, *Creating Rosie the Riveter*, 135.

23. May, *Homeward Bound*, 20.

24. Weiss, *To Have and to Hold*, 17.

25. "Round-Up Is Certain to Have Huge Crowd," *Pendleton East Oregonian*, August 18, 1945.

26. "Donne's Crown Is 'Dream Come True' but She's Well Qualified for High Honor," *Pendleton East Oregonian*, September 14, 1945.

27. "Queen Donne Versatile Lady," *Pendleton East Oregonian* September 14, 1945.

28. Jameson, "Women as Workers, Women as Civilizers," 1.

29. "Queen Jackie of the Round-Up in Her Every-Day Life," *Pendleton East Oregonian*, September 13, 1946. The *Pendleton East Oregonian* gave less coverage to the 1947 Round-Up queen, Patti Folsom, and to the Round-Up in general, because of a paper shortage (see "R-Up Souvenir Edition May Be Ordered Now," *Pendleton East Oregonian*, August 23, 1947).

30. May, *Homeward Bound*, 101.

31. Bailey, *From Front Porch to Back Seat*, 80–82.

32. "Selected," *Pendleton East Oregonian*, February 29, 1929.

33. "Indians Big Bond Buyers," *Pendleton East Oregonian*, souvenir edition, September 14, 1945.

34. "Royal Court Headed by Virginia I," *Pendleton East Oregonian*, souvenir edition, September 17, 1948.

35. "Members of First Families Will Rule over 37th Pendleton Show," *Pendleton East Oregonian*, August 14, 1948.

36. Lear, *No Place of Grace*.

37. Weston, *Native Americans in the News*, 104.

38. Graebner, *The Age of Doubt*, 4.

39. Myrna Williams Tovey, personal correspondence with the author, August 30, 2001.

40. "Royal Court Headed by Virginia I," *Pendleton East Oregonian*, souvenir edition, September 17, 1948.

41. Green, "The Pocahontas Perplex, 701.

42. Green, "The Pocahontas Perplex," 710.

43. Athearn, *The Mythic West*, 272.

44. Williams Tovey, correspondence.

45. "Round-Up Queen Joan Fulfills All the Royal Requirements," *Pendleton East Oregonian*, August 20, 1949.

46. "Round-Up Royalty Returns from Calgary," *Pendleton East Oregonian*, July 18, 1949.

47. "Queen Kite Knows How to Rope Calves," *Pendleton East Oregonian*, July 29, 1950.

48. "Riding and Cooking Francine's Favorites," *Pendleton East Oregonian*, July 31, 1950. The article title emphasizes the two most impor-

tant characteristics for a Pendleton court member—riding and domestic skills.

49. "Queen Kite Knows How to Rope Calves," *Pendleton East Oregonian*, July 29, 1950.

50. Banner, *American Beauty*, 285.

51. "Queen Julie Sets Sights High for Real American Girl of Today," *Pendleton East Oregonian*, August 18, 1951.

52. "We, the Women," *Pendleton East Oregonian*, July 25, 1950.

53. Hartman, "Women's Employment and the Domestic Ideal," 86, 89.

54. See, for example, Walker, *Women's Magazines*; Walker, *Shaping Our Mothers' World*; and Leibman, *Living Room Lectures*.

55. Conner, interview.

56. Rupp, *Let 'Er Buck*, 61–64.

57. U.S. Census Bureau statistics for Pendleton, courtesy of Mary L. Finney, Pendleton Public Library, Pendleton, Oregon.

58. Rupp, *Let 'Er Buck*, 72.

59. "Round-Up Queen Leah Shows Royal Qualities," *Pendleton East Oregonian*, September 12, 1952.

60. Green, "The Pocahontas Perplex," 714.

61. Conner, interview.

62. "Queen Leah the First, Ruler of the 1952 Pendleton Round-Up," *Pendleton East Oregonian*, September 12, 1952.

63. Conner, interview.

64. Weston, *Native Americans in the News*, 104.

65. Weston, *Native Americans in the News*, 99–100.

66. Moses, *Wild West Shows*, 52.

67. See Ellis, *A Dancing People*, and Mellis, *Riding Buffaloes and Broncos*, for current studies on performance as a means of resisting assimilation.

68. Moses, *Wild West Shows*, 275.

69. Conner, interview.

70. "Round-Up Royalty," *Confederated Umatilla Journal* (Umatilla Reservation OR), no. 7 (September 2000): 15.

71. Heather Corey, personal correspondence with the author, March

21, 2002. Tony Minthorn was a Happy Canyon princess in 1978 (her mother was the first Happy Canyon princess in 1956) and a 1978 Round-Up princess; Debbie Weathers was a Happy Canyon princess in 1985 and a 1988 Round-Up princess. When asked about the switch from the All-Indian courts to the application process, Conner replied, "It was a good decision. Any way [Indian girls are on the court] it is good, but it's better if they select them as they come along" (Conner, interview).

72. "Queen Joan Pearson, 1954 Round-Up Queen," *Pendleton East Oregonian*, September 16, 1954.

73. "Queen Joan Pearson," *Pendleton East Oregonian*, August 14, 1954; "The Pendleton Round-Up Gets a Boost," *Pendleton East Oregonian*, August 17, 1954; "Dell Haverly of Benson, Ariz Holds Oregon Journal Trophy," *Pendleton East Oregonian*, September 19, 1954.

74. "Queen, Court Honored at Parties," *Pendleton East Oregonian*, August 10, 1954.

75. "Queen Joan Pearson of the 1954 Pendleton Round-Up and Former Queens," *Pendleton East Oregonian*, August 28, 1954; "The 1954 Round-Up Is Over," *Pendleton East Oregonian*, September 19, 1954.

76. "Queen Joan Pearson, 1954 Round-Up Queen," *Pendleton East Oregonian*, September 16, 1954.

77. "Queen Kathryn Reigns over Pendleton Round-Up," *Pendleton East Oregonian*, September 15, 1955.

78. "Pendleton Round-Up Princesses," *Pendleton East Oregonian*, September 1, 1951; LeCompte, *Cowgirls of the Rodeo*, 158.

79. "Queen Kathryn Reigns Over Pendleton Round-Up," *Pendleton East Oregonian*, September 15, 1955.

80. "Rodeo Queen Sought for Festival" *Grant County Journal* [Ephrata, WA], 13 July 1950.

81. Armitage, "Rawhide Heroines," 179.

82. "Fourth of July Celebration in Soap Lake," *Grant County Journal* (Ephrata WA), July 3, 1942.

83. "Broncs, Indians, Horses at Rodeo July 3–4," *Grant County Journal* (Ephrata WA), July 2, 1943.

84. Nancy Neumann Martini, personal interview with the author, June 10, 1999.

85. Garfield County Historical Society, *Garfield County Round-Up*, 19.

86. *Fifty Years of Nebraska's Big Rodeo*, 74.

87. Ruby Dearmont Purcell, telephone interview with the author, May 30, 2000.

88. Jeannette Clancy Rutledge, personal interview with the author, July 27, 2001.

89. Ann Dinneen Smith, personal interview with author, December 11, 2001.

90. Information courtesy of Ann Dinneen Smith, May 15, 1993.

91. Neumann Martini, interview.

92. Clancy Rutledge, interview.

93. Dinneen Smith, interview.

94. Williams Tovey, correspondence.

95. Neumann Martini, interview.

96. Conner, interview.

97. For example, see Burgess and Valaskakis, *Indian Princesses and Cowgirls*; LeCompte, *Cowgirls of the Rodeo*; and Wills and Artho, *Cowgirl Legends from the Cowgirl Hall of Fame*.

98. Burbick, "Romance, Rodeo Queens, and the 1950s," 126.

99. Burbick, "Romance, Rodeo Queens, and the 1950s," 130.

100. Burbick, *Rodeo Queens and the American Dream*.

101. Dinneen Smith, interview.

7. All-Girl Rodeos

1. "Queen Kite Knows How to Rope Calves," *Pendleton East Oregonian*, July 29, 1950.

2. "Queen Mabel Makes Throw Despite Hurt," *Pendleton East Oregonian*, 17 September 1927.

3. "Queen Mabel Arrives to Rule the Round-Up," *Pendleton East Oregonian*, September 12, 1927.

4. M. Allen, "The Rise and Decline of the Early Rodeo Cowgirl," 124.

5. LeCompte, *Cowgirls of the Rodeo*, 72.

6. "Golden Age of the Cowgirl," Cheyenne Frontier Days Old West

Museum, Cheyenne, Wyoming, analysis of newspaper articles from the *Wyoming State Tribune* and *Cheyenne (wy) State Leader*, 1927–29.

7. "Both Sides Suffer," *Yakima (wa) Republic*, October 3, 1929.

8. LeCompte, *Cowgirls of the Rodeo*, 78.

9. "Queen Mabel Makes Throw Despite Hurt," *Pendleton East Oregonian*, September 17, 1927.

10. Westermeier, *Man, Beast, Dust*, 94.

11. LeCompte, *Cowgirls of the Rodeo*, 96.

12. LeCompte, *Cowgirls of the Rodeo*, 101.

13. McGovern, "The American Woman's Pre–World War I Freedom," 333.

14. Cott, *The Grounding of Modern Feminism*, 272.

15. Articles in local newspapers describing sponsor girl contestants typically featured a studio portrait of the young woman, followed by a brief story discussing family history, scholastic and civic participation, and leisure activities.

16. According to John O. Baxter, pressure by humane societies to ban steer roping began in the late 1800s and had its earliest success in the Southwest. The event was banned in New Mexico in 1903, in Texas in 1905, and in Arizona in 1907 ("Whoopee Ty-Yi-Yo!").

17. LeCompte, *Cowgirls of the Rodeo*, 116.

18. "Vote for Isora DeRacy," Isora DeRacy Honoree file, National Cowgirl Hall of Fame Archives, Fort Worth, Texas (hereafter NCHFA, Fort Worth).

19. "Vote for Isora DeRacy," NCHFA, Fort Worth.

20. Jordan, "Cowgirls."

21. Fredriksson, *American Rodeo*, 73–74.

22. Cahn, *Coming on Strong*, 140–47.

23. Hurley, "Girls Rodeo Then and Now," 11.

24. "World's First All Girl Rodeo to Begin Friday," *Bonham (TX) Daily Favorite*, June 23, 1942.

25. "World's First All Girl Rodeo to Begin Friday," *Bonham (TX) Daily Favorite*, June 23, 1942.

26. "World's First All Girl Rodeo to Begin Friday," *Bonham (TX) Daily Favorite*, June 23, 1942.

27. *The World's First All-Cowgirl Rodeo—Official Program, Bonham, Texas, June 26–27–28 [1942]*, Kirkwood file, NCHFA, Fort Worth.

28. LeCompte, *Cowgirls of the Rodeo*, 129.

29. "Motley Cowgirl Is Rodeo Champ: Mary Ellen Barton Brings Home Many Wichita Honors," n.p, n.d., Mary Ellen "Dude" Barton file, NCHFA, Fort Worth.

30. "Motley Cowgirl Is Rodeo Champ," NCHFA, Fort Worth.

31. *The Flying V All Cow Girl Rodeo Official Souvenir Program, September 3–4–5 [1942] Paris, Texas*, Vaughn Kreig Honoree file, NCHFA, Fort Worth.

32. "The Flying V All Girl Rodeo" promotional flyer, 1942, Vaughn Kreig Honoree file, NCHFA, Fort Worth.

33. "The Flying V All Girl Rodeo" promotional flyer, NCHFA, Fort Worth.

34. LeCompte, *Cowgirls of the Rodeo*, 137.

35. LeCompte, *Cowgirls of the Rodeo*, 135.

36. LeCompte, *Cowgirls of the Rodeo*, 137.

37. Newspaper clipping, n.d., Binford Tri-State Rodeo scrapbook, 1996.010.001, NCHFA, Fort Worth.

38. Statistics on Texas Cowboy Reunion sponsors are compiled from West Texas newspaper records and information at the Texas Cowboy County Museum Archive, Stamford, Texas.

39. Of the 129 women who entered the sponsor contest, 33 (25 percent) were sponsored by ranches (information compiled from West Texas newspaper records, Texas Cowboy Country Museum Archive, Stamford, Texas).

40. This was the case with Mary Ellen "Dude" Barton, who was alternately sponsored by her home ranch and hometown.

41. "Cowgirl Organize Rodeo Group Here," n.p., n.d., Binford Tri-State Rodeo scrapbook, NCHFA, Fort Worth.

42. Willis and Artho, *Cowgirl Legends*, 84; "All Girl Rodeo Set for Fair," n.p., n.d., Binford Tri-State Rodeo scrapbook, NCHFA, Fort Worth.

43. Nancy Binford interview, Hereford, Texas, 1985, pp. 70, 71, transcript SR20, BBC Cowgirl Interview File, NCHFA, Fort Worth.

44. Binford, interview, 71.

45. Bailey, *From Front Porch to Back Seat*, 104–5.

46. "Balloon Parade to Open Fair," n.p., n.d., Binford Tri-State Rodeo scrapbook, NCHFA, Fort Worth.

47. Binford Tri-State Rodeo scrapbook, NCHFA, Fort Worth.

48. "Performers Prove Beauty and Rodeo Can Be Mixed," n.p., n.d. Binford Tri-State Rodeo scrapbook, NCHFA, Fort Worth.

49. "Performers Prove Beauty and Rodeo Can Be Mixed," NCHFA, Fort Worth.

50. Meyerowitz, "Beyond the Feminine Mystique," 234.

51. "All Girl Rodeo Set for Fair," n.p., n.d., Binford Tri-State Rodeo scrapbook, NCHFA, Fort Worth.

52. LeCompte, *Cowgirls of the Rodeo*, 168.

53. "Cowgirls Organize Rodeo Group Here," n.p., n.d, Binford Tri-State Rodeo scrapbook, NCHFA, Fort Worth.

54. "Cowgirls Organize Rodeo Group Here," NCHFA, Fort Worth.

55. LeCompte, *Cowgirls of the Rodeo*, 157.

56. Girls Rodeo Association Handbook. Binford Tri-State Scrapbook, National Cowgirl Hall of Fame Archive.

57. LeCompte, *Cowgirls of the Rodeo*, 169.

58. "The Tactless Texan," 1948; "Girls Set to Open Rodeo," 1949; "All Girl Rodeo a 'He-Man' Show," *The Quarter Horse Journal* 1, no. 1 (September 1948) (all from the Binford Tri-State Rodeo scrapbook, NCHFA, Fort Worth).

59. Queen Kite Knows How to Rope Calves," *Pendleton East Oregonian*, July 29, 1950.

60. "Performers Prove Beauty and Rodeo Can Be Mixed," n.p., n.d., Binford Tri-State Rodeo scrapbook, NCHFA, Fort Worth.

8. From Local Community to National

1. "Pendleton's Vickie Pearson Takes 'Miss Rodeo of America Title," *Pendleton East Oregonian*, November 16, 1959; "Miss Rodeo Oregon," *Pendleton East Oregonian*, September 18, 1959.

2. Miss Rodeo America Web site: http://www.missrodeo.com.

3. Westermeier, *Man, Beast, Dust*, 341–42. Westermeier notes that

the two organizations did not compete against each other for members, rather encouraged cowboy athletes to join both groups if they competed in rodeos falling within the two areas. The Southwest Rodeo Association changed its name to the NRA in 1942.

4. Westermeier, *Man, Beast, Dust*, 100. In 1945 the Cowboy Turtles Association changed its name to the Rodeo Cowboys' Association, and later to the Pro Rodeo Cowboys' Association.

5. Westermeier, *Man, Beast, Dust*, 348.

6. Westermeier, *Man, Beast, Dust*, 348.

7. "Boylen Rides Herd over 200 Rodeos," *Pendleton East Oregonian*, April 30, 1946.

8. Sherrie Vincent Scott made the first Miss Rodeo America appearance at the Pendleton Round-Up in 1968 (Sherrie Scott, personal correspondence with the author, July 15, 2001).

9. "Queen Vickie Heads for Las Vegas," *Pendleton East Oregonian*, November 10, 1959.

10. Westermeier, *Man, Beast, Dust*, 285–91.

11. Gitlin, *The Twilight of Common Dreams*, 96.

12. Information on gay rodeos from the International Gay Rodeo Association Web site (http://www.igra.com).

13. Dallas Hunt George, personal correspondence with the author, July 6, 2001.

14. Susan Cox Valley Stauffer, personal correspondence with the author, July 2, 2001.

15. "Beauty, Personality, Horsemanship Mark Queen," *Pendleton East Oregonian*, September 14, 1959.

16. "Royalty Runs in Harvey Family," *Pendleton East Oregonian*, August 25, 1959; "Talented Lynda Ferris to Ride with Royal Court at Round-Up," *Pendleton East Oregonian*, September 2, 1959; "Princess Ruth to Reign at R-Up," *Pendleton East Oregonian*, September 7, 1959.

17. See list of women who responded to the rodeo queen questionnaire in appendix B.

18. Cahn, *Coming on Strong*, 239.

19. Cahn, *Coming on Strong*, 239.

20. Elsa Neumann Jensen, personal conversation with the author, December 7, 2001.

21. Benedict R. Anderson used the term "imagined community" in his discussion on emerging nationalism, but it applies well to the enlarging sphere of rodeo queens. With the advent of the Internet, the "imagined community" of rodeo queens continues to develop, with listservs, Web sites, and chat rooms, in which rodeo queens keep each other informed as to upcoming queen contests, winners, dress and appearance advice, and all matter of information pertinent to "queening."

22. Anderson, *Imagined Communities*, 6.

23. See, for example, "Europe's Prettiest Princesses Come of Age," *Pendleton East Oregonian*, August 16, 1951.

24. Susan Talbot, personal interview with the author, July 31, 2001.

25. Rodeo Royalty listserv message dated February 24, 2002.

26. "Martha Lehmann, Runner-up in National Contest, Replaces Ineligible Oregonian," no newspaper listed, 1960. My thanks to Darla Willbanks, office assistant at the Miss Rodeo America headquarters, for bringing this article to my attention.

27. Harvey, *The Fifties*, xv.

28. Moore, "'She's My Hero,'" 478.

29. Douglas, *Where the Girls Are*, 5.

30. LeCompte, *Cowgirls of the Rodeo*, 115; Burbick, "Romance, Rodeo Queens, and the 1950s," 130.

31. Slatta, *Cowboys of the Americas*, 212–13.

32. Westermeier, *Man, Beast, Dust*, 310.

33. Savage, *Cowgirls*, 95.

34. Douglas, *Where the Girls Are*, 7.

35. Willis and Artho, *Cowgirl Legends*, 14.

36. Patricia Limerick, qtd. in Moore, "'She's My Hero,'" 477.

37. Cahn, *Coming on Strong*, 237.

38. Walter E. Houghton, in *The Victorian Frame of Mind*, gives an excellent description of the social and cultural changes that encouraged the development of this dichotomous worldview in the 1800s, one that continues to reassert itself whenever a society feels threatened.

39. Karen Passion, Rodeo Royalty listserv message dated March 10, 2002.

40. See Shields and Caughlin, "Performing Rodeo Queen Culture," 183.

41. Eisner, *Rodeo Cowgirl*, 1.

42. Eisner, *Rodeo Cowgirl*, 1.

Bibliography

Abbott, Carl. "Boosterism." In Neil L. Shumsky, ed., *Encyclopedia of Urban America: the Cities and Suburbs*. 2 vols. Santa Barbara: ABC-Clio, 1998.

———. *Boosters and Businessmen: Popular Economic Thought and Urban Growth in the Antebellum Middle West*. Westport CT: Greenwood Press, 1981.

Allen, James Sloan. *The Romance of Commerce and Culture*. Chicago: University of Chicago Press, 1983.

Allen, Michael. "The Rise and Decline of the Early Rodeo Cowgirl: The Career of Mabel Strickland, 1916–1941," *Pacific Northwest Quarterly* 83 (October 1992): 122–27.

———. *Rodeo Cowboys in the North American Imagination*. Reno: University of Nevada Press, 1999.

Allmendinger, Blake. *The Cowboy: Representations of Labor in an American Work Culture*. New York: Oxford University Press, 1992.

Anderson, Benedict R. *Imagined Communities: Reflections on the Origin and Spread of Nationalism*. London: Verso, 1983.

Armitage, Shelley. "Rawhide Heroines: The Evolution of the Cowgirl and the Myth of America." In Sam B. Girgus, ed. *The American Self: Myth, Ideology, and Popular Culture*, 166–81. Albuquerque: University of New Mexico Press, 1980.

Athearn, Robert G. *The Mythic West in Twentieth-Century America*. Lawrence: University Press of Kansas, 1986.

Bailey, Beth. *From Front Porch to Back Seat: Courtship in Twentieth-Century America*. Baltimore: The Johns Hopkins Press, 1988.

Banner, Lois W. *American Beauty*. New York: Alfred A. Knopf, 1983.

Baxter, John O. "Whoopee Ty-Yi-Yo! Cowboy Tournaments, 1855–1905: A Changing Vision of the Southwest." Paper presented at the Western History Association Conference, Fort Worth, Texas, October 9, 2003.

Behling, Laura L. *The Masculine Woman in America, 1890–1935.* Urbana: University of Illinois Press, 2001.

Bledstein, Burton J., and Robert D. Johnson, eds. *The Middling Sorts: Explorations in the History of the American Middle Class.* Routledge NY: 2001.

Blevins, Winfred. *Dictionary of the American West.* New York: Facts on File, 1993.

Boylen, E. N. "Pink." *Episode of the West: The Pendleton Round-Up 1910–1950.* Pendleton OR, 1975.

Britt, George. "Women in the New South." In Schmalhausen and Calverton, *Woman's Coming of Age,* 409–23.

Brumberg, Joan Jacobs. *The Body Project: An Intimate History of American Girls.* New York: Random House, 1997.

Bull, Debbie. *Hillbilly Hollywood.* New York: Rizzoli, 2000.

Burbick, Joan. *Rodeo Queens and the American Dream.* New York: Public Affairs, 2002.

———. "Romance, Rodeo Queens, and the 1950s." *Frontiers: A Journal of Women Studies* 17, no. 3 (1996): 124–45.

Burgess, Marilyn, and Gail Guthrie Valaskakis. *Indian Princesses and Cowgirls: Stereotypes from the Frontier.* Montreal QB: Oboro, 2001.

Cahn, Susan K. *Coming on Strong: Gender and Sexuality in Twentieth-Century Women's Sport.* New York: The Free Press, 1994.

Carlson, Paul, ed. *The Cowboy Way: An Exploration of History and Culture.* Lubbock: Texas Tech University Press, 2000.

Cheyenne Frontier Days Old West Museum, Cheyenne, Wyoming. "Golden Age of the Cowgirl," exhibit.

Cooney, Terry A. *Balancing Acts: American Thought and Culture in the 1930s.* New York: Twayne Publishers, 1995.

Cott, Nancy F. *The Grounding of Modern Feminism.* New Haven: Yale University Press, 1987.

Crandall, Judy. *Cowgirls: Early Images and Collectibles.* Atglen PA: Schiffer Publishing, 1994.

Dary, David. *Cowboy Culture: A Saga of Five Centuries.* New York: Knopf, 1981.

Derry, Kathryn. "Corsets and Broncs: The Wild West Show Cowgirl, 1890–1920." *Colorado Heritage* (Summer 1992): 2–16.

Douglas, Susan J. *Where the Girls Are: Growing Up Female with the Mass Media.* New York: Times Books, 1994.

Eisner, Lisa. *Rodeo Cowgirl.* Graybull Publishing, 2000.

Ellis, Clyde. *A Dancing People: Powwow Culture on the Southern Plains.* Lawrence: University Press of Kansas, 2003.

Fass, Paula S. *The Damned and the Beautiful: American Youth in the 1920s.* New York: Oxford University Press, 1977.

Fenin, George N., and William K. Everson. *The Western: From Silents to the Seventies.* New York: Grossman Press, 1973.

Fifty Years of Nebraska's Big Rodeo. Burwell NE: Rodeo Book Co., 1975.

Fischer, David Hackett. *Albion's Seed: Four British Folkways in America.* New York: Oxford University Press, 1989.

Flynn, Shirley E. *Let's Go! Let's Show! Let's Rodeo!: The History of Cheyenne Frontier Days, The Daddy of 'Em All.* Cheyenne WY: Wigwam Publishing Company, 1996.

Fowler, Loretta. *Shared Symbols, Contested Meanings: Gros Ventre Culture and History, 1778–1984.* Ithaca NY: Cornell University Press, 1987.

Frazier, Jules. "Rodeo Queen." *Cowboys and Indians* 3, no. 4 (Winter 1995): 60–67.

Fredriksson, Kristine. *American Rodeo: From Buffalo Bill to Big Business.* College Station: Texas A&M University Press, 1985.

Freedman, Estelle B. "The New Woman: Changing Views of Women in the 1920s." *The Journal of American History* 61, no.2 (1974): 372–93.

———. "Separatism as Strategy: Female Institution Building and American Feminism, 1870–1930." *Feminist Studies* 5, no.3 (1979): 512–29.

Frink, Jayne. "Pendleton Round-Up Royalty of 1910." *Pioneer Trails* 6 (September 1981): 11–12.

Garfield County Historical Society, *Garfield County Round-Up: A History of the People, for the People, by the People of Garfield County, Nebraska, 1867–1967.* Ord NE: Quiz Graphic Arts, 1967.

George-Waren, Holly, and Michelle Freedman. *How the West Was Worn.* New York: Harry N. Abrams, 2001.

Gilman, Charlotte Perkins. "The New Generation of Women." *Current History* 18 (August 8, 1923): 731–37.

Gitlin, Todd. *The Twilight of Common Dreams: Why America is Wracked by Culture Wars.* New York: Metropolitan Books, 1995.

Glenn, Susan A. *Female Spectacle: The Theatrical Roots of Modern Feminism.* Cambridge: Harvard University Press, 2000.

Gordon, Susan. "Any Desired Length: Negotiating Gender through Sports Clothing." In Scranton, *Beauty and Business*, 24–51.

Graebner, William. *The Age of Doubt: American Thought and Culture in the 1940s.* Boston: Twayne Publishers, 1991.

Grafe, Steven L. "Lee Moorehouse: Photographer of the Inland Empire." *Oregon Historical Quarterly* 98 (Winter 1997–98): 426–477.

Green, Rayna. "The Pocahontas Perplex: The Image of Indian Women in American Culture." *Massachusetts Review* 16, no. 4 (1975): 698–714.

Haddow, Robert H. *Pavilions of Plenty: Exhibiting American Culture Abroad in the 1950s.* Washington DC: Smithsonian Institution Press, 1997.

Hanesworth, Robert D. Cheyenne Frontier Days scrapbooks, American Heritage Center, University of Wyoming, Laramie, Wyoming.

———. *Daddy of 'Em All: The Story of Cheyenne Frontier Days.* Cheyenne WY: Flintlock Publishing Co., 1967.

Hartman, Susan M. "Women's Employment and the Domestic Ideal in the Early Cold War Years." In Meyerowitz, *Not June Cleaver*, 84–100.

Harvey, Brett. *The Fifties: A Woman's Oral History.* New York: HarperCollins Publishers, 1993.

Haywood, C. Robert. *The Victorian West: Class and Culture in Kansas Cattle Towns.* Lawrence: University Press of Kansas, 1991.

Hearn, Cynthia W. "The Texas Cowboy Reunion: 1930–1983." Master's Thesis, Hardin-Simmons University, 1983.

Higham, John. "The Reorientation of American Culture in the 1890s." In *The Origins of Modern Consciousness: Essays*, 73–103. Detroit: Wayne State University Press, 1965.

Hobsbawm, Erick J., and Terence O. Ranger, eds. *The Invention of Tradition*. Cambridge: Cambridge University press, 1983.

Honey, Maureen. *Creating Rosie the Riveter: Class, Gender, and Propaganda during World War II*. Amherst: University of Massachusetts Press, 1984.

Houghton, Walter E. *The Victorian Frame of Mind, 1830–1870*. New Haven: Yale University Press, 1957.

Hoy, James F. *Cowboys and Kansas: Stories from the Tallgrass Prairie*. Norman: University of Oklahoma Press, 1995.

Hurley, Jimmie. "Girl's Rodeo Then and Now." *This Is Girls' Rodeo* Official Publication of Girls Rodeo Association, 1977.

Iverson, Peter, and Linda MacCannell. *Riders of the West: Portraits from Indian Rodeo*. Seattle: University of Washington Press, 1999.

Jameson, Elizabeth. "Women as Workers, Women as Civilizers: True Womanhood in the American West." *Frontiers: A Journal of Women Studies* 7, no. 3 (1984): 1–8.

Jordan, Teresa. "Cowgirls: How the Fairer Sex Succeeded in the Rough World of Rodeo." *True West* (July 1983): 19–23.

———. *Cowgirls: Women of the American West*. Garden City NY: Anchor Press, 1982.

Kertzer, David I. *Ritual, Politics, and Power*. New Haven: Yale University Press, 1988.

Kesey, Ken. *Last Go-Round*. New York: Viking Penguin, 1995.

Kimmel, Michael S. "The Cult of Masculinity: American Social Character and the Legacy of the Cowboy." In Michael Kaufman, ed., *Beyond Patriarchy: Essays by Men on Pleasure, Power, and Change*, 235–49. Toronto: Oxford University Press, 1987.

King, Mary. "Cowgirls Have the New Look Too." *The Quarter Horse Journal* 1, no. 3 (November 1948).

Kleinberg, S. J. *Women in the United States, 1830–1945*. New Brunswick: Rutgers University Press, 1999.

Latham, Angela J. *Posing a Threat: Flappers, Chorus Girls, and Other Brazen Performers of the American 1920s*. Hanover NH: Wesleyan University Press, 2000.

Lavenda, Robert. "Family and Corporation." In Manning, *The Celebration of Society*, 51–64.

———. "It's Not a Beauty Pageant!": Hybrid Ideology in Minnesota Community Queen Pageants." In Colleen Ballerine Cohen, Richard Wilk, and Beverly Stoeltje, eds., *Beauty Queens on the Global Stage: Gender, Contests, and Power*, 31–46. New York: Routledge, 1996.

Lawrence, Elizabeth Atwood. *Rodeo: An Anthropologist Looks at the Wild and the Tame*. Knoxville: University of Tennessee Press, 1982.

Leach, William. *Land of Desire: Merchants, Power, and the Rise of a New American Culture*. New York: Pantheon Books, 1993.

Lear, T. J. Jackson. *No Place of Grace: Antimodernism and the Transformation of American Culture*. New York: Pantheon Books, 1981.

LeCompte, Mary Lou. *Cowgirls of the Rodeo: Pioneer Professional Athletes*. Urbana: University of Illinois Press, 1993.

———. "The Hispanic Influence of the History of Rodeo." *Journal of Sports History* 12 (Spring 1985): 21–38.

Leibman, Nina C. *Living Room Lectures: The Fifties Family in Television and Film*. Austin: University of Texas Press, 1995.

Mahood, Mrs. R. F. "Cowgirl Sponsors from Various Towns and Cities: Colorful Notes in Cowboy Reunion." *Badford Grocery News*. n.d. Texas Cowboy Country Museum, Stamford, Texas.

Manko, Katina L. "Depression Proof Business Strategy: The California Perfume Company's Motivational Literature." In Scranton, *Beauty and Business*, 146–68.

Manning, Frank E., ed. *Celebration of Society: Perspectives on Contemporary Cultural Performances*. Bowling Green OH: Bowling Green University Popular Press, 1983.

May, Elaine Taylor. *Homeward Bound: American Families in the Cold War Era*. New York: Basic Books, 1988.

McFadden, Bernarr. *The Power and Beauty of Superb Womanhood: How They Are Lost and How They May Be Regained and Developed to the Highest Degree of Attainable Perfection*. New York: Physical Culture Publishing Co., 1901.

McGovern, James R. "The American Woman's Pre–World War I Freedom in Manners and Morals." *Journal of American History* 55 (September 1968): 315–33.

Mellis, Allison Fuss. *Riding Buffaloes and Broncos: Rodeo and Native Traditions in the Northern Great Plains.* University of Oklahoma Press, 2003.

Meyerowitz, Joanne. "Beyond the Feminine Mystique: A Reassessment of Postwar Mass Culture, 1946–1958." In Meyerowitz, *Not June Cleaver*, 229–62.

———, ed. *Not June Cleaver: Women and Gender in Postwar America, 1945–1960.* Philadelphia: Temple University Press, 1994.

Moore, Laura Jane. "'She's My Hero': Women's History at the Cowgirl Hall of Fame." *Gender and History* 6 (November 1994): 474–80.

Morris, Robert C. *Collections of the Wyoming Historical Society.* Cheyenne: The Wyoming Historical Society, 1897.

Moses, L. G. (Lester George). *Wild West Shows and the Images of American Indians, 1883–1933.* Albuquerque: University of New Mexico Press, 1996.

O'Neill, William. *A Democracy at War: America's Fight at Home and Abroad in World War II.* Cambridge: Harvard University Press, 1993.

Peiss, Kathy. *Cheap Amusements: Working Women and Leisure in Turn-of-the-Century New York.* Philadelphia: Temple University Press, 1986.

———. "Going Public: Women in Nineteenth-Century Cultural History," *American Literary History* 3, no. 4 (1991): 817–28.

———. *Hope in a Jar: The Making of America's Beauty Culture.* New York: Metropolitan Books, 1998.

———. "Making Faces: The Cosmetics Industry and the Cultural Construction of Gender, 1890–1930." *Genders* 7 (Spring 1990): 143–69.

Pioneer Ladies Club. *Reminiscences of Oregon Pioneers.* Pendleton: East Oregon Publishing Co., 1937.

Powell, Eyre. Untitled essay on Helen Bonham, c. 1925. National Cowgirl Hall of Fame Archive, Fort Worth TX.

Pratt, Gretta, and Karal Ann Manning. *In Search of the Corn Queen:*

Pictures from the Heartland. Washington DC: National Museum of American Art, 1994.

Remley, Mary L. "From Sidesaddle to Rodeo." *Journal of the West* 17, no. 3 (1978): 44–52.

Riley, Woodbridge. "Historical Perspectives on Marriage." In Schmalhausen and Calverton, *Woman's Coming of Age*, 91–109.

Roach, Joyce Gibson. *The Cowgirls*. Denton: University of North Texas Press, 1990.

Rotunda, E. Anthony. *American Manhood: Transformations in Masculinity from the Revolutionary to the Modern Era*. New York: Basic Books, 1993.

Rupp, Virgil. *Let 'Er Buck: A History of the Pendleton Round-Up*. Pendleton OR: Master Printers, 1985.

Savage, Candace. *Cowgirls*. London: Bloomsbury, 1996.

Schmalhausen, Samuel D., and V. F. Calverton, eds. *Woman's Coming of Age: A Symposium*. New York: Horace Liveright, 1931.

Schwantes, Carlos A. "The Concept of the Wageworker's Frontier: A Framework for Future Research." *Western Historical Quarterly* 73 (July 1982): 39–55.

———. "Patterns of Radicalism on the Wageworkers Frontier." *Idaho Yesterday* 30 (Fall 1986): 25–30.

Scranton, Philip, ed. *Beauty and Business: Commerce, Gender, and Culture in Modern America*. New York: Routledge, 2001.

Searcey, Mildred. "History of Pendleton Round-Up Association Queens." *Pioneer Trails* 6 (September 1981): 3–10.

Shelton, Hooper. *Fifty Years a Living Legend: Texas Cowboy Reunion and Old-Timer Association*. Stamford TX: Shelton Press, 1979.

Shields, Vickie Rutledge, and Colleen Caughlin. "Performing Rodeo Queen Culture: Competition, Athleticism, and Excessive Feminine Masquerade." *Text and Performance Quarterly* 20 (April 2000): 182–202.

Slatta, Richard W. *Cowboys of the Americas*. New Haven: Yale University Press, 1990.

Sloan, Dorothy. *Women in Cattle Country*. Austin TX: Self-published, 1986.

Stoeltje, Beverly. "Females in Rodeo: Private Motivation and Public Representation." *Kentucky Folklore Record* 32, nos. 1–2 (1986): 42–49.

———. "Gender Representations in Performance: The Cowgirl and the Hostess." *Journal of Folklore Research* 25, no. 3 (1988): 219–41.

———. "Power and the Ritual Genres: American Rodeo." *Western Folklore* 52 (April 1993): 135–56.

Walker, Nancy. *Shaping Our Mothers' World: American Women's Magazines.* Jackson: University of Mississippi Press, 2000.

———. *Women's Magazines, 1940–1960: Gender Roles and the Popular Press.* Boston: Bedford/St. Martin's, 1998.

Ware, Susan. *Holding Their Own: American Women in the 1930s.* Boston: Twayne Publishers, 1982.

Webb, Walter Prescott. *The Great Plains.* Boston: Ginn and Company, 1931.

Weiss, Jessica. *To Have and to Hold: Marriage, Baby Boom, and Social Change.* Chicago: University of Chicago Press, 2000.

Welter, Barbara. "The Cult of True Womanhood." In Lucy Maddox, ed., *Locating American Studies: The Evolution of a Discipline*, 43–70. Baltimore: John Hopkins Press, 1999.

Westermeier, Clifford P. *Man, Beast, Dust: The Story of Rodeo.* Lincoln: University of Nebraska Press, 1947, 1987.

Weston, Mary Ann. *Native Americans in the News: Images of Indians in the Twentieth-Century Press.* Westport CT: Greenwood Press, 1996.

Wills, Kathy Lynn, and Virginia Artho. *Cowgirl Legends from the Cowgirl Hall of Fame.* Salt Lake City: Gibbs-Smith Publishers, 1995.

Wooden, Wayne S., and Gavin Ehringer. *Rodeo in America: Wranglers, Roughstock, and Paydirt.* Lawrence: University Press of Kansas, 1996.

Zelinsky, Wilber. *The Cultural Geography of the United States: A Revised Edition.* Englewood Cliffs NJ: Prentice Hall, 1992.

Zunz, Oliver. *Making America Corporate, 1870–1920.* Chicago: University of Chicago Press, 1990.

Index

Engendered Encounters:
Feminism and Pueblo Cultures, 1879–1934
By Margaret D. Jacobs

Riding Pretty: Rodeo Royalty
in the American West
Renée M. Laegreid

The Colonel's Lady on the Western Frontier:
The Correspondence of Alice Kirk Grierson
Edited by Shirley A. Leckie

A Stranger in Her Native Land:
Alice Fletcher and the American Indians
By Joan Mark

So Much to Be Done: Women Settlers on
the Mining and Ranching Frontier, second edition
Edited by Ruth B. Moynihan, Susan Armitage,
and Christiane Fischer Dichamp

Women and Nature: Saving the "Wild" West
By Glenda Riley

The Life of Elaine Goodale Eastman
Theodore D. Sargent

Moving Out: A Nebraska Woman's Life
By Polly Spence
Edited by Karl Spence Richardson